To Joan & Paul,

Happy travels !

SWIMMING TO ANGOLA

... And Other Tips for Surviving the Third World

CHRISTOPHER S. BLIN

Christopher Blin

Bloomington, IN Milton Keynes, UK

authorHOUSE®

AuthorHouse™
1663 Liberty Drive, Suite 200
Bloomington, IN 47403
www.authorhouse.com
Phone: 1-800-839-8640

christopher.blin@gmail.com

P.O. Box 83312
San Diego, CA 92138

First published by AuthorHouse 11/24/2008

ISBN: 978-1-4259-9749-6 (sc)

Printed in the United States of America
Bloomington, Indiana

This book is printed on acid-free paper.

To my parents

Helen and K.C. Blin

My sincere appreciation goes to all those who helped with this book, especially Mark Ribowsky, Eric Gibson, Tony Puntar, Brett Cottrell, and Franklin Reed. The help with editing was invaluable.

Also, respectful thanks goes to Paul Sutta (in memorium) whose encouragement helped get the story told.

INTRODUCTION

I didn't set out around the world with lofty goals – not wanting to change the world, only to travel it. This obsession was probably in the blood, with the first trek coming right out of college after traveling cross-country, then just continuing... for the next ten years. I studied in Germany, played pro basketball in England and Australia, roamed across India, Kathmandu, Southeast Asia, became an Australian citizen (while retaining U.S. citizenship) and lived in the land down under for eight years.

After returning home to California, there came more arcane journeys, with sights turned toward the Third World. A word here about the use of that term. It is used in this book for familiarities sake and because it endures in the vernacular of the West. However, for many in the two-thirds of the world that is underdeveloped, the words could in fact be perceived as being derogatory.

A little history is instructive in understanding why. The term 'Third World' was first coined in the modern era in 1952, borrowed from French statesman Emmanuel Joseph Sieyes' 1788 pamphlet "Qu'est-ce que le tiers état?" or "What is the Third Estate?" which became the manifesto of the French Revolution. It included, "...because at the end, this ignored, exploited, scorned Third World like the Third Estate, wants to become something too."

Sieyes' heart was in the right place, as he later drafted the "Declaration of the Rights of Man and Citizen", expounding on theories like national sovereignty and popular representation. However, the greater Third World enjoyed few of these noble concepts. As the term evolved, it came to define nations with a low UN Human Development Index. A half century ago, such a definition meant that the People's Republic of China, Russia and Cuba were all 'Third World.'

In truth, there is no objective definition of a Third World country. Many geopolitical scholars regard the term as a synonym for the colonialism that has left many of these countries in tatters and scarred by their colonial masters to this day, decades after the last European overlords pulled out. In general, Third World countries are not as industrialized nor as technologically advanced as free-market nations of the West, leading many in academia to adopt the more politically correct terms "developing nations," "less wealthy nations," "global south," "least developed countries," and even "majority world," which all can seem a bit glossed-over for my tastes.

The term Third World is also disliked as it may imply the false notion that those countries are not a part of the global economic system. Even so, it is undeniable that these nations – which carve out huge land masses in Africa, Asia, and Latin America – suffer from the Cold War economic, political, and military maneuverings of the most powerful Free World, and Slave World, powers. And so I think it appropriate to continue to use the old term Third World, not just for familiarity, but as a reminder of why they remain so rooted to an environment so different than our cushy and spoiled-rotten world.

The journeys you will be part of will take us through six separate phases of travel – part of a 20-year odyssey that has set my boots down at the borders and beyond of 96 different countries as of this first publication. I will continue to explore countries until having seen them all, and have a full lifetime in order to accomplish the lot. In fact, the Third

World phases did not begin in earnest until well after satiating the 'civilized' wanderlust by traveling through Europe and settling down in Australia.

The phases that center on the Third World excursions, however, comprise the shank of the book, and are rich with detail and adventure. They break down this way:

1985: Overland from India to Australia.

1999-2000: Driving from California to Panama.

2002: Driving from Capetown, South Africa to northern Kenya, and return.

2002: Treking through the former Soviet Bloc countries of Eastern Europe.

2004: Installing a computer center at a hospital in Nigeria, and travels through north-west Africa.

2006: Crossing South America from Chile up to Venezuela by car.

You may call me a nomad, if you like. I prefer to be called universal, a traveler along the endless road looking ahead at an endless horizon. For the record, I do have a home base in San Diego, someplace to hang my hat and keep my golf clubs cool between hitting the road again. Which would be in my current vehicle of choice: a 40-mile-per-gallon car, a Honda CRX. A two-seater. As you'll learn, this is the perfect kind of wheels to ride on through the dirt roads of the Third World. You don't want to try it with that snazzy Land Rover, which might be smooth on rough terrain, but will be useless in places where there are no gas stations for a hundred miles. And it may be hundreds of miles away from you when you wake up, having been driven off by one of the local thieves who had measured you as a quite visible target of opportunity, and ripped you off during the night.

The lesson here is that to travel heavy, you must travel light. In the pocketbook, that is. These pages will provide all the information you need to get where you want to go and back, and never have to carry more than a couple hundred dollars in your wallet, as well as how to play the exchange-rate game to your advantage. Understanding these guidelines will put you miles ahead – literally – of less worldly travelers whom local con artists will pluck of their dollars like the feathers off a Thanksgiving turkey.

You will even learn one of the best secrets of world travel: how to make money along the way that will pay for your journey. For instance, I've spent as little as the equivalent of two U.S. dollars for a hotel room – that is, when I wasn't spending the night under the starry sky in my ever-present light-weight tent. One friend of mine, a fellow Westerner whom I became friends with in Africa, shared a home with meals included in Dar Es Salaam, Tanzania for five dollars a *week*!

The sections of this book printed in Italics are actual diary entries and e-mails sent back home to report on my whereabouts at the time. They give a real time look as to what was happening right then and there in those countries as I was experiencing it. Some national currencies are also listed with the exchange rates to the US dollar at the time of the visit. These allow the reader to get a general idea of monetary values as well as inflation rates in these countries.

The unofficial theme song might be Ricky Nelson's one about the "Traveling Man" who has "made a lot of stops all over the world." I won't get into whether the rest of that song applies, about how in every port the traveling man owns the heart of at least one lovely girl. I'll take the Fifth about how many "pretty senoritas" are waiting for me down in old Mexico. Perhaps that's for another book. However, let's just say this traveling man has enjoyed a full and satisfying menu. And, like the proverbial Chinese meal, I often find myself hungry again an hour later. I do consider the world to be my oyster.

Which is why I'll soon be back on the road again, going over the hundred mark in countries visited, making more good friends, swimming, riding, dodging bullets, and hopefully sinking that hole-in-one somewhere where very few Westerners have ever seen the sun rise and set. The destinations may be a bit different, but as ever, the Third World will still be the first choice.

Crossing the Strait of Gibraltar into Morocco.

ROUTES AND YEARS

1982

1999

2006

1995

OF OVERLAND TREKS

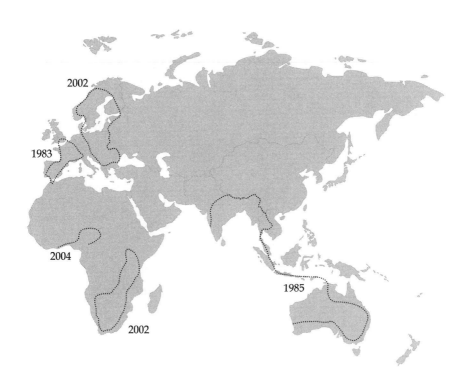

Bartering with merchants in India.

*A ship in the harbor is safe... but that is
not what ships were made for.
— Anon.*

Elephants are great jungle transportation.

CHAPTER ONE

The time was February of 2002, the place Namibia, in southwestern Africa. I had just made it safely through the country and gotten to the border with Angola, located just to the north. But between here and the next step of the journey stood a border guard – one of the fraternity that world travelers come to know as the ultimate gate keepers for any movement to and fro. These fellows usually don't present themselves as helpful, which is only because they aren't there to be helpful. Instead, they are usually there to give you a hassle, or possibly pick up something for their back pocket in the process.

This one played the role of the stone wall. He didn't look as if he was going to wish me a good stay in Angola. Not with a particularly belligerent attitude, but more like a matter of fact fatalism, he gave the bad news.

"Sorry sir," he said, "this is a war zone."

There had been a civil war raging in Angola for three decades, but I assumed they would allow at least some tourists into the country. I assumed wrong. They were not giving out any tourist visas, at any price.

I like to go places where there is action, and am not generally scared off by war zones. After all, are people trapped in the ravages of war any less of human beings? In my experience, having been in countries torn by violence, refugees of war – those breathing the stench of death, rousted from their homes at a moment's notice, being caught in crossfires they have nothing to do with – are the very people who need affirmations of hope and reassurance that their lives still mean something. I wished to do some kind of goodwill work in Angola. Right now, though, it seemed good enough to at least leave my footprints there.

Little did I know that this was possibly the worst time to tempt the country's wariness about outsiders, given that tensions were running particularly high. An insurgent leader was killed in combat with government troops, and there was grave concern about minefields and an outbreak of the Marburg virus. This would rapidly become the worst outbreak of a haemorric fever in recorded history, with over 237 deaths recorded out of 261 reported cases, and having spread to seven out of the 18 provinces in the country. Maybe it was best I wasn't fully aware of the crisis. Ignorance is bliss, they say. Which may have explained the border guard's initial perplexed reaction.

Driving a little farther until coming upon the Okavango River, there was a little beach area on its banks. I pulled onto the hard sand, near where some people were washing their cars, and looked across the river. Could this be my 'back door' to Angola? The river was only something like 100 yards wide, but it wasn't a calm river by any means. It had rushing water, not quite like rapids, but a quick current just the same. Still, I am a good swimmer and had been through strong currents in the Amazon.

A local man happened to be sitting there, obviously looking for something to do. When he saw this big white guy approaching, one could read his mind: there's got to be some money here somewhere. I then got the idea of paying him to watch the car while making my foray into Angola.

"Is this water safe?" I asked.

"Oh yes, quite safe."

"No crocodiles?"

"No."

"Okay, great. Do you mind watching my car while I swim?"

"No problem."

While stripping down to my trunks, I gave the mission some thought. Swimming straight across, the current would certainly pull me down-stream far away because it was that strong. So when diving in, to the amazement of the people on the shore, I had to start swimming into the current, and swam basically at a 45 degree angle. Swimming as hard as possible would compensate for being pushed sideways by the current.

But I was never in any real danger, and made it across to the Angolan side in a matter of minutes. I finished pretty much straight across from the starting spot on the other side. Looking around to make sure there weren't any border guards waiting with guns drawn, I found instead there weren't many people around at all. Trading some souvenir coins with the locals was my main activity, being only in a pair of trunks and not able to wander around very far.

Having cheated the Angolan interdiction against tourists, I wasted no time going back across the river before someone could get wise, utilizing the same maneuver: swimming against the direction of the current as it pushed me down-stream. But because of fatigue, I was pushed past the beach area into some reeds which line the sides of the river. These reeds were a good six feet tall and quite thick, and cut off any movement to and from the river. A perilous situation, indeed.

I was standing in about four feet of water, with the water up to my chest and rushing at me. Knowing drowning was a possibility if unable to extricate myself, I grabbed the reeds hand over fist, pulling myself into the oncoming current. It was only about 15 yards, but I pulled myself back to the safety of the little beach area. Just then while wading ashore, another local man who was washing his car looked a bit surprised to see me.

"You're a brave man," he remarked in English.

"Why is that?"

"You could have been a crocodile's breakfast."

I said, "A man told me earlier that this water is safe."

He explained, "Oh yes, it is safe – here at the beach. But down there by the reeds, that's where all the crocodiles live!"

I thought, gee, thanks for that critical bit of information – which had been offered just a bit late. Needless to say, it is good to get a consensus of opinion before doing something on impulse. One man's idea of safe is another man's peril. The postscript, as I found out later, was that there had been nine deaths on that very section of beach – all having been eaten by crocodiles! I might have been number ten if luck hadn't been with me.

Luck aside, however, the lesson had been learned, as it had and would be for as long as my feet hit the long road through the Third World.

Be aware.

* * *

The aforementioned story underscores that this is not your grandfather's, or even your father's, idea of a travel book.

It is, in fact, the most unlikely travel itinerary you'll probably ever read. Some of the destinations in these pages have rarely, if ever, made it to those high-gloss volumes of global travel literature. And for a good – or at least logical – reason: most people in so-called 'advanced' countries looking for 'exotic' locales to spend time in, normally wouldn't want to go here. These are places that we might consider deep in poverty and hopelessness, where civil wars rage, where dictators confiscate land for their own use, where babies starve, and where travel itself is crimped by men in battle fatigues carrying automatic rifles.

On roads paved and unpaved leading to the four corners of the globe, the ones in the Third World are the very least traveled. Where the scent of stability and higher living standards can be whiffed, and tour-guided safaris through safely-made 'wild' jungles and nature preserves can be offered for a pretty price, that is when the roads begin to get crowded.

This book, then, is testament to the folly of those stereotypical Third World incursions, and the fiction inherent in their premise. In reality, in a decade of journeys through the darkest outposts of Africa, South America, and Eurasia, I have found some of the most exhilarating scenic wonders on the globe, and some of the nicest, friendliest people in *any* World, First and Second included, in an adult life dedicated to enhancing standards of living all around the globe.

I also have encountered some real danger, moments when less luck or less wise on-the-spot decisions might have been life threatening. However, this is an occupational hazard for any hardy world traveler with a yen to veer off the well-beaten path. Even so, such is the inviting nature of even the most rugged terrain in these still-primitive environments, and the generally helpful attitudes of the natives there, that never did I feel powerless or left to the whim of people out to do me harm. On the contrary, I have made enduring and endearing friendships everywhere the road has taken me. Indeed, people whom most would assume to be threatening turned out to be more solicitous and accepting than might be found waiting in line at the supermarket or in cars impatiently tailgating on the Hollywood Freeway.

The underlying purpose of this book is to encourage others to discover the same world I did, a world of endless fascination and joy and adventure. People can go around the world, with the pride of doing it independently and with the sure-fire result of writing new chapters on world travel that no one else has ever written. If there is one thing I wish to see banished from our planet, after wars and hunger and famine, is xenophobia – fear of the outside world.

Just remember a few basic rules in order to come back home in one piece. Be aware. And, be gracious. Quite simple and to the point. Following these two rules will help insure a better than average chance at a successful trip. That is, coming back with all limbs hopefully attached in the right places.

People will say, "Gosh, we live in the best world around, why would we want to go anywhere else?" Think of it this way: yes, we enjoy the best that life has to offer, and we should treasure that. But there are a lot of people out there who were not lucky enough to be born over here. We can help them by telling them about us, our natural goodness as a people, and they can help us by shedding light on things we don't know about. When you meet up with people, you find out that they're not much different than we are.

There is a lot of hatred in this world because we've never sat down and talked with other people. All they hear is second hand about what Americans are about, but they haven't seen us. You go and shake their hands and their ideas start to change, in a hurry. You may even, in a small but significant way, change the world. I have actually done that, as you will read.

These pages are meant to convey the aspect of hope and reclamation shared by the people who live in the Third World, who after all never asked to be colonial pawns or slaves to rich nations, and the natural scenic beauty that is common to all of these diamond-in-the-rough nations. Indeed, the journey through these pages will surprise as to the extent of civilization in the Third World. In short, there is more of it than imagined, though one wonders whether perhaps becoming civilized is worth it.

For example, there are McDonald's restaurants in just about all the big cities out there. On principle alone, combined with the fact that native food staples are much more economical than a Big Mac, I will routinely keep my distance from a fast-food joint that pops up along a pristine landscape such as the Serengeti Plain or the rising majesty of Kilimanjaro. Still, progress is progress, and it's probably beneficial that Internet cafes also can be found on many Third World streets, bringing these countries information from the global superhighway.

You may be saying: okay, so here's a rich guy who could afford to indulge a travel hobby. If so, let me disabuse you of that notion. I am neither rich nor poor, but certainly haven't gotten around the world and back by boarding first-class champagne flights. Just an average guy who wanted to prove to himself that he could see all in the world he wanted to see, and do it in the spirit of the old-time explorers, pretty much blind (sometimes even carrying a map, but more often relying on the directions of the locals), not knowing what was waiting around the next corner.

And with generally no more than a couple hundred dollars in cash and some traveler's checks and credit cards, I would set out in whatever local transportation that would wait until getting home before breaking down. Traveling light in the pocketbook, in fact, is one of my rules of travel – the reason being that you don't want to become a target, especially in the Third World. I'm tall and white enough as it is, I don't need a sign around my neck reading: "Free money for everybody, right here."

In fact, another aim of this book is to put to rest the notion that one must be a moneybags to travel the world. It really doesn't take much, although you must know a few tricks to stay solvent in lands where the exchange rates will literally bleed you dry if you're not aware. It comes down to common sense and not living beyond your means. Self sufficiency is what I'm all about. A buddy in Las Vegas likes to tell me, "Christopher, how can you do all this traveling? You've never had a job." The response is, jovially and honestly, "I don't know – but I keep working at it."

That means working hard and plugging away and doing jobs here and there that add up to a comfort level. Some people have a job for 40 years. I'm not averse to that, everyone has their life choices. But to do that, I'd have to start now and keep working until age 80. I've never had a 'same old daily grind' job – knock on wood. My real job is to keep living a dream.

Thus, I admit to having a perspective different than most folks. Some people must have all the material things, the DVDs, the VCRs, the big-screen TVs – all of which are built to become outdated. Planned obsolescence means going out and buying those same luxury items over and over. I just don't buy them at all. I'm not the ideal American consumer, buying gasoline and my daily bread and a little bit of semi-stylish clothing once in a while.

My one concession to the 'upscale' life is my passion for golf, but even this has a broader explanation than the desire to be seen at the local country club with the Joneses. I am a physically fit guy, a real fitness freak – which is helpful considering that the world is full of mountains to climb and deep rivers to swim. And golf is a game one can play all over the world – and even in the Third World – on courses in the most unlikely of places. I played 48 courses on the trip through eastern Africa alone. Indeed, guys just like me have gotten together for worldwide golf tours, their great calling in life being to notch as many rounds on great, scenic links in postcard-like settings. While paying the big bucks for it.

My calling is a little less ornate. While I would love to walk the main course at St. Andrew's Royal and Ancient Club in Scotland, I get just as big a rush finding a public course in, say, Swaziland and playing nine holes with the local citizenry. Hanging around a golf course with a six-foot-five *mzungu* – as they call a white guy in Swahili – is something that doesn't happen much for the locals in those countries.

And it's worth lugging my golf clubs around in the back of the car, which may be the only violation of my general rule to travel light, but well worth the extra effort. When playing the Elephant Hills course in an unfenced area in the jungles of Zimbabwe, I was but a few feet from what may have been a lion, hidden in some brush along the fairway. Brave-hearted, I shooed whatever it was away – with a five-iron. All in a day's work out there in the real world.

As this incident would suggest, the biggest rule of the road is that nothing is predictable except that something unpredictable will happen. That makes it imperative to develop a certain set of 'sixth senses' about devoting one's life to travel and adventure. And in so doing, helping those people with whom you come into contact.

To choose this path is definitely *not* to be a tourist, or to even think like one. Through the lessons gleaned from these pages, one learns precisely how to avoid tourist-speak – which is another dead giveaway and an invitation to be ripped off for a lot of money. The result leads to an exhilarating path into the unknown that will create memories to last for a lifetime that few among us actually have the opportunity to rack up.

The tragedy is that in a world so big and so amazing, most of us will see so little of it. Many people literally never leave the town in which they were born. Others will leave only for their annual two week vacation – to the same exact place each and every year. The usual trip abroad consists of the good old group package to Paris or Rome, while being squeezed into an airplane, then buses, then hotels, with pretty much people like ourselves. Often with people we go through life with at home, have lunch with at Denny's, play poker with on Friday night, ride with to and from the PTA. Again, if this is your choice, off you go.

Friends are a wonderful thing, and I've made many of them. But I'd rather know them for their special place in a special environment, celebrating their differences from me rather than their similarities with me. And I wouldn't enjoy traveling with just any packaged group around the world. Or they with me, for that matter.

* * *

The Essence of Today –
I expect to pass through this world but once. Any
good I can do, or any kindness that I can show, let me
do it now, for I shall not pass this way again.
– William Penn

* * *

Everyone learns their survival skills in their own personal ways. I learned my share as a kid growing up with Boy Scouts of America. At age 14, I was the youngest Eagle Scout in the history of my troop in California. Now, over 30 years later, I still wear that badge – okay, in spirit rather than on my chest, but wear it I still do. And at the risk of sounding like a Norman Rockwell painting come to life, I owe many of my survival instincts to those hallowed scouting principles which became burned into my consciousness and remain there to this day.

The Scout motto is: "Be Prepared."

The Scout slogan is: "Do a good turn daily." (A good deed.)

The Scout Law is: "A scout is trustworthy, loyal, helpful, friendly, courteous, kind, obedient, cheerful, thrifty, brave, clean, and reverent."

The Scout Oath is: "On my honor, I will do my best to do my duty to God and my country, and to obey the Scout Law; to help other people at all times; and to keep myself physically strong, mentally awake, and morally straight."

Okay, so I am the proverbial Last Boy Scout – or was that Bruce Willis in the movie of the same name? But before you laugh, keep in mind that those principles have fueled my travels, because these ventures are my own sort of humanitarian missions. And on more than one occasion, in more than one town that never made it to a map, and in more than one threatening scenario, those principles may have even kept my trip, and my life, from ending right then and there.

There are opponents of Scouting – believe it or not. They try to trash the Scouts' good name or tarnish their reputation. Why? First of all, everyone seems to want to trash something. Usually we only 'bad mouth' things we perceive as bigger than us. A threat to us. Ever want to cut down a group you see as inferior to you? What fun would that be? Pity them maybe, but attack them? Not really. Groups opposing the Scouts seem to want to teach their own agenda to little kids. The Scouts have other ideals to teach.

The USA gets its share of 'bad mouthing' all the time. Big churches, big corporations, as well. If you are perceived as being big, you are automatically a target. Australia on the other hand, hardly ever gets 'trashed' when world discussions come up. Who wants to cut down a bunch of guys who are perceived as beer drinking, good natured, sport loving blokes?

It is all part of life. Learn to deal with it.

If life itself is a journey, and of course it is, mine began in Los Angeles, where I was born and raised, the son of an engineer and a homemaker who took me and my three sisters every summer to San Diego on vacation for two weeks. For me, that 90 mile journey to an ocean-side resort planted a seed. That feeling of an engine in front of me, gliding over roads, with trees and mountains whizzing by the windows while the sun hung in the sky, seemed to be what life should be about.

The notion of being sedentary, seeing the same things routinely, effectively opposed what I came to see as man's primal instinct: to live as many different life experiences as possible. Think about that old adage about a rolling stone that gathers no moss. That is an enlightening piece of philosophy, and it probably was conceived back when cavemen roamed the Earth. After all, if those guys didn't keep moving, they would surely have been a saber-tooth tiger's lunch.

While there aren't many tigers in L.A. – though there are more than a few reptiles of the human kind – I wanted no moss to grow under my feet. Though I'd have to cool my heels a while. First came education, which I completed after studying economics and attaining a degree in Business Management. I had no intention, however, of going through the usual ritual of pounding the pavement looking for a job in the smog-choked downtown L.A. business district. If pounding any pavement, it would be on sidewalks on distant roads.

After graduating, while hanging around the fraternity house one day, some of the guys spoke about going to the regional convention in

Arizona. They needed someone to drive them, and I got the hint. "I'll drive you one way," was the response, "but I'm going to keep on going, somewhere, anywhere."

That was anywhere the road took me: Texas, Florida, Key West, up to New York City, back across the continent through Chicago, Denver and San Francisco. This was in one car – a sporty Chevy Nova – and with practically spare change in my pocket after gassing up the car a few hundred times. Of course, I was hardly the first 22-year-old kid right out of college to live on a car and a prayer. Youth is a great time to be young, before little things like 'accommodations' and 'food bills' and 'plans' begin to matter.

All that was really needed was the local Pi Kappa Alpha fraternity house in each college town. I'd introduce myself and say, "Hey, I'm a brother from California, can you put me up?" After the required mystics and hand shakes, I'd get a nice place to stay, and most of the time, meals, booze and babes. You remember the road trip in the movie *Animal House*? I had a road trip like that, all summer long. The only things missing were Otis Day and the Knights, and Fawn Lebowitz's roommate.

Not to claim complete irresponsibility. Remember, I'm a proud and loyal Eagle Scout. I'm also, for reasons never quite figured out, the kind of guy who naturally seems to be able to find what is needed, be it lodging on the road, good companionship, or even a ride to get there and back. It seems to be a knack, a built-in adapter (no plug-in necessary, thankfully) that allows me to fit in with strangers in strange lands. The knack also covers earning enough money to really live – and no, this does not include pan-handling or picking anyone's pocket!

There was once a TV show where struggling medical students were all bitching and moaning that they didn't have any money and were down to the dreaded option, borrowing from their families. And there was this one guy who was saying, "Oh man, I can't believe it. I just dropped below the $3,000 minimum on my savings account. I'm going to get charged a fee." Everybody's looking at him, bewildered, as if thinking, "How does this guy do it?" Well, I could be that guy. Not being born rich, I just got to know what to buy and where to buy it at a good value. Some people just throw their money around and wind up not having two sticks to rub together. And then there are folks who figure out ways to be sensible and still have all that is needed.

Some people come out of school $90,000 in debt. But why? I made money in college working at the pub in the student center. You sell textbooks in the school store, you flip burgers for pay and to feed yourself. I was a dorm resident adviser, and got free room and board. And when traveling, frequently have done so under the aegis of a business, as a consultant, a researcher. There are many people who can't do these jobs because they have families. So it can pay well.

Indeed, my first international trek was in this same vein, starting off as a courier to transport documents across the country on free plane flights. Being a courier is a truly inspired way to travel on the cheap. It got me all the way to New York. Once there, instead of going home, again I just kept on going. Not into the Atlantic Ocean, but over it. I bought a one-way ticket on Icelandic Airways from New York to Reykjavik to Luxembourg, for the simplest of reasons: at $115, it was the cheapest flight around.

* * *

Honor is something no man can give you, and no man
can take away. It is a gift that you give to yourself.
– Rob Roy MacGregor

* * *

Luck can also play a big part in just about anything. Getting off the plane and proceeding to the passport control, a few people ahead of me in line was a young black guy, who was being questioned at length by the man in uniform. When I heard him say, "How was I supposed to know I had to have a return ticket?" my ears perked up. When they took him to the back room for further questioning, I started to sweat. He may still be there, for all I know. When it came my turn, my passport was stamped without even a second glance. Was it really just luck, or had I seen my first sign of international profiling or even racism? In any event, welcome to Europe. Onward and upward.

There probably weren't very many frat boys living in Luxembourg, but I still played the college-boy card. With my backpack carrying not much more than a change of clothes, I made my way to a youth hostel, and was put in a room with three other guys and four bunk beds. So at least there was room for me on the top of one of the bunks.

This was my first encounter with non-Americans and the plan was to pick up bits and pieces of whatever language was being spoken. One of the guys in the room I just couldn't understand when he greeted me. He sounded German for some reason, so I used the sprinkling of that language from college to ask what it was he just said. One of the others laughed and said, "He's talking to you in English, can't you understand?" It turned out they were all from Liverpool, where English may as well be a foreign language. So for the rest of the day when he would speak to me, the others would translate into the 'other' brand of English or I would just nod in agreement with my glazed look. I came all the way to Europe and couldn't even speak English with an Englishman. That was a little foreboding.

Accents can be a little tricky. Much later I stumbled upon a way of finding the jist of the meaning, when getting stuck on one word can make or break the conversation. One gentleman said I should go stay at the "Hotel Fairmow." I said I'd never heard of it. "You have never heard of the Hotel Fairmow?" he said, "It is a state in the USA. You are American aren't you?" So I asked him to please spell that out, and he wrote out on paper V-e-r-m-o-n-t! That is how he pronounces it. Always get them to write it down.

This worked well most of the time, and I was getting quite good at it, until trying it with someone who explained that he couldn't read or write. Sometimes you just have to move on to the next topic, and throw that last one in the 'Too Hard' basket.

Everything can be a challenge, and I was very eager to rise to it. For train travel around Europe, I bought a Euro Rail select pass – which is the next tip for shoe-string train travel. A Euro Rail pass can be used in any of 18 European countries. The pass took me all around Europe, and I had a ball making friends at many a youth hostel, playing sports, camping-out on the occasion, and seeing enough thousand-year-old churches and museums to last a lifetime.

The trains rolled down to the south of France, to Spain, to Portugal. The first night in Spain, a youth hostel seemed to be the best bet. Traveling with a beautiful French girl, we went into the hostel in San Sebastian, right in the northern Basque country. It was all filled up for males because they were hosting a soccer tournament there. They did have rooms for females, so I said to my lady, "Why don't you just stay here tonight and I'll go pitch my tent out on the lawn." I'd meet her in the morning at 7 a.m., when the hostel opened.

I walked out and asked myself, where is the safest place to pitch a tent? The best place seemed to be the back yard of the hostel, so I jumped over the fence, pitched my tent, and went to sleep. At about 2 a.m., I began to hear the sound of barking dogs, incessantly. They were guard dogs, German Shepherds. There were four of them around my tent, and only one of me. They had me surrounded, and they were barking and snarling, taking a break, then back for more barking. It went on for several hours of intense intimidation. In fear, I instinctively curled up in a fetal position, but kept my senses and told myself that it would have to end, and that the barking was just sound, it wasn't a physical attack. And as long as they're not biting the tent, I'd be okay. So of course, just then one of them did just that, biting right through the tent and nipping my leg in the process.

That pretty much determined that I'd have to do something proactive, not wanting to be a sitting duck for a German Shepherd to tear apart. Not taking the time to think about it and change my mind, I jumped to my feet, zipped open the tent door, and began swinging a blanket and chasing the dogs away. It was kind of funny because as menacing as dogs like these are, they looked totally bewildered. As if they had no idea what to do with this blanket-swinging lunatic. It really was the element of surprise that worked for me.

Seeing how well it worked, I became Conan the Barbarian, continuing to chase these sharp-fanged dogs – which realizing in five seconds, was really pushing my luck. And as soon as getting to the fence, I veered off and leaped over it, leaving the tent sitting abandoned on the lawn. Going back would have been the lesser part of valor, so the rest of the night was spent sleeping under the blanket that had been my weapon, plopping down across the street in a stadium park on the grass. I wrapped myself 'taco style', half the blanket below me and half above, a technique since employed frequently. Up until that four dog night, when man almost bit dog, that was the scariest thing I had ever encountered. As I'd find out over the coming years, it was a mere warm-up.

The next morning, in the safe harbor of a bright sunny day – and with the guard dogs having been put in their pens – I went back and collected my tent and young French girl. And we went on our merry way. And I do mean merry, indeed. I might as well point out the obvious by saying that such companionship is one of the better fringe benefits of world travel. American women are not generally prone to open up to strangers they've just met. It is part of the American conditioning process in which people are generally taught to be scared to death of anyone they don't know. This xenophobic quotient is reduced to nearly nothing once one goes abroad, and thank goodness for that.

Accordingly, the most meaningful relationships I've had seem to have happened on foreign soil. This includes the adventurous woman I lived with in London, who traveled with me over four continents. I look back in joy and sadness, recalling the good times, and the let-down when we had to part. I also recognize the oft-time folly of stoking long-term relationships when on the road. Of course, the case can be made that world travel and service is a kind of marriage. And full of love, to boot.

By this time I was on the move again, down the Spanish coast, across the Strait of Gibraltar to Tangier, Morocco. These first scenes of Africa had camels roaming around placidly, bustling ancient markets, smoke filled dens where people made deals for exotic rugs, and cafes where unhurried residents sipped tea on the floor, propped casually on pillows and dickering with the merchants. This was the front door of the Third World.

It was also the introduction to a different kind of toilet facilities. A flush toilet here is not much more than a hole in the tile floor with two foot pad markers on either side to help with the aim as you squat. In poor countries with not many resources, instead of toilet paper there is generally a little plastic tea-pot of water right near by. It is for hand washing, and that is why it is an insult in desert countries to touch someone with your left hand. The right hand is used for eating – don't get them mixed up!

But in a more modern accommodation, I had the luxury of a regular Western toilet. When a local friend came to help me move my luggage, he spied it, and asked about the plastic thing on the top of the bowl. He had seen a toilet before, but never a toilet *seat*. I proceeded to tell him about all the male/female arguments where I come from about toilet seat up, toilet seat down. He said if it is such a problem, why not take the darn thing off? He had a point there.

With great reluctance, I had to settle for a mere sample of the 'dark continent.' But I had already begun counting the hours until returning for further exploration of Africa in depth and detail.

* * *

In Germany, even though not speaking the language like a local, I enrolled in a few courses at a school in Munich. To pay for it, I took a job in the restaurant industry, starting out as a professional 'Spuehler', then advancing all the way up the ladder to 'Kellner' – which is the fancy way of saying from dishwasher all the way up to table waiter.

The amazing thing was, after a few weeks, I woke up and was speaking German, not fluently, but enough to make conversation. That is a common phenomenon, and by far the best way to learn a foreign language. Not having many friends there who spoke English, I was hanging around with Germans, listening to the language almost exclusively. And then one day, boom, you fall right into it.

A friend in that school was a Spanish guy named Pepe. We used to speak German together because he couldn't speak any English and I couldn't speak any Spanish. Twenty-five years later, I still speak better German than Spanish, even having been through Central and South America twice. Why? Because, for example, when studying in Panama, I worked with many English speaking people, and didn't really have the burning need to 'sink or swim' in Spanish alone. This is a flaw to be resolved.

That Euro Rail pass was like a magic carpet ride. I went up to Scandinavia and then came down through Eastern Europe, including Poland, Czechoslovakia, and Hungary. Having to get back to Germany, and my classes, made it a big loop through Eastern Europe. The last leg through Austria was an overnight train that would get into Munich by morning. At about 2 a.m., the conductor made his rounds, coming through the cars to check all tickets. He said my pass had just expired and pointed it out to me.

"Really?" I deadpanned. "Hmm, how'd that happen? How much do I pay?"

"Just wait here," he replied. "I'll finish and come back to you."

Before he could get back, the train made a stop for a signal right out in the middle of nowhere. I didn't know if a fine was imminent, but certainly did not want to trouble the conductor with more paperwork. So, being as much as I was into the adventure of the game, I said, "What the hell," and got off the train right then and there. It was in the middle of a warm moon-lit summer night, and very peaceful. When the train pulled away, I was about to pitch my tent, content to sleep right there in the velvety grassy field.

Within a few minutes, another train lumbered by. Not a passenger train but a box-car train, carrying loads of huge shipping containers. When it stopped in the same spot, a light went on in my head. I swallowed hard, telling myself, "I'm gonna jump on to this thing and tell my grandchildren about this someday." And I did, although having no idea where this train was going! I felt much like Butch Cassidy without the Sundance Kid, not with stolen loot, but just a backpack.

Between two of the large containers was a space of no more than three or four feet. That's where I eased my large frame, settling-in between the containers. As the train began to roll again, it was an incredible feeling.

The containers kept the wind off, and made it a comfortable ride in the balmy night air. It was quite a beautiful starry ride, and the night air was so invigorating. I used my backpack as a head rest and reclined, watching a parade of mountains and forests going by. As the sun came up, the beautiful horizon was fanning out. Eventually we pulled into the Munich station – as it happened, exactly where I wanted to go! I took my back pack, climbed down from the car without being seen, and started walking out onto the platform.

To get out of the station, you need a ticket to show that you'd just come off a train. Worse, I was in a section of the station off-limits to passengers. Within minutes, someone in a uniform called to me, "Hey, what are you doing over there?" After responding, "I'm a tourist and I'm lost," he never even asked to see a ticket, and just showed me right to the exit. "Danke schoen," I chirped and walked out, with a small but significant victory under my belt.

* * *

After the courses were finished, I was experiencing something as never before – what cold weather really feels like. It was a particularly bitter winter in Germany, and the first time I'd actually lived in snow in my life. Now it was understood why people get depressed in the cold of winter. Not used to such feelings myself, I looked for a quick way out, and with a usual knack for falling into a good situation, I found one.

Providentially, an Australian buddy was living in London at the time, and he invited me to come there for Christmas. That winter in London town was paradise by comparison – as the Gulf Stream can dump warm air there right at the appropriate time. I wound up staying for the next year, and with a modicum of fame, at least in certain circles of London. Chalk that one up to the fact that I grew up to be six-foot-five. In England there was a semi-pro basketball league, and as always, basketball teams need tall men who can play. So, in short order – or tall order – I was signed by a team called the Tower Hamlets Basketball Club.

There wasn't a ton of money involved, but the league teams did find jobs for the players. Mine was with a financial company in the downtown banking district, and it kept me quite comfortable. Even better was the side benefit of playing ball – getting to go to parts of western Europe on road trips. The team played on nights and weekends.

I was a power forward, and may have been the team's missing puzzle piece, because we began to beat everybody after filling the league's set maximum of two foreigners per team. The other American was good enough to get a tryout with the Philadelphia 76ers, and while we played together, we won a number of tournaments around England, France and Holland.

London, then, was a jolly good experience, though it was darkened by one very unpredictable event around Easter time, 1984. My job at the finance company was in an office building that bordered St. James Square in central London. As it happened, the Libyan embassy was situated two doors down. On that day, there was a huge demonstration of Libyan expatriates opposed to Mohammar Qaddafi, the brutal Libyan dictator. The demonstrators were out in the middle of the park in the square, which is ringed by four block-long buildings. They were wearing masks so as not to be filmed and identified by the embassy workers, which would have meant retribution would be taken on their families back home

Everyone in our office was watching the commotion just outside. One of the girls in our office said, "Open the window, let's hear what they're chanting." And just as the window slid open, we heard a series of shrill, sharp noises – pop pop pop, as if someone had lit some firecrackers. But then we saw people were falling like bowling pins. Someone in a window of the embassy was training a machine gun on the crowd and firing, the smoke of the shots wafting past our window. Suddenly, there was pandemonium, with people trampling each other to get out of the square, which emptied in a matter of seconds! They dragged several lifeless bodies that had blood seeping from them.

It turned out that thirteen people were hit, and one died – a British bobby named Yvonne Fletcher, who ironically was there to keep the peace, and lost her life in the process. In the confused minutes after the shooting, the perpetrators holed-up in the embassy, resisting demands from the police to come out. Dozens of bobbies, in shooting position behind trees, pointed their guns up at the embassy building – right next to us. While the siege was on, nobody could get out of our building because our entrance opened into the square, and no one was allowed there.

That meant the cops had to get us out of there, one way or another. A few hours after the shooting, the bobbies led us onto the roof, where they had placed planks across to an adjoining building maybe ten feet away. They had made a little makeshift bridge – five stories up. Looking at it made me a little queasy, but also a tad excited by the idea of having to become a pirate walking the plank to get to safety. There was only room on the narrow planks for one person at a time, lest the weight of several people might cause the wood to break and send us down into the dark alley. But we were all good pirates. We got across to the other building and then down the stairway to a back exit facing away from the square. Mission accomplished.

We were away from our offices as the stand-off lasted a week, but since it coincided with Easter week, the buildings would have been closed a few extra days anyway. At that time, the basketball team went on a road trip to Paris and Holland for tournaments. Upon getting back, I read that all the Libyans had diplomatic immunity, had been escorted to the plane, and flew off to Libya – having quite literally gotten away with murder. They were even treated as heroes back home.

A few decades later, it is said that Qaddafi quietly executed the trigger man, apparently as a signal to the West that he wasn't the same guy who exported terror in the eighties. Of course this was long after Libya's involvement in the Lockerbee, Scotland plane explosion. When remembering these incidents, I think back to officer Yvonne Fletcher, who died in clear view of my sight, and who was standing where I could have been on a lunch break, had fate taken me into the crowd in St. James Square that eventful day.

I stayed in Europe for two years, traveling, working, studying, playing basketball. I did return for the 1984 Olympic Games that were held in my home town of Los Angeles. While there, my parents didn't even try to talk me out of going back. They knew that world travel was in my blood, telling me, "Go for it, live your dreams." I'm still living them, to this day.

CHAPTER TWO

The trip back home served as a kind of punctuation mark for what had been two years of 'get-your-feet-wet' journeys through Europe and North Africa. Now taking stock of where to go next, I was absolutely riveted by the sights and sounds left in my consciousness by too-brief forays into the outer edges of the Third World. My priority became to go deeper and deeper into that world, almost as a calling, since such travel would pique both a curiosity to plumb foreign lands and a desire to make a humanitarian difference wherever the road took me.

Thus, when returning to London in the late summer of 1984, I looked for an opening that could fuel these objectives. Fortunately, it happened rather quickly. Several of my roommates in London were Australians who were going back home soon, and they invited me to come and visit them. In essence, they said, "You've got to see Australia before you go home, mate." They didn't have to twist my arm. So of course I dusted off my backpack and hiking boots and was off on another circuitous adventure – now into the heart and soul of the Third World. With my English girlfriend coming along for the flight to India, from there I would then continue overland through Nepal, Thailand, Malaysia and Indonesia before reaching the land down under.

India, $1 = 45 Rupees

We landed in New Delhi at Christmas time, a mere two months after Prime Minister Indira Gandhi had been assassinated by her Sikh bodyguards. This was retribution for her sending troops into the state of Punjab, when they invaded the Sikhs' holy Golden Temple – where rebel Sikh separatists had been holed-up in a stand-off. The bodyguards later took their vengeance, plunging a knife into her heart.

Thus, we could not have chosen a more exciting time to come to India. The Sikh community was marked for retaliation. We would hear tales of them being beaten and burned to death, with the charred bodies left in the streets to rot. Fortunately we did not come upon any. When we arrived, Mrs. Gandhi's son Rajiv Gandhi had been installed as a caretaker prime minister after his mother's death. He was formally elected and confirmed as the ruling prime minister, only to be killed himself a few years later.

The first thing I recall about India – the country that most people think of by reflex when they hear "Third World" – is the acrid smell of smoke. Not from gunfire but from fires around which people would congregate. Now years later, whenever smelling the smoke of a campfire, in the middle of nowhere, I immediately think back to India. But also remembered are the people, lots of people, seemingly as far as the eye can see. Rather than being threatened by such a profusion of humanity, I was struck by how eager everybody was to help me. We traveled by plane, by train, by bus, sometimes by private car. I got off the train one night in some small town and a young guy said, "Come with us. My brother-in-law has a hotel, you can stay with us." At the same time, another person was saying, "No, no, come with us, use our hotel." Soon the argument escalated into a full-blown fist-fight.

Finally, I threw up my hands and said, "We're not going with any of you guys if you're going to fight over us. Forget it." We walked off in the other direction, where we ran into more people, all of whom wanted to take us to their brother-in-law's house. Obviously, they were going get a commission from bringing a paying customer into the hotels. The result is that if one is at the center of these arguments, the prices offered will de-escalate downward, to almost nothing in American dollars. We were fortunate to run into that all the time (not the fights), and we stayed at some very nice places along the way for a song. We also stayed at backpackers' places, which can be found everywhere.

For all of the goodwill we encountered, we felt at times as if we were walking on egg shells, hoping to avoid the areas where the violence was raging. The authorities did not close off travel to foreigners – not with so much tourist money invested in trips to the Taj Mahal. But they widely closed off any travel north of New Delhi to Punjab. So we went in the other direction, moving south to Agra – where the Taj Mahal is located.

It was here that we spent New Year's Eve. We had taken one set of dress clothes with us, and now was the time to break them out and live 'high on the hog.' We found a place near the Taj Mahal where there were many people in tuxedos and long elegant saris, the traditional wrap-around dress of Indian women. The charge was the equivalent of ten dollars per person, which only the well-to-do in India can afford, but clearly, a great value for a visitor. For the ten bucks you got an all-you-can-eat meal and drinks, and dancing until the wee hours.

And we became the floor show. We were out there dancing up a storm, and I was twirling my lady around, just having a ball. At midnight, after they counted down to the new year, they made an announcement that, "We've been having a secret dance contest, and we've been secretly judging you all night." Then they said, "And the prize goes to the American couple." I looked around and said, "I didn't see too many Americans out there." And she whispered, "I think they mean us." Just then, we were being motioned to the stage. Seeing my bewilderment, they said, "Yes, yes, come up," and we were given two Swiss watches. There was just one catch. They said, "In order to collect your presents, you have to do a dance for us. Do you want a slow dance or a fast dance?" She said a slow dance, so they turned out the lights and shone a spot light on us, and we did a waltz. Halfway through, I motioned for everybody to come and dance with us, and they all did.

The next day out on a golf course, the pro came up and said, "Say, didn't you win a dance contest last night?" Which was amazing because he hadn't even been there. Word sure got around fast. Maybe it was in the local paper. Whatever, we had become somewhat like visiting celebrities. What was all that fame really worth? Heaps in my memory, but not enough to get a free round of golf out of it.

Next on the journey south came the old Portuguese colony of Goa, where there is a profusion of stately old Catholic churches and comparable architecture, the sight of which is a formidable contrast with the Hindu temples in the rest of India and in the entire region of southern Asia. One would almost swear you're in Mexico by the adobe arches and sweeping verandas. In fact, the surprising thing about India – and as I would come to see, in nearly all of the Third World – is that things are rarely as they had been depicted to us back home. Perhaps the best example of this is how we got around Goa those few days – on rented motorcycles, after spotting a motorcycle place right in the middle of town.

* * *

A word to the wise: since there are generally no price tags in developing countries, always ask the price first, no matter how small the item. If you ask they will give a price. Then work down from there. I can't paint a picture about how to go about playing – and winning – the dickering game with the locals, but I can give a diagram of the parameters:

1. Think of what they want you to pay – as eye level.

2. What you want to pay – chest level.

3. Where you are after bargaining – somewhere around the neck.

4. What the locals would pay – knee to ankle level.

5. What they will charge if you forgot to ask the price beforehand, and you went ahead and received, say, a cab ride or a meal – above the top of your head.

Remember this: a merchant is going to ask you to pay at eye level and you're going to want to pay down at chest level. And if you didn't ask before you consumed, the price is above your head — maybe way above. And that price you cannot bargain from, since you cannot give the merchandise or service back. You didn't ask, so they figure you don't really care. And if they get a cop to enforce that price, that cop will take you down to the station and he will get something extra for himself, just for the inconvenience. If they have to lock you up for a little while, just to make you think about it, they'll do it in a heartbeat.

You win the game if you can keep your gaze on the 'strike zone' – knees to chest. If it helps, think "Roger Clemens, Roger Clemens" over and over.

* * *

The biggest thing learned upon my first sight of India was the long-delayed potential it has to become a thriving country. For many years, the incongruity was that the nation with the second largest population on Earth – 1.1 billion people in 2006 – had one of the world's worst standards of living. Yet, I saw signs of a sea of change, in its people. There was an eagerness to serve and to get ahead, with people hustling all the time, committed to providing for their families, and educating themselves to hold good, stable jobs. The economy of India is today the fourth largest in the world, with a gross domestic product (GDP) of $3.63 trillion in U.S. dollars. Full development won't come about right away. But in the far foreseeable future, it will happen. They're getting there, because they're working hard to get ahead.

A question to make the point: If asked which country on the planet makes the most motion pictures each year, what would you say? It would have to be America, right? Except that it's not. Not even close. The correct answer is...India. Movie billboards, in fact, are everywhere. Cinema production is based in Mumbai, where they produce mainly commercial Hindi films. This operation is referred to as "Bollywood." There are also strong cinema industries based on the Bengali, Malayalam, Kannada, Tamil and Telugu languages. Think about how much a "blockbuster" makes in a population almost four times that of the U.S.!

Seeing the potential for India to at least become 'Second World,' I did whatever possible, sharing expertise I had, explaining how things worked in my country and how they could be applied in India. Most people in India speak at least some English, as they were once the jewel of the British Empire. They are also fairly well versed in events happening in America. This is also true, I found out later, for most countries. They all know much more about us than we do about them. I sat for long hours in give-and-take discussions about politics – far more learned and civilized discussions, I might add, than I might have thought back home.

Of course, not all the stereotypes are wrong. In India and neighboring Nepal, we saw many beggars on the streets. After all, there is still rampant poverty in this part of the world. You can't pretend otherwise. Even so, I was convinced that India was on its way to fruition. In the twenty years since being there, it has fulfilled a great deal of the promise

I saw. The gap between rich and poor isn't as wide, and the imbalance between the two not as stark.

Yet, its national pride is such that every effort is made to preserve its established traditions and way of life. In America, the lyric sung so famously by Joni Mitchell – "They paved paradise and put up a parking lot" – is a sad but perfect metaphor. In India, it would be unheard of. It is a land of sacred cows, but also some rivers and islands are sacred, as well. Yes, the cows do roam around freely. I have seen cows in an ally ever so gently shooed away by an elderly lady with a broom, just to let local cars pass.

When I come back, it will be to celebrate another New Year, and dance again with people who earned their place on the world stage.

* * *

Nepal, $1 = 72 Nepalese Rupees

Nepal had a longer way to a modern-day conversion. Just as in India, this rectangular shaped sliver of land along India's northeast border buffering China was suffering growing pains after the splintering of the monarchical governments of the past. Pains that would only grow worse. In fact, a quarter-century after I was there, on June 1, 2001, the Heir Apparent to the Nepalese throne, a fellow named Dipendra, reportedly went on a killing spree in the royal palace. This was in response to his parents' rejection of his choice of wife. His parents were killed along with many others, and he died 3 days later. The details of this incident are still shrouded in mystery.

Nearly eighty percent of the population of 22 million people in this predominantly Hindu country exist below the poverty line. And its lack of natural resources, landlocked location, technological backwardness and a long-running civil war with Maoist rebels have also prevented Nepal from fully developing its economy.

While we were there, in January of 1985, we heard tales of a beggar's mentality. Sometimes beggars will put their children to work as beggars, as well. And this defeatist way of thinking goes beyond sad, when a parent might even disfigure a child by cutting off a limb – just so it will be a 'better' beggar. More income for the family coffers. I made it my business not to get involved in people's begging. As one of the natives explained to me, "You Westerners are nice people, but your hearts are in the wrong place. If you give someone five dollars, that person will never work again because he'll just wait and wait for another white person to come around and give him another five dollars. It is a tremendous disincentive to work."

This is because five dollars to us is, well, five dollars. But five dollars to them might have the purchasing power of hundreds of dollars in their local economy. Because they get by on so little, giving them just a little pocket change actually is a lot of money to them. So you have to temper your sense of goodness. You can give people hope, give people encouragement, give people ideas, give people a helping hand – but don't give beggars money, because it defeats the whole purpose. Buy a small trinket instead. You keep an artist employed, help the local economy, and actually have a nice souvenir to take home to show friends. With begging, it is buying pity. Not really helpful.

Nepal is synonymous with mountains, most famously the barren and arid Himalayas. Lesser known are the low ranges in the hilly belt of the Kathmandu Valley. This is the country's most fertile and urbanized area that includes the political and cultural center of Nepal – the capital city of Kathmandu. For experienced hikers, of course, the challenge is to scale the peaks of the world's highest mountain, Mount Everest ('Sagarmatha' in Nepali), which rises 8,850 meters high along the border with Tibet. But dedicated climbers will also look further, as eight of the world's ten highest mountains are located in Nepal.

I took my mandatory hike up one of the ranges near Kathmandu, where we stayed. Mounting my way up thousands of steps, upon reaching the zenith, there was a wonderful Hindu temple overlooking the valley. Completely out of breath, and while kneeling on one knee waiting for my heart rate to return to normal, I looked up and saw a boy whose face was alarmingly disfigured. His lower lip was deformed to the point of being non-existent, and he was begging for money. Adhering to what I had been told about the beggars, I at first refused, but he wouldn't take no for an answer. He was getting right in my face. This, I realized, was his act: grossing people out until they gave him money. So I gave in, just to get rid of him. He immediately ran and dropped the coin with the sound of a clank into the family pot. If he could get cash from me, he must be the cream of his profession. In the game of begging, everybody's got their own little angle.

Another time, we decided to ride motorcycles to the border of Tibet, the annexed plateau province of China. A German traveler teamed up with the group, and came along as well. We made it all the way out to the Kanma border, and even crossed into Tibet. We wound up on roads that were impassable for cars, even four-wheel drives, because of the many gullies that turned the road into something of a roller coaster ride. We could just about navigate the gullies with the bikes, by walking them down one side of the gullies and running along side and gunning the engine on the way back up the other side. This was the main road to Tibet, and it was just then being upgraded to accommodate cars, instead of just foot traffic. Finally, we made it back to Kathmandu by nightfall, though we were freezing. Being so high in altitude, Nepal is very bright during the day. At night, it cools off immensely.

The next day we went southward, to the Royal Chitwan National Park, a magnificent 932 square mile tract of forests and private land in the subtropical lowlands of the inner Terai region. The area was declared Mahendra Deer Park by the late King Mahendra in 1959. Soon after, south of the Rapti River was demarcated as a rhinoceros sanctuary. Recognizing its unique ecosystems of international significance, UNESCO declared Royal Chitwan a World Heritage Site in 1984.

We decided to take a public bus to get there, and when we hopped it we had it pretty much to ourselves. Fairly soon though, as the driver let on more and more passengers, the bus was packed like a can of sardines. We could not breathe; the air was thick and smelled as horrible as all the tiny people packed around us. I saw that there was a ladder attached to the side of the bus and I asked the driver, "Is there any way we can go sit up on top?" He said, "Sure, go ahead." He stopped the bus and we climbed the ladder on the side of the bus. The passengers surely thought we were insane. Their gaze was riveted to us, especially since my German friend and I were like something they'd never seen before: two white guys each about six and a half feet tall – just like super-heroes, we laughed to ourselves later.

Up on top, we saw huge bags of rice, a couple of goats, and more than a couple of chickens all clustered with their feet tied together. So we had gone from the smell of pent-up people to the smell of pent-up goats and chickens. It was a toss-up which was worse. But at least we had the fresh air all around us up there. We used the bags of rice as a windbreaker, sitting behind them as the bus rolled through the mountain roads, to the accompaniment of chickens clucking and goats baying. We were well aware that buses in Nepal were notoriously unsafe, and sometimes were apt to fall down a cliff as they are riding along. So we made a contingency plan: if the bus fell off a cliff that was on the the left, we'd jump to the right, and vice versa. Why not? We were super-heroes.

Chitwan is a huge tourist attraction, but I never was keen to pay tourist prices. They want you to pay up to fifty dollars to ride an elephant in the National Park. In a place like Nepal, I could travel for a week on that amount. The objective should be to pay what the locals are paying. We simply contacted the young guys who took care of the elephants. I asked one, "When do you feed the elephants?" He said, "At seven in the morning." I said, "If we got here at seven tomorrow, can we help you feed them?" He leaped at the thought. "Sure," he replied, "just give us a tip, and we'll even let you ride them." You know, he had a great idea there.

So we got there early the next morning and gave these guys a little something for themselves and their families. They are regular employees who don't get anything except a minuscule salary. They were overjoyed, and we got to ride these marvelous creatures through the jungle, looking down from on high at rhinoceroses and all manner of exotic animals. Riding atop an elephant reminds you of how unbelievably strong they are. They literally will make their own path through the jungle. Yes, by the way, there are jungles in Nepal, not just mountains. The south bordering India even has a 'Serengeti Plain' type look to it – with grass huts, to boot. If an elephant comes upon a tree in its way, the handler will give it a verbal command, and it will wrap its trunk around the tree trunk and just tear the tree to the side, then just keep on going. It's something like a New York City cab driver, the difference being that the latter will wrap his front fender around anything that gets in the way.

* * *

Wherever the road would wind, we stayed at small hotels or rooming houses. This is one of my own hard and fast rules of travel. Some may think of this as 'roughing it.' However, pointing out the obvious, you are perfectly welcome to go to a Sheraton or a Marriott and spend seventy-five, one hundred, even two hundred a night for a room. Or you can go right across the street and get a lesser-known hotel for half that price.

Or you can go around the corner to a 'word of mouth' lodging and spend five or ten dollars a night. It is up to each individual.

What's more, don't think the last means staying in a rat-hole. Some of the rooms I've called home are nearly on a par with those Sheratons, sans the exorbitant room service and swimming pools (which, as you will see a bit later, are not totally inaccessible). In over twenty-five years of travel, I have stayed at 'luxury' hotels maybe a handful of times, opting instead for a small hotel – that is if I'm not utilizing my sleeping bag or my tent. And in all that time, not often have I ever encountered a problem. On the contrary, the friendships made hanging with the natives is a priceless reward in itself. And they will lead to being told of – or even invited to – some of the best bargains found in food, lodging, transit, just about anything. For me, the bottom line is that, sure, I can stay in an American version of somewhere else, but prefer to go where there are regular local people. If I want to go see Americans, why would I be tens of thousands of miles from the USA? It's not just a matter of taking in the local color; I want to fit into the local color, live with it, be it.

Okay, so that means living with tons of the local insects in your bed at night, right? Again, going by my own experience, there is only one time I can recall where I even had to think about critters. In Goa, India there was a religious festival going on with hordes of people streaming in, and all the hotels were booked solid. So the restaurants pulled out mats and let people sleep on the floor, including us. And that was the only time I've ever really encountered a few cockroaches as up-close neighbors. And they were big three inch monsters, to boot!

One night in Nepal, we were walking around and it had gotten dark and we were lost. We stopped at a farmer's house and knocked on the door. When he opened it, I explained that we needed a place for the night and that we had cash. I pulled out some money and said, "Would this much be okay?" And he nodded, "Yes, this much is good." And I handed him him the equivalent of what back home would have been pocket change, which thrilled him to no end. We stayed in his house and in the morning he gave us breakfast.

In the barnyard there was a rooster, which was to be the guest of honor at tonight's dinner. The farmer chopped off its head, and held it down until it stopped moving. He then poured hot water on the feathers, which made them stand straight up for easy plucking, then sliced and diced and chopped it into quarters. This all happened in about two minutes, and it looked like something one could find in a fine grocery store: a leg here, a thigh there, all cleaned and ready to go. It couldn't have been a more professional job.

More details about how to stretch money on a journey through the Third World are ahead, once getting into more extensive, and intensive, trips to Central America and Africa. The point to be imparted now is that it's not difficult to enjoy the luxuries of any stay in any foreign land, for pennies on the dollar. I won't say you can travel, say, Kenya, on a dollar a day. But it's not that far from the truth, either. The key element to keep in mind is not to be afraid of getting more information from the locals, who basically know there are high profit margins when dealing with unknowing Westerners. On balance, a lack of timidity will take you a long way. But always remember to be gracious.

* * *

Thailand, $1 = 36 Baht

In Thailand ninety-two percent of the country is Buddhist, and Bangkok is home to some 400 Buddhist temples. This ancient beauty contrasts with modern realities. The most telltale sign of the 'new' Bangkok was the thick smoke coming out of the autos, trucks and taxis on the bustling streets – an unwelcome example of how gentrification spews pollution. Like an ink blot, the urban sprawl – and dirty air – of

Bangkok spills beyond the greater Bangkok Metropolitan Area, which now teems with over 6 million people.

The first thing that happened upon entering Bangkok was that I got sick from all the smoky, foul, dank, humid air. But the pollution and humidity of Thailand aren't nearly as stomach-turning as a different form of annoyance – scams. The desire to rip off tourists is what sticks in my mind about Thailand. It seemed scams were being perpetuated everywhere. Westerners have been robbed of their dollars over the years, not usually in armed robberies, but in different more deviant ways.

Which is why I was asking for it when, on a lark, deciding the first night in Bangkok to do the 'when in Rome' thing. After weeks of living with ascetics in India, I reasoned it was time for something a little more arousing. That meant going to the infamous Red Light District. Bangkok has earned an unenviable reputation as one of the most depraved places in the world, which granted is taking in a lot of territory. Prostitution is openly negotiated on the streets, back alleys, musky bars, massage parlors, saunas, parks, and hourly hotels along a thoroughfare called Pat-pong Road. It is modeled on the famous Red Light District of Amsterdam, but with no behavior seemingly regarded as taboo. Indeed, Amsterdam's sex trade seems like a Mormon convention compared with the muck and mire of Bangkok.

It is estimated that some 300,000 women and children are involved in the sex trade. Some are ethic Chinese nationals seeking a better life in Southeast Asia. They have no money, and many have lost their families – or have been sold off by them. They march through malaria-infested jungles in Laos and Burma, and then ride in cramped vans into the big city. There, pimps and other shady characters bargain for their ownership and services. Some women will be traded as much as seven to ten times between pimps and criminal gangs.

This ugly reality is the product of two inherent conditions: Thailand's high poverty rate that breeds desperation even at the cost of selling their own children's bodies, and the bustling market of wealthy Westerners eager to have sex with young, and younger girls. Not that this practice is legal in Thailand, but the money flow – complete with kickbacks to the local police – is just too abundant to enforce laws against such 'victimless' crimes. Which of course are anything but victimless, corrupting and destroying the lives of thousands of young girls. Academic studies have valued the trade as being worth more than 100 billion baht (US$2.5 billion) a year, one third the size of the construction or agricultural cropping industries. A good chunk of that comes from the profusion of organized 'sex tours' arranged for Western businessmen by local hustlers in concert with club owners and pimps.

How ugly is the situation? Consider that not only are young girls abused by this atrocious trade, but in many cases young boys are as well. They become pimps – sometimes for their own sisters – at equally young ages. Walk along Pat-pong Road and you will see cliques of these young boys scurrying around, hustling johns with come-on pitches, haggling with them over price. If we are in the last throes of civilization as we know it, the end will be hastened by what goes on in the depths of the hell on Pat-pong Road.

When deciding to check out the Red Light District, I was as naive as anyone. I had been to Amsterdam and while not partaking in the action, the entire milieu was exciting, but unyieldingly adult, with age of consent laws strictly enforced by the Dutch authorities. Bangkok, I discovered, was something entirely different, and disturbing. In retrospect, the conditions were all in place for the most tawdry of activities, most notably in the rip-off attitudes of the bar owners and the hands-off compliance of the police to keep things spiraling. The reptilian nature of business became instantly obvious when I journeyed with three of my Australian mates to Pat-pong Road, again, not to do anything untoward but to watch, listen, learn.

We went from place to place asking how much does it cost to get in, the cover charge, how much is a beer, and so on. We decided on a small cafe where we were told there was no cover charge and a beer would cost the equivalent of about two dollars. We went in, sat down in a room well attended by Westerners, mainly Germans, judging from the accents I heard. Not really prepared for what went on in these joints, we watched in astonishment as on a small stage in front of us, young women performed acts that defied the laws of gravity and biology. The act culminated with a tourist having sex with one of the women on stage. Talk about audience participation.

During the show young ladies would come to our table, sit in our laps, play with our chests and rub our crotches as they coyly asked if we wanted to come back into private rooms with them, or at least buy them a drink. We demurred on both counts, as their drinks had no price tags and could be assumed to be inordinately expensive. Yet, even though we had begged off of buying any drinks, somehow by the end of the show there were about twenty shot glasses on our table. This was in itself a rather amazing feat, a real sleight of hand trick worked in tandem by the girls and the bartender while they'd been distracting us. And I knew what it would mean. "I bet they're going to try to make us pay for these," I told my friends. Our trick was how to get out of there without being ripped off.

"Are you guys ready to leave?" I said under my breath, anticipating a quick getaway. We'd had one beer each, and at the price we'd been quoted, that added up to eight dollars. I pulled a ten out of my shirt pocket and we all stood up to go. Just then, as if on cue, the waiter appeared. "Here's ten dollars," I said, "keep the change." As we started walking for the door, the waiter put up his arm. "No, here's your bill," he said with a smile as he handed me a bill for $168! I could hardly believe it. "That is someone else's bill," I said, knowing we hadn't been quick enough – and likely couldn't have been even if we were world-class sprinters.

He insisted that the bill was right. I said, "What about the cover charge? You told us there was no cover charge." Still smiling that oily smile, he said, "Oh no, there is a cover charge. Can't you see it written down here," pointing to a tiny, barely visible sign on the wall, placed in the most obscure spot possible. He went on, "And what about all those drinks you bought for those girls?" I said, "We didn't buy any drinks for those girls." Without arguing the point, he did what he no doubt had been trained to do, and had done a thousand times – he started negotiating. Which meant lowering the sky-high rip-off price to a lower rip-off price.

"No," I said firmly, by now the stigma of being caught in a scam dissolving into anger about it, "here's your ten dollars," and we went for the door. But it was locked. And out of nowhere about a dozen small but wiry Asian guys in kickboxing outfits emerged, and stood face to face with us four big white Westerners. It was *Gunfight at the O.K. Corral* transferred to a Bruce Lee movie.

No false bravado on my part, but I believe any other person would have panicked in that situation and gave these crooks as much money as they could just to get the door open. I'm not a tough guy nor especially fearsome, but I am big. And – as you will find at various stages of this book – tend to stand my ground when my dignity is being violated, no matter where or how. I've found that the worst thing you can betray when in such situations is fear, and the scent of fear will be picked up by predators and will make you a target. In every culture, respect that you earn will work in your favor. There are exceptions, of course, when discretion – or a fast U-turn away from trouble – is the better part of survival. This, however, wasn't one of those times.

Refusing to panic, I said to the waiter and the Bruce Lee clones, "You know guys, it looks like we're not gonna get out of here tonight. But it also looks like you're not gonna get any other customers coming in here, either. It's gonna be a standoff and you're gonna lose money because no one else is gonna be coming through that door. As a matter of fact, I'm gonna tell every white face in here that you're gonna extort more money from them on the way out." Sometimes ya gotta talk like dat.

Having talked the talk, I then went up and down the aisles telling the German couples that they were going to be a target of extortion on the way out. And when our gracious hosts saw that a lot of the other tourists were looking a bit peeved, the waiter went back to the negotiating tactic. He worked his way down from 168 to 92 to 75 dollars, trying to get as much as they could from us. I kept saying, "Forget it, ten dollars, that's how much it is." And so we stood there for a few uneasy minutes, toe to toe, with the equally trapped Germans saying that they too weren't going to get ripped off. The crooks cracked first – the only thing they could do, or else risk a riot. They agreed to take the ten dollars. Still, I wasn't letting my guard down.

"Open the door first," I said.

"No, first pay the money," came the reply.

We went back and forth on that issue as I held out the ten dollar bill. The waiter reached, got his fingers almost around it, when I pulled it back, just to make sure the door was open. He then went and unlocked it and I dismissively flicked the ten dollar bill at him, adding a parting verbal shot: "We're leaving, but were going straight to the police."

He grinned more defiantly than before. "We own the police in this town," he said smugly. It was, again, like a really bad movie. But it was one with a happy ending.

* * *

Before leaving Thailand, in the northern area outside of the city of Chang Mai, I found myself standing squarely in the 'Golden Triangle', region where Thailand intersects with Laos and Burma (now Myanmar). This happens to be where a good percentage of all the world's opium is produced. Some Australians and myself went on a tour that included a boat ride, an elephant trip, and a trek through the jungle. On the first third of the trip, the boat once stopped right in the middle of the river because the water was a little low at that point. So we had to actually get out and push the boat. Once we were able to push it out into the deeper water, we then got back in and continued on our merry way.

Right after we brought it in to shore, we got on large Asian elephants and rode them through the jungle. We had three elephants following each other down the path, and were riding in a basket on the elephant's back. Well, that didn't quite make it for me. First, I prefer driving elephants to riding in the 'rumble seat.' Second, with the elephant's shoulders lumbering from side to side, I was getting sea-sick up there in the first five minutes. I wasn't going to last long on this thing, so I tapped the driver on the shoulder. "Is there any chance we could switch places?" I asked. He agreed, and he got into the basket and I straddled the elephant's neck with one leg on either side. And I got to drive the elephant, which the elephant liked, too. As I'd found out in India and Nepal, elephants are happy when there are no sticks beating them.

When the elephants stopped, we got off and found the hill tribes village where we met with the natives and hung out in little huts that are propped up on stilts. This is to prevent flooding in heavy jungle rains. So we were up there in one of those stilted huts watching a young girl dancing to the music of an old lady playing a flute. Have you ever felt like a sultan? That was the feeling I got when another young village girl brought me a pillow to sit on. Or at least I thought it was a pillow. It was actually a bag full of marijuana, or ganja, as they say locally. They also brought out their locally harvested opium, as well.

I'll just repeat my favorite adage: when in Rome do as the Romans do. And, today, the Romans were smoking the opium pipe. It did not have a bowl, but rather a rounded ball with a little hole. For those with some expertise on these things, it wasn't a hookah pipe, which filters opium with water. This was just a simple little bamboo shaft attached to a little ball at the end. The opium is like a paste and spread on the ball around the hole, then you light that thing up. I'd never experienced opium before, so this would be an adventure. The last part of that picturesque tour was a hike through the jungle to get back to where we started, and we were laughing and having the time of our lives as we went, happy as a lark. We were literally skipping through the jungle half the time.

We came to a waterfall and went swimming underneath it. We took pictures of us and the beautiful Japanese girls and beautiful native Thai girls that were all with us on the tour. This is what paradise is all about, the experience was so good and so unique. Just as any other similar experiences, I will do practically anything the natives do, at least once, within reason.

* * *

Against my usual rule of never eating at a Western restaurant while in the Third World, I agreed to have at least one meal at a McDonald's in Bangkok with an Australian mate of mine named Phil who'd also been traveling through Thailand. We both had been eating local, native food for months now and needed a taste of the Western world. Then, too, with everybody and his brother seemingly coming up to you on the streets asking for money, it can get a little bit intimidating. In a place like McDonald's you can sit in a relatively calm place and clear your head. In the middle of our meal, a young Thai man sitting next to us struck up a conversation, saying, "Oh, you guys are Westerners" – not a difficult guess since we were the only tall white guys in the place.

"Yes, we are – and we don't have any money. So don't even bother asking us," I said, my coarseness caused by the experience in the Red Light District that made me extremely jaded about all the begging and scams around me.

"Oh, no problem," he said. "Oh, by the way, do you guys like beer?"

"Yeah, we like beer."

"Have you guys ever been in a movie or a commercial?"

"No."

"Would you like to be in a commercial while you're here?"

This was a good one, I thought. Again, I reiterated, "We don't have any money."

"No, this would pay you money."

"Oh really?"

"Yes, we have a beer, the local Singha beer of Thailand, and they want to market it for export to the outside world. And they need some Westerners to be in some commercials. Can you ride a motorbike?"

"Yeah."

"Do you like pretty girls?"

"Who doesn't?"

"Great. If you do this thirty-second commercial, just say 'Singha beer is great,' then drive off into the sunset on a motorcycle with a beautiful Thai girl on the back. They will pay you money for that, and they will pay you royalties every three months for a year." I must admit I was a little intrigued, although my gut still told me it was a con. But it could be an adventure. So I went along, telling the guy okay, as long as we don't have to invest any money because we didn't have any. He reassured us it didn't matter, and we went outside and got into a taxi cab with him. He took us to the other side of Bangkok and we waited in an office for the 'producer' to come, as the man kept telling us. He even opened us some bottles of Singha beer to drink. So the whole thing looked like it could be legitimate.

As we were sitting around drinking beer, I noticed there was a pack of cards on the table. And within seconds, the guy asked, "Do you like to play blackjack?" I said yes. He then explained that there was a game in Thailand called pontoon, which is very similar to blackjack, but it also combines the action of a poker game where you can build a pot. He claimed he'd been a croupier at a very plush government casino in Singapore, and that he'd made a lot of money down there.

All of a sudden, red lights began to flash in my head, along with the growl in my gut. As it happened, I had recently read that there is no gambling in Singapore because the government there is very strict about such vices. I told myself that for the rest of the time I'd be with this fellow, he was going to lie to me. Still, I was into this caper, and wanted to see how far it would go.

He then proceeded to tell me that he would work with a man from Switzerland, and they had a system where they could always win at pontoon. That while he was dealing, he could spy the opponent's face-down card, and he would communicate with his accomplice using a combination of his fingers and knuckles on the table. Meaning that it would be virtually impossible to lose. But I knew he was telling me about his 'foolproof' system of cheating, only to draw me into a 'sting.' However, Phil had this look of complete fascination, and I thought he could use a good James Bond kind of adventure. So I waded further into the plot, waiting for the right moment to cut bait.

He continued, "I know a guy around here, and if you guys are interested, he's a wealthy businessman from China and he's a real a-hole. He never tips me at the table. If I got him here we could take a lot of money from him and split it." Again, like a broken record, I said we didn't have any money, and again he said no problem. And now it really got interesting.

"Here's 200 US dollars, put it in your wallet right now," he instructed. I did and he made a phone call. He then said that a wealthy Chinese businessman would come over in the next fifteen minutes, and we would get a game going and make as much money as we possibly could. Now I was intrigued just where this was going.

While waiting for the arrival, the Thai hustler explained that I'd play one-on-one against the businessman, who would be the house bank. Hand signals would tip off what the businessman had. Then, when we were about to play the last pot of the night, he'd tell me what to do with a simple utterance: "Would you like a cup of coffee?" That would mean I was to bet everything on that hand.

The 'pigeon' came over, right on time and ready to play some pontoon, for big stakes. He had a briefcase obviously full of cash. The hustler took up his position as dealer and asked me how many chips I wanted. I said $200 worth of chips and pulled out the money he'd given me. The Chinese businessman took from his briefcase a roll of bills and said, "I'll take $3000, please." But was it really $3,000? The roll of bills was wrapped in a rubber band, so you couldn't see what was inside the hundred dollar bill wrapper.

"Are you going to count that?" I asked.

"Oh, no, it's an insult to count it," my 'friend' replied, looking offended. "He is a very honorable man. This is a very honorable profession in our country. Do not question him, he has been a regular here for a long time." So it was his word for it. That was another alarm bell. As was the fact that, within twenty minutes, I had won most of his chips on my own. Far too easily, I believed, to be on the up and up.

The next hand, my two cards totaled 14. The businessman's up card was a 10. The dealer was signaling that the down card was also a 10, and that meant that his total was 20. "Hit me," I said, and he gave me a 7. What luck! My 21 beats his 20. If only all this was for real.

Then came the words I'd been waiting for: "Mister Christopher, would you like a cup of coffee?" Bingo! I was to bet my entire winnings – $3,000. I said no thanks to the coffee and re-checked my hand. "I'd like to bet it all," I duly intoned, pushing my pile of chips into the middle of the table.

That's when the Chinese man's eyes perked to attention. He was looking at the table, looking at all the cards, apparently lost in thought. Then he said, "Okay, I see you – and I raise you," pulling from his bag $50,000 in US currency! It was a stack with a hundred dollar bill on the top and bottom, and about three inches worth of hundred dollar bills (so he said) wrapped like a brick with rubber bands.

Now, knowing the fix was in, I wasn't going to bow to his 'status.' I told him, "Obviously, sir, you can't just pull out more money like this, because I don't have any more money to bet. I can't possibly win if you keep raising above what is on the table. In Las Vegas, Monte Carlo, wherever, you play with the money showing. You can see me, not raise me."

Ready for this, my con man just tried to placate me. "Take the bet," he whispered, as though I were to understand the pot was in the bag. "No thank you," I said calmly. Meanwhile, several other associates of the Thai hustler who we had met earlier were all trying to get me to equal the bet. "No. I don't have that kind of money."

"We can work something out," the con man said. He tried to hand me a piece of paper. "Just write that you owe $50,000 and sign it and put it in the pot. No problem." He was getting a little frayed, as if I didn't know why. "No thank you," I said again. By now, even my friend Phil wanted me to do it. He was nudging me in the ribs with his elbow and saying "Go for it, Christopher! Sign the I.O.U."

"No thank you," I maintained. With that, I quit [who won the game?] and got up and walked into the bathroom. When I came out, they were pressuring Phil to sign in my place and take over my hand, anything to keep the farce going. I said, "Lets get out of here." As we walked out, and down the street, having not a clue as to where we were, he was still bewildered by what I'd done. "How could you walk away from $50,000?" he asked. "That would help buy a house back home."

"Because I knew it was a scam. All I had to do was sign that paper and throw it in the pot. And if he flips over an ace for his down card, his natural two-card 21 beats my three-card 21. And all of a sudden instead of being a very rich man, I then owe a lot of money."

Phil said, "Well, if they pulled a scam, we could have just run out of there." I laughed, "Run to where?" And the next thing out of that guy's briefcase isn't a stack of cash – it's a gun! And they'll hold one of us there until the other guy can come up with some kind of money, just to make things go away. And that's when people come out of the woodwork, a whole mess of other people, intimidating people.

We got home that night by taxi. And when leaving Thailand I had the satisfaction of surviving against Bangkok rip-off artists, with my life intact. All in all, it was a helpful hint that there would be similar challenges in the future.

A postscript: years later, a Dutch man shared a plane ride with me, and related that a friend of his had been stung in Thailand for something like ten thousand dollars. A slap of recognition hit me. "How did it happen?" I asked, and he said that the friend was so embarrassed that he didn't even want to talk about it. But he knew it was something about a card game.

"I know exactly what happened to him, as I know the people he was dealing with," I said, and proceeded to tell him how his friend lost ten thousand bucks. This may be a big, wide world. But when it comes to the scam artists of Bangkok, the world might as well be one small room with a deck of cards on a table.

* * *

Cambodia, $1 = 4000 Riel

A bus eastward from Bangkok took me to the border of Cambodia. At the time, no tourists were allowed into Cambodia. In the 1970s the communist Khmer Rouge had conducted a genocide of at least a million people, while forcing mass evacuations of people from the cities out into rural areas. Thereafter, civil war and unimaginable torture and death raged in the killing fields through the seventies and eighties.

Upon reaching the border, a democratic monarchy was still twelve years away, and while the fratricide had died down a bit, it was nowhere near over. In fact, the Khmer Rouge, though dislodged from the government, had not yet ended its terror reign. They were still scattered in the jungle and still a force to be reckoned with. There were scores of refugee camps along the border because people were afraid to go too far into the country.

With a thirst for adventure and observation, and wanting to perform some form of humanitarian service, I wanted to brook the danger, and at the very least to go to some of these refugee camps. But without an official organization's sponsorship, the border guards weren't going to let anyone across. Down the roads and into the jungle one could see machine gun nests beyond the border. Mine fields were all around the area. The best that I could do was rent a motorcycle in a small border town in Thailand and cruise around, looking perhaps for some way that was either unfenced or unmined to safely stray across the border.

For a while I hung out at the doorstep of Cambodia, listening to stories of those who had escaped the gunfire in the distance, and hearing rockets bursting in the air where there was still scattered fighting. Another example of mankind's utter stupidity. Like the old folk song says: when will they ever learn? In the case of Cambodia, where grandeur was replaced by bankrupt notions of violence, it would be another twelve years before they did.

* * *

Malaysia, $1 = 3.6 Ringgit

We then took the train south through Malaysia down to Singapore at the very bottom of the Asian continent. Both countries can be very strict places. They take their laws seriously. At the border of Malaysia, there is a sign reading: "Drug smuggling is a capital offense in Malaysia. DEATH TO ALL DRUG SMUGGLERS. Remember, you have been warned." Another sign next to it read: "Bonafide tourists are more than welcome in Malaysia, but hippies are not."

That got me to thinking. When was the last time I ever saw the word 'hippies' used in an official context? I couldn't remember where or when in America, but in Malaysia time seemed to run a couple of decades behind. Helpfully, the sign went on to define: "If you are of unkempt or scraggly appearance, you will be asked to leave Malaysia."

While we were on the train, a man explained the protocols of the dreaded hippie status, for which one can be denied a normal 90 day tourist visa, and will be ushered out of the country, unceremoniously. "They will give you the option of getting a shave and a haircut right there at the border," he explained, "If not, they'll give you a 24 hour transit visa and let you ride the train – straight through to Singapore. But they will stamp on your passport: SUSPECTED HIPPIE IN TRANSIT." You may have already deduced that the acronym for that is S.H.I.T., and they line it up so as to have maximum effect. That can work in two opposing ways. For some, it will have the intended effect of stigmatization. For others, it is a priceless cultural badge of honor.

The reason for the Malaysians' extreme paranoia about 'hippies' is that they freely associate any counter-culture lifestyle with drug trafficking, which is a crime in the country on the same level as murder. They will make an example out of any case of drug smuggling. A few years after my visit, there was a huge cause celebre when two Australians were caught smuggling drugs and were sentenced to be executed – the first Westerners ever convicted of the crime there. In Australia, there was an uproar, with the prime minister and even the Queen of England writing letters to the Malaysian government begging to spare the two men's lives. In the end, however, they were hung from the gallows. To the Malaysians, there is no mercy for drug dealers, period. Everybody knows it. I wouldn't recommend taking the challenge of trying to get away with it.

In Malaysia, I was intrigued at how they have remained peaceful and live in common cause despite a huge cleft in religious identity. Given all the sectarian violence in many Third World countries, Malaysia gets along split nearly equally in thirds, between the Malays who practice Islam, the Chinese who are Buddhist, and the Indians who are Hindu. It's officially an Islamic country but there seems no tension between religions. In fact, some folks even sang Christmas carols when I was there! The rest of the world could learn a whole lot about living in peace and harmony from the example of a developing nation such as Malaysia.

Outside of the Malaysian capital city of Kuala Lumpur, there happens to be a little Hindu temple up in a local mountain. I went up to see it, and got myself a coconut to take along. They sell these big green coconuts, slice off the top, poke hole in it and stick in a straw. In tropical lands, it's a popular alternative to the globally ubiquitous Coca-Cola. I was sipping from it very contentedly while climbing up the mountain steps, glad I had gotten it because it was a steaming hot day. Halfway up, a group of four of five wild monkeys came out of nowhere and actually jumped me, screaming like banshees and scaring the heck out of me!

Reflexively, I dropped my coconut, which clearly was what the monkeys wanted. They seemed ready for just that possibility, since one of them picked it up and ran away with it! Yes, they had planned this out. The monkeys have learned a lot about humans – especially those that look like tourists. They know that people get tired halfway up and will be easy targets. They jump you, pick up your coconut and make off with it. Evolution in process.

But they picked the wrong human this time. Why, I don't know, but some reflex inside me jumped the trolley. I immediately started running after them, yelling, "Come back with my coconut!" This must sound like a scene from a Three Stooges movie, but in my value system, you don't steal someone's coconut – especially if you're not even on the same level of the food chain! And I got it back. Apparently my own mad dash scared them, and several yards away, the one with the coconut dropped it. Pleased with my victory over the simian gang, I merrily continued my journey to the top.

Only later did it occur to me that those monkeys might have chewed my face off. But in the flush of the moment, my instinct was the same as if they'd been a human gang. One of my precepts is to stand up for yourself. All I knew on this day was that it was right to get my coconut back, and that those monkeys were going to have to fight me for it.

In southern Malaysia, riding around the coastal resort area with a friend on rented motorcycles we came upon the local golf course and decided to play a round of 18 holes. At the club, they rented us golf clubs and charged a green fee. Then they said we had to have a caddy, even though we didn't want a caddy. And we would have to buy some golf balls and tees. Just as we were walking out toward the tee, someone stopped us and said, "Oh, sorry, you can't go out with those shorts and white socks you're wearing. You must have socks that go up over your calf up to your knee. Those are course regulations."

Then they added, "Don't worry, we'll sell you those at the shop." That ripped it for me. It was the straw that broke the camel's back. "You know what," I said, steaming, "we're not golfing. Give us ALL our money back." When they heard this, they had to stop and think. They already had us for some pretty exorbitant 'tourist' fees. So finally, they said, "You know, we'll let those regulations slide for today. You can golf in your short socks."

Just another notch on the belt for standing up for what is right and proper. You simply must not allow hucksters and hustlers to intimidate in these far-off places. They are like locusts and will rip you off only if you let them. You might want to practice saying this: "I am not an ATM machine for people who want to hustle me."

* * *

Singapore, $1 = 1.6 Singapore Dollars

In Singapore, at the bottom of the peninsula, one is struck by how clean everything is. This is a very small island country, but a very modern and very clean and conservative one. A few years ago, they noticed that too many people were spitting gum on the sidewalks and leaving those icky dried gum droppings that are a pain to clean up. So the government simply outlawed chewing gum!

Now, Valley Girls take note, if you want to chew bubblegum in Singapore, you are officially a criminal. I would strongly recommend leaving the gum home and bringing Lifesavers instead.

Mr. Clean would love it in Singapore. The modern beautiful skyscrapers rise majestically from those pristine streets, and palm trees are planted all in a row, each exactly equidistant from each other. Yet there are still some throwbacks to an earlier era when civilization was slow in coming. Because Singapore has a tropical climate where a lot of seasonal monsoon rain comes down in a short time, the streets can have gutters that are massive: sometimes four feet deep and two feet wide. And they often don't have grates on top of them. So if you're staggering home in a drunken stupor some night, and you fall into one of these things you can easily kill yourself. In the Western world, this would be a lawsuit waiting to happen. So Singapore is almost a First World country, with Third World attachments that are hard to break.

* * *

Indonesia, $1 = 9100 Rupiah

In Indonesia, I met a German girl who was stranded. She was dazed and confused, and when I asked what was wrong, she explained that she had been riding in a boat with a ship captain who had promised her money for being in the crew. But the guy became a pirate of sorts, and dropped her off in the middle of nowhere and drove off without paying her. As a firm believer that chivalry is not dead, on an island or anywhere else, I came to her rescue.

I could speak some German, and gave her a shoulder to cry on. After getting her to the appropriate authorities, she then got back on her feet. I don't know what would have happened to her all alone in this still rather primitive area had our paths not crossed. It was my good deed for the day.

* * *

China, $1 = 8.3 Yuan

Hong Kong was my gateway to southern China and the neighboring city of Gwangchow (formerly Canton). There was a huge market at the edge of a wide muddy river where all manner of exotic foods came into port. A man was processing a huge basket of frogs by holding one at a time, slicing around the neck, cutting off the arms, pulling the skin off from the neck to the feet, and throwing the skin in one pile and throwing the rest into another pile. The rest of the frog meant a body of pink frog meat and its little green head. It reminded me of the farmer in Nepal who had done such a professional job skinning his chickens. But at least those chickens died a quick death. The frogs had to carry on flopping around for a few minutes, literally with half their bodies stripped away. The chef did this for several hundred frogs, skinning them while they were still alive.

While going through this market, if you wanted to buy half a fish, they would bisect it and you could take half of it with you. The other half of it was gasping for air and still throbbing, half cut-away and half still alive before it died. There were huge salamanders two or three feet long that had been harvested from the river, as well. Also, little kittens were kept in cages, not to be sold as pets, but to be a course for the evening meal. People were reading newspapers or chatting about their lives, and lifting forks full of dog and cat meat to their mouths.

Third World or not, what is seen when traveling will make you sit up and take notice. Sometimes it will make you want to sit down, to keep from tossing your cookies.

CHAPTER THREE

The plane ride from Southeast Asia culminated at Darwin on the top end of Australia. I arrived in one piece and still hale, hearty and tall – a fact that hit me immediately in Australia. After spending three months with tiny Oriental people, I was suddenly amongst all these tall white people. Not that the first jaunt through the Third World wasn't exciting – even exhilarating, and certainly enlightening. But perhaps I should settle down for a while in a developed nation.

Australia, $1 = 1.4 Australian Dollars

Indeed, Australia seemed to be the place. I could repeat the enjoyable way of life of London: working at a lucrative day job that stoked the professional side, and playing basketball at nights and weekends to stoke the physical side. It wasn't a bad deal. In fact, it was so comfortable that I wound up spending eight nearly uninterrupted years doing it.

It was a bit more cushy than in London, actually. Basketball is a much bigger deal in Australia, which has exported a number of top-notch, quality players to American colleges and the NBA. I saw the Australian leagues really begin to burgeon in talent and influence, not to mention their budgets and payrolls. Even back then, the teams would get you a place to work and a place to stay, even a car to get around in.

Working in some pretty darn good jobs, they mainly centered in the financial markets: the Sydney Stock Exchange and the Sydney Futures Exchange. I was actually down on the trading room floor at times, plying skills as a foreign exchange broker, buying low and selling high. They hired me because of my experience from the banking institutions in London, as they liked anyone with international financial connections.

There I was, Mr. Khaki Shorts and White Socks wearing a suit and tie. And then, after changing and putting on a cape in a phone booth, being Mr. Power Forward at night and weekends. The need for a change of scenery was fed by road trips across Australia and New Zealand. Our home games would be packed with fans. My team was the Manly-Wahringah Sea Eagles, so named for a very famous beach in the northern suburbs of Sydney, Manly Beach, as well as the adjacent town with the aboriginal name of Wahringah. We would fly to Melbourne, for example, for a Friday night game, a Saturday night game, and a Sunday afternoon game. And then fly home Sunday night, ready for office work the next morning.

By then, I had the opportunity to become an Australian citizen. That happened in 1991 when the USA changed its stance, and allowed dual citizenship. Now, you don't have to give up your citizenship to take on a second one. I didn't know this was possible until one of my teammates, a fellow American, showed me his Australian citizenship paper. I said, "Mate, now in order for you to go home to the States, you have to go get a visa." He said no, it's not like that; the US said you now can take on a second citizenship.

So I called up the US Embassy in Sydney and asked, what's all this about getting dual citizenship? And they said yes, you can do that now. To make sure, I had them send me the documentation, a four-page government brochure. And, in essence, the entire first page said, no, you can't do it. But then flipping the page, three quarters of the way down it said the equivalent of, oh by the way, none of that applies if you decide not to renounce your US citizenship. I had no intentions of renouncing anything.

No matter where you are in the world, you will encounter this kind of government double-speak. They will want people to think you can't do something, and leave it for the fine print to inform you that you actually can. If you're not reading the whole thing, if you just read the first page, you will assume you can't do it. And most people will throw it away and say forget about that.

The Australian government also had its own rules about dual citizenship. This meant that I was an Australian citizen at a time when one of the most famous Australians on the planet, publishing baron Rupert Murdoch, wasn't. Murdoch had to renounce his Aussie citizenship when he brought his media empire to America. Only US citizens can own a television station in the USA, and he made the switch. He finally got to re-apply for Australian citizenship in 2003 when they changed their own rules. Welcome to the club, mate.

After being a permanent resident there so long, the hardest part about the citizenship procedure was only the paperwork. Although there was this one requirement about knowing Australian history. Just what I need, a history test. Basic facts were a cinch, but how much more in depth should I really study? The day of the big appointment came, and I was interviewed by a stately older policeman who said he had been out on the beat for the past 20 something years, and was about ready to retire from the force. They gave him this cushy desk job for his last six months of service. In fact, this was his first interview he was to do. I promised I'd be gentle.

When it came time for that history test, I was sweating, just a little. He said, "You know all about Australian history, don't you?" I said, "Of course." He checked off the box.

Yes, *that* was the test! On to the next item. And, yes, that is exactly what I like about Australia. No worries, mate!

* * *

Life Down Under was good. I had a car, a motorcycle, a windsurf board, and a wonderful place in Sydney's northern suburbs. Got to travel, sporadically and close to home. So settled in that I nearly got married – nearly, not quite – to my lady, a beautiful Australian nurse. This was the happiest time of my life, with a string of memories such as going to the outback to her family ranch, lots of sport and sailing. Alas, we just never quite made it to the alter, and it seems I've faced that a few times.

Eight years notwithstanding, I had to get back out there, to see more of the world again. The itchy restlessness was always there. I couldn't pack quickly enough when a job would take me to New Zealand on assignment, or to Southeast Asia where we had offices in Kuala Lumpur, Singapore, and Hong Kong. These sojourns were not approached as luxury tours, as I didn't expect, or ask for, a room-service trip.

On one such local trip, I was driving up along the coast of northern New South Wales, on the way to Queensland, and I happened to meet a beautiful girl at Byron Bay. For me, that frequently means trouble – and I mean that in the nicest way.

Byron Bay is a little bit of a sanctuary for the flower power counter-culture that survived from the 1960's. They are still there, and it's always the summer of love. Paul Hogan, from the *Crocodile Dundee* movies, has a place out in the back of Byron Bay, so the place has its star power, as well. This particular girl was a little bit of a flower child, and very free willed. I said, "I'm going to Queensland, and can give you a ride," so she hopped in.

After we talked a while she said, "Oh, have you ever tried mushrooms?" I deduced she was not talking about the kind mama puts in the spaghetti sauce. More likely the kind that produces a mind altering euphoric effect. I said no, not really, and she ventured, "Well, let's go pick some." She took me to a cow pasture and said, "Just look in the old dried cow dung." I wondered, "Is this sanitary?" She said, "Oh yes, it's all natural. You see little mushrooms growing out of it once in a while, and then you find the kind with the little collar around the shaft." It was a bit more information than I needed to know about what can be found in a cow pile. And perhaps luckily, we couldn't find any. After driving further north and dropping her off, I continued on the merry way to Queensland.

About three days later, I happened to be playing golf with some friends. At one point I hit my ball out of bounds, jumped over the fence to go get it, and – you guessed it – landed right smack dab in a cow pasture! Piled right in front of me sat an honest to goodness dung heap, along with what looked exactly like the mushrooms the girl had described. So I picked a couple, and walked back to the fairway. I showed them to my partners and told them the story.

"I don't know. It could be dangerous," one of them said.

Getting that old familiar do-anything-once feeling, I replied, "Why don't I just try a tiny little bit?" After a small sample, we played the rest of the hole. As we were walking to the next tee, I turned to my buddy and said, "It's starting to kick in." The rest of the game went by quite pleasantly, like playing in a cloud. At the end of the round, I went back to that cow pasture with a pillow case and stuffed it full of mushrooms, which I wanted to give to my friends. I know what you're thinking: so that explains why he has so many friends!

* * *

Subject: Merry Christmas - Australian Style

22 Dec 1992

G'day Mates!

Happy Christmas (as the Aussies like to say) from the land where Santa Claus arrives in a sleigh pulled by 6 White Kangaroos! (Not too many reindeer around here!)

Actually, I have seen quite a few wild kangaroos who have become accustomed to humans, and they hang around on the golf courses, as well as here at the University where I am writing this. They love to chomp on the well-manicured grass, and rest in the shade where they know the humans won't chase them off. Pretty cushy existence.

Speaking of golf, I went to the Jack Newton Celebrity Pro-Am event here on the Sunshine Coast of Queensland (home state of the Great Barrier Reef). Got to rub elbows with the former Prime Minister (Bob Hawke), an international super model (Kristy Hinze), and a PGA champion golfer (Brett Ogle). Partied til after the sun came up, as the Aussies sure know how to drink.

Water skiing and catamaran sailing keeps me busy here at the resort town of Noosa Heads. Been staying aboard a friend's luxury catamaran that is moored in the bay. What a way to spend the summer!

Merry Christmas and a Happy New Year! Cheers, Christopher

* * *

Brazil, $1 = 8 Reals

Working for an international company definitely has its advantages for an avid world traveler. On a trip to Brazil, I went to all the big cities of Rio De Janeiro, Sao Paolo, Brasilia, and all the way up to Manaus, which is a port on the Amazon River in the middle of the largest rain forest on earth. I got to take a day trip on this, the most magnificent of rivers – at 4,049 miles second in length only to the Nile. This included canoeing, penning for crocodiles at night with a flashlight, fishing for piranha, and also having a big meal with the local Indians of the Amazon.

I got a little bit sick after the lunch, and was getting hot and sweaty. We were rowing the canoes, with our fishing poles at the ready, and my skin felt like it was burning up. So I just jumped into the Amazon and swam around a bit before jumping back in the boat. And the people looked at me like I was absolutely insane. Like, "Hey, this is where we fish for piranha! And you're swimming here?" Well, I just went with instincts. Nobody had caught any piranha right where I was, so I briefly jumped in to cool myself off. I also, admittedly, had a strong desire to take a dip in the Amazon!

The irony was that I wound up getting sick, and that night had a plane to catch! I had business to attend to at the south of the country in Porto Allegro, where meetings were scheduled for the next three days. People were waiting to wine and dine at all those fancy Brazilian barbecues, and I got through them all, no doubt looking somewhat green in the gills. But I couldn't hold down what was in my gut for long, and made constant pilgrimages to the bathroom. I'd eat some and go to the rest room, and come back and eat some more. It's not something that has happened often, or even more than a handful of times when on the road. I like to eat just about anything the locals do. After all, it hasn't killed them yet.

Still, I wouldn't trade that day on the Amazon for anything. Just seeing the huge expanse of the Amazon is breathtaking. At certain points during the rainy season – November to June at its peak – the river can grow to over a mile wide. Alongside its banks there are cliffs about twenty feet high, from where vegetation grows on top to where water flows at the bottom. During the rainy season, the water will fill the Amazon to the very top of the cliffs – a twenty foot wall of water, over a mile wide! That is a lot of water that eventually drains into the ocean.

On the same trip, as a teaser, I also crossed into Argentina and Paraguay, visiting another spectacular waterway: Iguasu Falls, 800 miles north of Beunos Aires, the largest group of waterfalls on the planet. It actually marks the confluence where Argentina, Brazil and Paraguay meet. A bridge is built over the Iguasu River just a few meters from the Garganta do Diabo (Devil's Throat), the most dazzling of the falls. As with the Amazon, Iguasu Falls' essential character changes according to the water volume of the river, as it can widen to three times its normal size, or in the dry seasons thin to small streams.

* * *

Inevitably, perhaps, I moved back to California after having been away from home for a decade. Plotting a future course of serving the world in earnest, I wanted not only to visit the Third World, but to become part of its lore, its customs, its people. To achieve that, I would have to fuse into the very marrow of the world's developing nations. And squeezing in an elephant ride or a swim in piranha-infested waters in the folds between rushing to business engagements hundreds of miles away was just the beginning. Those truncated experiences did more than just whet my appetite for wanderlust. They helped determine my fate as a human being, and what I wanted to do with my life was to be of service as a cultural humanitarian.

As far as that pertaining to my professional life, I began working as an independent contractor, as my own boss, with a wide range of responsibility. Doing jobs for telecommunication companies, legal entities, information processing groups, I always helped companies with the way they do things and making them run a little bit more efficiently. I do a lot of that, as an organizer.

After buying my first home in the Del Mar Heights area, I was, in the words of some old songs, mister business man and a well respected man about town. Being voted 'Mr. Tall San Diego,' I escorted Miss Tall at the televised Holiday Bowl Parade. That was in 1998 when the town hosted the Superbowl, and I got jobs for 40 friends of mine at the Superbowl Halftime Show. We were down on the field 'dancing in the streets' with the stars of Mowtown Records. Again, life was good.

But how to explain such blessings? At the pool party after buying the house, one particular friend seemed a bit uneasy. I asked him what was wrong. "I have to be honest with you, Christopher," he said. "I've never known you to really have a full time job, and here you are traveling around the world. And now you are buying your own house. I just think that someone like that has got to be involved in drugs or something similar." I had to laugh, saying, "That's the farthest thing from my mind, and if you knew some of the places where I've stayed, the whole image would change completely."

It's funny, though, because other people think that I am CIA or DEA, or something clandestine in the government sector. I must admit, sometimes it's fun when people think you're an international man of intrigue. That may be a better pickup line than pretending to be a movie producer. But rather than indulging some fantasy role playing, my yen to travel was completely reality-based, and after three years building up contacts in business, I cashed them in. I could now offer services to the world, to do intensive population and sociological studies, or pioneer long-term connections in developing nations where franchise opportunities for big business are virtually endless.

So, in March 1999, I culled together a few of these assignments which were essentially open-ended, rented out my house, and made plans to go deep within the fiber of the Third World. I would drive from California to Panama, which would take me through Mexico, Guatemala, El Salvador, Honduras, Nicaragua, and Costa Rica. When telling friends what I was about to do, they all asked, "Why?" I would say, "I'm going walkabout." That's what they call it in aboriginal Australia when you uproot and go on to different more fertile hunting grounds: you've gone walkabout. And in a flash, I'd gone.

* * *

Mexico, $1 = 10 Pesos

The starting route of the journey was easy to choose. I had always wanted to go to the tip of Baja California driving overland instead of just flying to Cabo San Lucas. I jumped in my Nissan Sentra and hit the road southward.

About half way down the desert peninsula, I met some US military guys who were on leave and enjoying a vacation on the crystal clear waters of the Sea of Cortez. We had a few beers, and I told them about my plans to drive to Panama. When we parted, I got their email addresses and promised to keep them informed of my progress. These emails were the first of a list that grew to over 300 people around the world. I would type a letter home every couple of weeks, and send a blind carbon copy to everyone on the list. I regularly keep in contact with many of them, to this day. These original guys told me years later that they thought I'd never make it to Panama. That was after the second trip through Africa!

After getting to the tip of Baja and wanting to go further, I took a ferry boat to the Mexican mainland, and then drove down to Guadalajara. Stopping to do some work for a school of retarded kids was my first project, as they happened to be needing some organization and structural refurbishment. I did a lot of construction work with them.

And the way we met points to how easy it is to fall into these things. I saw a taco shop with a sign that said "Ricos Tacos," which in Spanish means rich or fantastic tacos. I ordered a taco and then stuck out my hand saying, "My name is Christopher, you must be Rico." I shook the guy's hand as everyone in the place laughed and set me straight. I laughed at my faux pas, too. In fact, telling that story all the time in Latin America, the locals always get a kick out of it. We became fast friends, and he introduced me to the school.

* * *

Subject: Sunny Day in Acapulco

17 May 1999

Greetings Amigos,

Speaking of the sun, it is hot and humid here. Lots of sweat dripping down whenever in direct sunlight. That is why when walking around town, I am constantly zig-zagging from one shady spot to another. It is 43 degrees Celsius (that is 109 degrees to you and me), but we saw a weather report on TV that said down south of here there was a place reporting 52 degrees Celsius (yes, that is 125 degrees Fahrenheit!). Sheech!

I swam out to the two islands here in Acapulco bay, about one kilometer away. On the swim back to shore from one, I got swept next to a rock and got a bit of a scrape on my leg, plus stepped on a spiny little sea urchin at the same time. Took me a day and a half to get all those little spikes out of my toes. No word on damage suffered by the sea urchin.

In Mexico City, the famous pyramids are over 2000 years old, and the culture that built them just died out around the year 700 AD. They left fantastic monuments for us, but you have to walk over 4 kms (2 miles) to get to the far pyramid, then climb it and turn around and head back. Yes, I am staying fit. Soccer and basketball with the locals are regular occurrences, as well.

I am staying sane with a smattering of English spoken with a few travelers now and then, but my Spanish is getting much better. Here in Acapulco there is even a radio station with English songs. A toast to the limes of Mexico! They have limes to squirt on everything, not just their cervesas (beers). Limes help kill off any germs, I guess. They have been good for me. Still feeling great.

Adios amigos, Christopher

* * *

Driving south, the next stop was Mexico City and then down past Acapulco, to the state of Oaxaca (pronounced, believe it or not: 'wa hawk uh'). In the town of Huatulco, right on the beach there are lots of resorts, including the Club Med vacation resort. A light bulb went on in my head, as several people have told me that I would be a great person to work for Club Med. I didn't even know that Club Med was a 'swinging singles' vacation spot. I asked, "Why would I be a great person to work for them?" and was told, "Because it's an adventurous kind of a place," and they left it at that. So here I was, at the adventurous place looking to find out just how adventurous.

I knocked on their door and said to no one in particular, "Hey, people tell me I should be working for you guys. Do you think you could put me to work?" And they hired me for the summer. I became a 'G.O.' which are initials for something similar to gracious organizer. The job was basically teaching windsurfing, sailing, and basketball. But I got to partake in all the other things like volleyball, softball, snorkeling, boat trips, tennis, etc.

It is a job that keeps you running from 8 a.m. to midnight daily. And you are expected to lead dances, parties, beach bonfires, theatrical performances, and generally socialize with all the guests to keep them happy. You run around so much that during the first few days, I was in a zombie-like state. The only thing it compares to is either training camp for a sports team, or going through Hell Week at the fraternity house all over again! But you hang with it and get to work with some exceptionally talented people from all over the world. All activities are in French, Spanish, and English... if not more.

For me it was a dream job. All you have to do is just be friendly to people and if you see somebody sitting at a meal alone, you go over and schmooze with them. And, oh yes, they had these gorgeous Brazilian girls in some of the skimpiest bikini swim wear I have ever seen. Those were nice side benefits. All guests are looking for the G.O.'s to take care of them, you might say. But I was really the one who was well taken care of, including all the food you can eat and all the drinks you can drink. Can't beat that.

* * *

Guatemala, $1 = 7 Quetzals

"A MAN, A PLAN, A CANAL - PANAMA"

22 Jul 1999

This palindrome says it all, backwards and forwards. After working the summer at Club Med Huatulco in southern Mexico, I am taking my plan and headed south to Panama. Current greetings come from Guatemala City, in the middle of the rainy season. Lots of water coming down every afternoon. Got to time it right to stay dry.

This country finished their civil war 3 years ago, and are trying to put all those former guerrillas to work doing something new. It is a country that uses gallons for their gasoline (not liters) and pounds for their produce (not kilograms), but kilometers (not miles) for their road distances. Kind of a mixed bag of things. The people are really friendly, and will help you any way they can.

Adios, Christopher

* * *

El Salvador, $1 = 8.7 Colon

Honduras, $1 = 14 Lempiras

When it was time to move on, the trail went through Guatemala, El Salvador, then Honduras. At the Honduras border, you realize the fun is over and you are knee-deep in a typical banana republic. They wanted to get some extra money, and could not show any paperwork requesting it. It was a bribe just to get in, a sure sign of corruption among the border guards. Well, I don't have a habit of paying bribes. I said, "That's ridiculous, where is that money going?" One of the guards replied, "It's going to someone's pocket."

That made no difference to me. I said, "Being a tourist with no definite itinerary, I'll just stay here awhile with you guys and practice my Spanish." Thus, I was a willing participant in my own delay – because there was a rainstorm happening and I didn't want to go out in the rain. They started to close the place down at six o'clock at night, and the rainstorm had become a flood. I helped them with the mop up, and even tossed them some spare change for the language lesson. They had a cash drawer, not where you put everything in stacks, twenties here, fives there, ones here. They had a cash drawer that contained a menagerie of currencies, all crumpled, unsorted, and strewn all over the place. It was the most unorganized thing I have ever seen – and sadly, this is par for the course in many parts of the world.

It was easier at other border places. In fact, seeing me approaching in my silver Sentra, people would flock to me like flies to... fly paper. They all try to sell their wares, or help to change currencies. It was like Asia all over again, you have to beat them back with a stick. All around this part of Central America you see military people with guns all over the place, but I felt relatively safe because I just drive away from anything that gets too out of control.

I had learned by now that there is absolutely no reason to pay through the nose for a perfectly comfortable room, wherever you may be. You drive through and ask somebody where a hotel is. Everyone knows at least one, it's that easy. It is no surprise that hotels can be real cheap. On the journey to Panama and back, I never spent more than five or ten bucks per night.

* * *

Nicaragua, $1 = 11 Cordobas

Managua, the capital of Nicaragua is a unique place. They do not have street numbers on the houses or buildings. They just have the name of the street. To get to any particular home, you need specific directions based on proximity to landmarks such as the railroad station, the local Exxon station, etc. You wonder how people ever get their mail!

There is real, gnawing poverty in Nicaragua. I was having a meal right on the shore of Lake Managua in a little park area, and I just had a quarter of a chicken. As I finished, the chicken bones were on the plate and a young guy came up to me and asked, very politely, "May I take your plate?" I said sure, thinking he was a waiter. He took the plate, scooped up the chicken bones and started to pick at them, before eating the bones themselves. It was rather a sad sight, one that immediately contrasts with the bloated excesses of fast food restaurants in the West. Also, because I really cleaned those bones bare, myself. If I would have known, I would have at least left a little more meat on them. That sort of incongruity, and how blase Westerners are about their good luck, can be a real eye-opener.

* * *

Subject: Rural Central America

27 Aug 1999

Traveling out in the countryside, I recently got to visit a village of indigenous people that was quite primitive, with no electricity, phones, nor running water. The river and lake at the edge of town was their main highway, and source of income. They told me they sometimes had soccer matches against a rival village one hour away by boat. They play at the school soccer field which had sparse grass, and wooden goal posts. So, we broke into a competitive soccer game!

Some even played without shoes, if they had none themselves. But they were good! They also rented me a dug-out canoe for a song, to explore the lake for the day.

Earlier, a little beggar girl of 9 years of age named Ana Cecelia came into my cafe as I waited for the rain to stop, over a cup of coffee. She was begging for the equivalent of 10 cents. I wanted to give so much more than that. I asked why she was not in school. The cafe owner said schools are expensive, and some kids are sent out to work the streets instead. Ana could write her first name. I sat with her for half an hour and wrote out the ABC's, which she copied nicely. Then her full name, plus mine, plus phrases in Spanish like: hello, how are you, fine thanks, I love school, and I love mommy and daddy.

She was so proud of herself, and we folded that paper so nicely for her mom and dad to see. I was proud of her too. It made me feel so good inside to see her take this very important first step. I hope her parents got the hint and get her off to school, for a chance at a better future. I gave her my pen to get her started. It is one that clicks open and shut. Hope that is special for her. She was really special for me.

Adios amigos, Christopher

* * *

In Nicaragua I found some work to do that was greatly rewarding in every way. Spotting a building with a United Nations logo on it, I went in and asked if there were any voluntary type of projects that needed a hand. They gave me a list of things and I chose the women's shelter in Granada, the largest city in the south of the country. Some people with good hearts pay big bucks to go to a Third World country and work as a volunteer. It is a growing industry. DO NOT FALL FOR THIS.

Just go there and do it yourself. The money you spend on these junkets could easily feed the whole village for years. Find the information about these projects on the Internet, or any other place that is much more cost effective.

I drove down to Granada the next day, and knocked on the door of *Casa De La Mujer*, or House of the Women. It was a complex that allowed women to be trained in different things like beauty shops and typing, and there was also a women's health clinic, a class for learning English, a computer learning center, and so on. Women can use it as a sanctuary, but it is a training school and a medical center, as well.

The mobile medical team took me along to different villages to help out with their medical services. They were giving out drugs for people who had illnesses of some sort due to bad water, viruses, whatever. I also cleaned up the place. This was my trademark, going into a place that was a mess and hauling several truckloads full of trash to the dump in the first two days. I made the place look really spic and span, and helped them install some of the computers they had, but were unaware of how to use.

They had a big mango tree in the middle of the compound, and I arrived during the summer season. Everyone would eat the mangoes and then throw the peel right on the ground. There were so many fruit flies there you'd have to swish them away all the time. Nobody would think twice about throwing trash on the ground. All through the Third World, people just throw trash all over the place. Which is how we used to be in America back before the 1960's. Then there came a public service commercial on TV that said you have to pitch in to clean up America. That was our big thing: get out the word to help out, and low and behold, now nobody throws trash out the windows of their car. Yet they do that all the time in the Third World. It's a real mess wherever you go, and they just do not seem to see any of it. So I cleaned up the entire place, put a trash can or a little box in every room, and also got someone assigned to empty them all into a communal trash can every couple of days.

Years passed without a thought of it. Then at around Christmas time 2005, just before going to a project in South America, I was speaking with a woman who had just recently got back from Nicaragua. I said, "You know, I used to work in Nicaragua, too." She asked where. "In Granada," I replied. And she related, "Wow, I was there, too. And now the mayor of the town is on this real kick. He is in the process of putting a trash can everywhere in the city."

I couldn't believe it! This was six years later, and perhaps what started in my small school had bloomed into a city-wide requisite. I felt so proud of that. It is never my intention while traveling to the Third World to interfere, but I do want to lead by example to change parts of it for the better. Apparently, I had left a legacy in Granada. I felt like Johnny Appleseed, planting little ideas in place of little seeds. Then all of a sudden the idea grew, was adopted from one person to another, and on to the mayor and to the entire city. No one can tell me one person cannot make a difference. Because perhaps I am one person who did. In Granada, Nicaragua for instance.

* * *

Costa Rica, $1 = 284 Colones

The next country on the way down to Panama is Costa Rica, and I was driving through the southern part of the country at night. This was before resolving never to drive at night because you can get in so much more trouble. People sometimes drive without their lights, and it's really dangerous. Plus, you can get robbed a lot easier. I had yet to realize this and was driving at around 11 o'clock on a pitch dark road. It was a main road, one lane in one direction, one lane in the other. While passing a truck in the middle of the road, all of a sudden I heard bang, bang, bang, bang. I didn't know what the heck it was, and looked back and saw that I had just run over four of those official orange traffic safety cones. And one was now wedged under the car, scraping along and sounding horrific.

Worse yet, I had sped right past a police checkpoint! Oh man, I had to be in big trouble now. So pulling over about 50 yards down the road, I got out and tried to get the cone out from underneath. And right then in the dark, the outlines of three figures came running forward with flashlights. Uh-oh, I thought, these are cops from that checkpoint. Two of them came up to me, along with another shortly thereafter, a roly-poly sort of guy who was really out of breath. They weren't there to welcome me. They told me not to move and began interrogating me in Spanish, their hands fingering the guns in their holsters.

Obviously, they believed I had run their checkpoint on purpose. I tried to be respectful and friendly, but to no avail. They went through the entire car and all my personal papers, and couldn't find anything wrong. So they went into the trunk of the car and took everything out. They were still sure that I was doing something wrong. Finally, after twenty minutes and having found nothing, they took the flashlight and shined it on the cone with all the scratches that had come out from under the car.

"You've got to give us something for the cone," one cop said. They, like the Honduras border cops, were going to put the screws to me for some money. And standing there in the middle of a dark night in Costa Rica, I wasn't about to argue the point. I said, "You know, you're right. I did ruin your cone." For compensation, I just happened to have a stash of girlie magazines in the car – just for this sort of occasion. I told them, "Here guys, have three of these." They were most appreciative, as apparently these are hard to come by in Costa Rica and are as good as smuggled gold to the red-blooded Latin males there. In fact, it's a world-wide currency. The cops all politely and contently went back to their checkpoint. I drove away, having come through yet another scrape undamaged.

This should underscore a point made earlier: you can barter with just about anything. T-shirts, magazines, compact disks. Any item like this just might get you out of a sticky situation – in the dead of night, too. It might even keep you out of the pokey.

* * *

Panama, $1 = $1 (The US Dollar is the national currency of Panama)

My corporate connections came into play upon arrival in Panama. I had arranged to meet with executives of an offshore banking company, to investigate legitimate options for client asset diversification. The whole area of offshore banking can be a mystery to many. The interesting thing about the Panamanian offshore companies is that they were not created merely for drug cartels to launder their ill-gotten money. These companies made their pitches openly at an anti money laundering convention that was actually attended by the Treasury section of the US government, as well as Interpol.

This industry is a way for Western businessmen to be quite good corporate citizens. They can diversify assets, and it is monitored closely so it is all legal, and completely free of any drug money. I took a business trip back to Costa Rica to run some seminars for affiliate companies who wanted information on the same plans. This is an object lesson that investing in these countries may be one more option for any Western corporate board to make a win-win contribution for both.

* * *

Subject: Panama Canal Greetings

23 Sep 1999

As I sit here at the computer, I am literally 20 yards away from the Panama Canal – at Pedro Miguel Boat Club, right at the canal locks of the same name. Getting ready to be a 'Line Handler' on a cruise through the canal in 2 day's time. And am I ever excited! Better not get too giddy, and go skipping around the canal banks, especially at night, as crocodiles abound in these parts.

It is truly amazing to see these huge ships from all over the world congregate in such a small area and move around so orderly. There are 40 each day that pass through here, 24 hours a day. Last night we watched many vessels rise and get lowered and it was all so quietly done, in the flood-lit lights that allow for safe waters. Each complete passage takes about 24 hours including waiting time, and releases 52 million gallons of water. All this water is rain water and river water that would flow naturally anyway into the oceans. The canal just dams it up for awhile, and releases it in a timely manner. No pumps at all are used. Amazing!

Panama is an interesting place. They use US dollars as their national currency. First time I have seen greenbacks in months. Quarters, dimes and nickels are used interchangeably with equal sized coins with the conquistador Vasco Balboa on the front. My laundry machine took both easily.

Makes me wonder what happens when the US completely pulls out on December 31 of this year. No armies for either Panama or Costa Rica. It is great to have friendly relations with a big northern neighbor. Speaking of which, everyone down here calls us 'North Americans'. When I ask where the North American continent actually begins, I get answers like, "Never really thought about that"; or the more common, "There is only ONE continent called America."

Costa Rica's National Parks and waterfalls were breathtaking, and while walking through a jungle near the Caribbean, I got the pants scared off me by a ferocious growl just meters away. I ran to the water's edge, just shy of jumping in. Thought it was either a panther or a wild boar. Turns out that the 'Howler Monkey' really lives up to its name!

You would think they could spend some of that eco-tourist earnings on better ROADS. Pot holes 4 feet wide and 8 inches deep are not uncommon. Worst main roads I have seen, and it was there I got my first fender-bender. With a supposed higher standard of living, they should have better transportation routes.

For everyone who emailed me, mucho, mucho thanks! For the last 2 countries, I am in the land of the s-l-o-w Internet, and just reading things is a chore. I will try some responses later on. Hope all is well where you are. Adios, Christopher

PS - News reaches me slowly down here, but I heard John Kennedy Jr. was in a plane crash. Any truth to the rumor that Ted was driving???

* * *

The most memorable thing about Panama was the life of a sportsman one could lead. I would go to one of the two big five-star hotels, the Caesar Park Hotel, to play tennis on Sunday mornings. Introducing myself to a group of people, they let me play tennis with them. These were all real corporate bigwigs who were leaders in the community. I was just a regular kind of guy, but was good at tennis and they liked having me around. They invited me to come back the next week too, and we played together the entire summer. We always had a little bit of a buffet of drinks and pastries at court-side, just to make it nice.

There was one black guy who played with us who spoke with a French accent. His name was Philippe and he was a big guy with a rotund physique and a jolly laugh, very outgoing, very funny. Towards the end of the summer my tennis partners said, "You know who Philippe is, don't you?" Then they added, "He's the ex-dictator of the country of Haiti!"

That knocked my socks off. If it was true, then our tennis partner was none other than Jean-Claude Duvalier, or 'Baby Doc' as they called him in Haiti. At age 19, he succeeded his dictator father Francois 'Papa Doc' Duvalier. Baby Doc evidently was corrupt and inept, a pampered playboy, and had been in exile after being ousted from Haiti in 1986. He had been in France, living a life of luxury until losing everything in a divorce settlement and apparently leaving France in 1998, just a year before this 'sighting.' A year after, he announced his intention to return to Haiti and run for president after the ouster of President Jean-Bertrand Aristide, but never did re-surface.

Our little tennis clique was willing to give 'Phillipe' a break. "He may have been a bad guy in the past," one of them said, big-heartedly, "but he's okay now." I wonder if the Haitian people would agree with that sentiment. That was a common refrain in Panama: they will take in anybody. They got the Shah of Iran his own little island after the rest of the world refused to allow him to stay, following the revolution that installed Ayatollah Khomeini. And any Latin American strongman that gets run out of his country after looting the national treasury also seems to end up here.

* * *

About a week before leaving Panama, I had my only untoward experience. It always seems to be that way: something bizarre happens just before leaving somewhere. I was driving in my car through Panama City and a taxi driver rather gently bumped me from behind, his front bumper to my back bumper. It was a little bump, nothing really happened so I didn't really react. But then the taxi pulled up next to me and the driver said, "Oh, we bumped." I said, pleasantly, "Yes we did. You hit me from behind. But it's nothing, forget about it." He disagreed. "No, no, it is a big problem," he said. "Got to get the police."

"No, thank you very much. It's fine. Goodbye," I said, and drove off. Not mollified, he followed and again pulled up to me at the next light and got out of his car. He was a larger man, probably over six feet tall, and heavy set. I saw no need to ignite the fire. Again I said, "There's nothing wrong." But he kept trying to make a big incident out of something that really was not.

That's when it dawned on me what was happening here. Obviously, he had seen my California license plates and pegged me as a pigeon. And he wasn't going to let the pigeon fly. When the light turned green and I started to drive off once more, he got in his car and followed me through the streets. Evidently he had gotten on the radio because soon four or five other taxi drivers were also following me.

It was quite a scene. Panama City has a New York City type of skyline, a cosmopolitan city with big huge buildings, and here we were having a high speed chase down the middle of this big city's streets. Their convoy caught up with me and, as if by plan, one taxi got in front and another behind, wedging me in. Now, cars were honking and a crowd developed watching all this, and the guy who'd bumped me got out. So I got out and we were going face to face, screaming at each other in different languages. We were trying to intimidate each other, but then it took an ominous turn when he pulled out a tire iron and waved it around like he was going to clobber me with it.

That was when I reached into my pocket and pulled out what looked like a felt pen about a half-inch in diameter, a utensil I'd been carrying in my pocket for the last couple of years – just in case. It was a small canister of pepper spray disguised as a pen.

"Let me write this down," I said. And as soon as taking off the cap, I sprayed him right in the eyes and all over his face. It was the first time ever actually spraying it, though I always traveled with it. I had no idea how it would work, and in fact, it seemed not to work at all. At first he simply wiped his eyes with his hands, barely blinking. So now I was thinking, "My God, it didn't work!" Maybe I'd made him even madder, and he'd wrap that tire iron around my head.

But pepper spray takes about five seconds to have an effect, and when it kicked in, he began clawing at his eyes, yelping in pain. It was reminiscent of the James Bond movie where he uses a delayed-reaction pen gun to shoot a villainess, who at first laughs then is blown away, with nothing left but her smoking shoes. This guy didn't quite suffer that much, but he had to flush his eyes with water and his pain lasted for the next two hours. I know because we spent four hours waiting for this absurd episode to play out. Policemen and even soldiers arrived, and weren't going to let us go, so I had to stay rooted there.

This is a common ritual of the Third World, where you don't only pay with money, but also with your time. People will wait forever if they think they can get something out of it, because they know the cost of their time is a heck of lot less than someone like me, supposedly a rich tourist. Meaning that I must have a lot of money and must have to go somewhere in a hurry, and will throw up my hands and say, "How much?"

Worse, it was a typically brutally hot Panamanian day. Luckily, a doctor's office was right there, and they let me wait in their waiting room and drink their coffee and read their newspapers for four hours. It was my

Spanish lesson for the day. All the while, the guy running the con was trying to intimidate me, looking through the window pretending he had a gun in his hand that he was pointing at me. I just laughed it off. At one point when heading toward the bathroom, I walked by him. He made some sort of threat, and I pulled out my pepper spray again and said, "*Uno mas?*" – as if to say, "One more, buddy? If you want one more I'll give it to you!"

Meanwhile, I was on the phone with the U.S. embassy. They knew exactly what to do, having gone through this no doubt numerous times. Somebody from the the embassy came and sorted it out. If the con got anything, he certainly earned every penny of it in pain.

I recommend that travelers carry pepper spray, but there are limits. If someone has a gun, they will be able to get off five or ten shots and kill you before it takes effect. I never carry a gun with me when on the road, for a simple reason: I'd probably wind up doing something stupid like getting shot with it. Moreover, lots of countries have laws against carrying concealed weapons, worried about the danger of revolutionary activities. A border guard could confiscate it and throw you in jail for it. For a long time. The pepper spray pen is something they don't even recognize. I carry many pens with me, so a cop will look at a stack of pens held together with rubber-bands and be none the wiser.

* * *

What struck me about Panama City wasn't just the heat but the lights. You drive by those huge glass palace skyscrapers at night and see nothing but a sea of light reaching into the skies. However, the lights can also indicate something darker about the town and the country. Passing many of the residential condominiums around the city, you are apt to see only one floor of lights that are lit, while the rest of the building is unlit and clearly empty. It becomes obvious that not many people actually live in these places, and that these buildings had been built from laundered drug money. Having some expertise in this area from time at the anti money laundering conventions, I knew how the game worked: someone has all this drug money and they need something to do with it, to hide it. So they say, let's build a building.

The results can be seen all around Panama City: brand new buildings that not many people live in. Where the common people do live, predominantly is in the poorer section of town where there are old buildings populated by many families. I couldn't help but think: is there anyone with any guts in this city who would condemn the old buildings, and put the families in those nice buildings over there? The case against it is that overnight this might turn a nice building or area into a slum; that people would be sticking their laundry out the windows, etc. There has to be a balance. Urban reform comes when people are not just given some new program. It comes when something is set up so they are allowed to invest and buy into a concept with their own resources, and show pride of ownership. They then have a stake in it, and can continue to prosper upwards.

* * *

The Panama Canal Zone is the 10 mile wide strip of land that runs from the Caribbean to the Pacific that was bought when the United States helped get the Panamanians their independence from Colombia in 1903. We used gun boat diplomacy back then. "Just sign these papers, and you guys are an independent country." "Great, where do we sign?" They have used the US dollar as their currency since then. The Zone is a beautiful place: well manicured lawns, beautiful military style housing, once full of Americans who all seemed to work for the government and all lived in the same splendid little area. Which made it seem like any working-class mid-American town. They were paid in US dollars, at regular US salaries – and a regular salary was probably four times of what an average Panamanian could make. They could go into Panama City and all of a sudden they'd be treated as if they were rich. The Panamanians loved the Americans coming in and spending their dollars, because it helped the economy.

I got to spend New Year's Eve in Panama. That was a double big day there because it also marked the official hand-over of the Panama Canal. The U.S. transferred ownership to Panama at noon on December 31, 1999, completing the deal worked out by President Jimmy Carter in 1980. So it took 20 years for the transition. The transfer, of course, meant all those Americans were going home. So, ironically, the national pride of assuming control of the canal had a flip side: the economy might take a hit. Not to worry. American subsidies came into play, and we actually paid them millions to take it away.

All the summer I was there, families gradually began heading north. Americans who had lived in Panama for two or three generations, whose grandfathers had built the canal in 1914, were going to a place they may never have been before – the mainland USA. Every Friday they had a barbecue at a local park, which included food, drinks and tossing the Frisbee around. By the end of the summer, instead of the earlier sixty or more people at this barbecue, it went down to four people. I looked around and wondered, where did everybody go?

Anticipating the historic moment of the hand-over, I went to the Canal Zone, which I had done so often during the stay. The transfer was at noon, then midnight was the turn of the millennium. All the celebrations and fireworks were viewed from the Pedro Miguel Boat Club right on the canal, where I had become a member. This club, in itself, was like a crossroads of the world, as there were people from Europe, Asia, everywhere crossing from one ocean to another. Usually, it would cost a pretty penny to become a member of that club. With the club looking for as many 'warm body' replacements as possible, I was allowed to join for a song. But then all too soon, alas, it was time for me go home, too.

Tanzanians transporting water at a well.

CHAPTER FOUR

There is an old Thomas Wolfe line that goes, "You can't go home again." As far as my life is concerned, that would read: "You can't go home again – for too long." For two years I resumed a comfortable lifestyle anchored by corporate consulting, and was enjoying life in that warm California sun. But I considered the travels up to now to be something like appetizers – very satisfying ones, to be sure – but in the main a mere gateway for more serious and intense journeys to Third World outposts. That is probably why my mind always drifted to thoughts of where the road would lead next, and what stimuli would get me on that road.

This is the benefit of making friendships all around the globe: there are people out there who will be able to facilitate future journeys. Thus, I had met some friends in Panama, who just so happened to be white South Africans, and they wrote me saying I should come and visit them in Capetown. I hadn't yet been to the southern part of Africa, only to Morocco at the very northern tip of the continent. And seeing the full conditions in this most unyielding area is essential for any traveler seeking to make sense of the realities and potentialities of people and lands that the 'civilized' world has pretty much swept under the rug. For me, it was a given. So I arranged with my Capetown friends to fly in. As usual, to help defray costs and to do some work helpful to small businesses while over there, I lined up some contacts in Capetown and

Nairobi, Kenya, the latter expanding the itinerary beyond South Africa in order to explore as much of eastern Africa as possible.

This work entailed doing business process improvements for small companies, including some in the restaurant industry. I was working on uncovering deficiencies, and getting the work flowing more easily. It's the kind of work few westerners care to do in developing areas, but which would kick-start many a business run by locals in nations that struggle to establish a business class. For me, being able to lend a hand is both a calling and a blessing.

The last detail was the flight to Capetown, no small jaunt from the west coast of the USA. I scouted the Internet for travel agencies to find the best prices available for a round trip ticket which would also allow for the longest stay. The flight was from Los Angeles to Amsterdam and then on to Capetown. There's a big connection between South Africa and Holland, because a lot of the white people of South Africa are of Dutch decent. There are generally two 'white tribes' of South Africa: one is Dutch and the other is English. The Dutch Afrikaners have been there since the 1400s, when explorers who came around the cape to go to the Far East settled down there and created Cape Colony. Thus, they have been there longer than the European people have been in America, and while they may be only one tenth of the population in South Africa they are certainly the most organized in all of Africa.

After securing a nice affordable fare, I was off on what would be my most ambitious journey to date, with no hard plan beyond landing in South Africa and following my nose. Leaving on January 4, 2002, I stopped over in Amsterdam for a day. The continent had just introduced the new Euro currency four days before, and with two sets of prices posted on everything, everyone was confused. I fit right in. The night flight then got into Capetown first thing in the morning.

South Africa, $1 = 10 Rand

You can't get much further south than Capetown, right at the bottom of the continent near the Cape of Good Hope. They have nine official languages here, and two of those are European-based: English and Afrikaans. This later one is similar to Dutch, and I can read it a bit (as it has German similarities), but it is really tricky to listen to. It had been cold and snowy in Amsterdam, but the middle of winter turned into the middle of summer in Africa when crossing to the Southern Hemisphere. It hits you like a sock full of humidity as you get off the plane. The first thing I did was change into short pants, after having a shower at the airport.

In South Africa the currency is the Rand, and it had just gone through a major devaluation, meaning that if you had US dollars to spend you could live like a king. Feeling kingly, I decided to go out and buy a car to get around. First, though, I had to use public transportation to get into Capetown's industrial area. The means of transportation were little minivans into which they would stuff 10 or 11 people like sardines before the van would drive out. The driver made stops whenever someone would call out a destination. Since most white people would usually have their own car, you can imagine the stares I was getting as the only white guy on the normally all-black transit system.

Dropped in the outlying industrial area of the city, I looked at the merchandise at a few used car dealerships. I was thinking about buying an older Mercedes, but it didn't quite look good, plus it had some oil leaks. Then I found a 1987 Ford Laser. It had a dent in it and a big chunk missing from the steering wheel, but I went ahead and bought it for a thousand dollars, and put it on my credit card. Before leaving, I said, "Do you mind if I fix this up a little bit before driving it out?" and the dealer said fine. I taped a little around that steering wheel, and then put a nice leather steering wheel cover on. Taking the inside of the back door off, I punched it out from the inside to bang the dent out of it. Before leaving that dealership, a little bit of polishing compound made the car look almost brand new. The dealer marveled at my work. "Man," he said, "if I would have done this myself it would have doubled the price!"

Later, I made one last modification before heading off into the African interior: removing the hubcaps. As good as it looked, I had actually made it a target for thieves. Without the hubcaps it looked a little bit rougher. That's another reason I passed on the Mercedes; something like that would be an invitation for every two-bit crook on the continent. Again, anywhere in the Third World, merely being a big white man would be invitation enough.

I met up with my friends from Panama who had invited me, and they took me to do all the tourist things such as hike to the top of the famous Table Mountain, film Zulu dancers, play tennis and golf, attend a cricket match, and so on. The beaches were spectacular, with the water temperatures differing depending on where you go. The Atlantic Ocean is cold, and the Indian Ocean is warmer and pleasant. After all, this is where the two oceans meet!

* * *

Like Rick's Cafe in the movie *Casablanca*, when you are in South Africa the feeling is palpable that everyone in Africa wants to come here. When I go around the world, people will say, "Oh, you're from America? I'm going to go there someday and strike it rich, then come back here and live like a king." In the U.S. people will say, "Oh, you're from California? I'm going to go there someday and strike it rich, then come back here and live like a king." In Africa, they have a different refrain – "I'm going to go to South Africa someday. I'm going to strike it rich there, then come back here and live like a king."

Everybody has their version of heaven. In all of Africa, that heavenly vision is South Africa. How did it happen? We in the West heard for many a year about the racist bastards of apartheid (separation of the races) and how bad they were to their black people, and no one in his right mind would argue that. Apartheid died a most welcome death, and the country has carried on as a 'zebra coalition' without major incident since black majority rule in 1992. A great deal of mutual cooperation between the races has stoked a stable economic environment. What helped lay the foundation for this development?

You will recall that I have previously made the point that economic progress thrives in a system where law and order is inviolate; however, the breakdown of law will undermine any attempt by local businesses to fend off corruption and anarchy. In South Africa, law and order rules with an iron fist as well as with an ingrained sense of conduct. Call it a kind of trickle-down effect. The white settlers of South Africa were clued in, and they understood how to build an infrastructure and have respect for the law. Again, the law was pretty bad as applied to blacks. But people did have respect for it, and still do. And ever since blacks were given their fair share of the pie, they carried on their innate respect for the law from the days when they were once being victimized by it.

You can observe the results of this dynamic. South African cities are nearly indistinguishable in standard of living from any Western city. The buildings are modern, the landscape is cleaner and more paved, and the creature comforts many. More impressively, it has an abundant supply of resources, well-developed financial, legal, communications, energy, and transport sectors, and a stock exchange (the JSE Securities Exchange) that ranks among the 10 largest in the world.

It is a place where there are roads and freeways, and there are beautiful hotels and resorts. You can drink water from the taps, and there are toilets that you can actually sit on. The farther away from South Africa you go, the roads get a little bit worse and there are no freeways. Pot holes sometimes are the size that a man could sleep in. There's a main road going north to south in Zambia, for example, with one lane in one direction and one lane in the other, with check points all over the place. They control the flow of people throughout the countryside, so it's a little bit less free and a lot more difficult to travel around.

And for instance, if you get a parking ticket in South Africa you will probably pay it within thirty days or else it will double, and you'll have to pay it sooner or later to get your car registration renewed. In other parts of Africa, the more likely it is that you probably won't even get a parking ticket. The policeman will just hang around until he catches you, and then he'll ask for money to put in his back pocket. However, if you try to bribe somebody in South Africa they'd probably arrest you just like they would in the US for bribery, so you don't generally do that in South Africa.

On the whole, South Africa is the crown jewel of the continent, with lessons that abound for the rest of Africa. The country is one of the few in Africa never to have had a coup d'état. They change governments by elections. And they will be the host nation for the 2010 FIFA Soccer World Cup – the first time the tournament will be held in Africa.

As an analogy, it is the equivalent of an organized and prosperous California having the poverty of Mexico right across the border. The reality here is an advanced South Africa has the 'rest' of Africa across it's borders – and even some places within it's borders.

* * *

Crime is becoming more of a problem, during this transition stage of the country. They deal with it in many ways. I was walking down the street in the inner city area of Capetown, and crossed the street in the middle of the block. On the opposite side was a black man with a large

German Shepherd guard dog on a leash. I actually surprised the dog because I seemed to come from out of nowhere. Fortunately the dog, which could have taken the meat off my bones if it had wanted to, merely sized me up, then calmed down.

I spoke with the owner briefly, and as we were talking, a local black woman came walking down the street, and the dog began snarling at her and barking aggressively until the owner had to forcibly yank the animal back under control. Racial stereotypes endure – even among black people themselves. Castes don't evaporate overnight, it seems. That dog had been trained by a black person to be aggressive towards black people, while whites could scare it silly and still get away with it. I could not quite get that little freeze-frame out of my mind. It bothered me for some time.

One white auto shop owner told me he was approached by three ominous looking guys who wandered into his shop after closing hours when he was all alone. He quickly put his hand behind his back, hiding an imaginary 'finger pistol,' and asked how he could help. Seeing this, the guys stammered that they had a flat tire down the road a bit. He said he doesn't do tires, but good luck with it. And they left without incident. One must be prepared to use whatever is at your disposal. Even if it is just a finger. Be aware.

* * *

There are many people in the country who are of mixed blood – who are called 'colored' people. Of course, racial mixing goes back some 400 years here. I happened to give a ride to one such colored person, a delightful young woman named Vanessa. I took her and her children out for pizza, and played some Frisbee on the beach.

We filmed the first day of school for Vanessa's daughter. It was a school that was taught half in English and half in Afrikaans. All the students were lined up by their room and grades, and they stood in a big assembly yard in their blue tartan school uniforms as the bell rang to start school in the morning. The principal was an older man who would speak in English for a few sentences, then start speaking Afrikaans for a few more. The kids knew their own language, and were learning the other one on the fly.

The next day I went to a hospital to get a vaccination for Hepatitis, which is required for travel through much of Africa. I had not gone for such shots back home before leaving, assuming that there would be money to be saved by getting the shots in Africa. Correct! It cost 150 rand, which is about 15 dollars. If I was to get that in the USA before coming, it would have easily been 75 to 100 dollars or more for the same thing.

Driving into a black township the next day, while it was a bit more down-trodden, people were still playing cricket on the street and acting just as normal people would in any neighborhood. Watching these scenes of everyday life, I recalled how some white South Africans had told me that it would be scary for me as a white person to go there, and that it should not be done alone. I would be taking my life in my own hands. Actually, I had let all that 'advice' play on my mind. I found that I was on my guard and not quite at ease, but this angst dissipated quickly. I had no qualm going to a township in Johannesburg later, and actually played golf at the Soweto country club. Everyone was quite nice to me, and I enjoyed the golf game which was a great value at only 15 rand, or the equivalent of $1.50 for the round!

Later, upon returning from a trip through the heart of Africa, as I looked around the townships I realized that the average local black people of South Africa had a much better standard of living than all the black people around the entire continent of Africa. They were able to build their houses with little yards around them with flowers and green grass. And they had the peace of mind security of knowing that when they are finished with their lifetime and they want to pass their assets on to their next of kin, that they can do so easily. In essence, the relative security of the government allows people to plan their lifelines much farther down the road than most African countries. Again, it was a matter of people having a respect for law, that is not really quite the same in the rest of the continent.

* * *

Namibia, $1 = 10 Namibian Dollars (stays pegged equal to the South African Rand)

Some friends in Capetown said I should look up their friends in Namibia, the dry desert country just to the north. They said they would call ahead and tell that I would be coming. So I set off north for Namibia, crossing the border at the Orange River, a muddy, murky body of water you wouldn't want to jump into. I found my way to where the friends lived, at the capital city of Windhoek, and phoned and asked if our mutual friends in Capetown had called to say I was coming. He said no they hadn't. So here I was, unannounced, and it was getting dark. They must have been in the mood to rescue a helpless urchin, as they said, "Come and stay with us!"

What's more, I ended up spending a week with them and they were just the nicest people. They were of Dutch-Germanic background, and I played a lot of sports with them. So I was living in hog heaven, playing golf, tennis, cricket, and throwing a Frisbee around that I'd taken with me on the trip. That last item was a revelation to me. Because when breaking out the Frisbee, I'd often get fifty kids and a whole village throwing it and having a great time, and it's like the circus coming to town. At the end of it all, the kids would all follow me as far as they could. It was almost like being the Pied Piper!

The moral is, if you travel through the Third World, do fun things with the locals. The amount of goodwill generated will be similar to that of millions of dollars in foreign aid, and put you in a place of high honor forever in the villages you visit. Be gracious.

* * *

The tourist industry around the world was affected by the September 11, 2001 bombings just months before. At Henties Bay Sports Club on the north coast of Namibia, I was the first tourist to pass through since the past November. That is at least three months dry, so I had to at least buy a beer or two to give them something in their coffers.

This was a small sea-side desert town with a water hole, started in 1969 with a guy coming to camp on his holidays. Thirty years later it's a cute little clean town. Gary Player, the internationally known famous golfer, is a member of their golf course men's club. It is a nine hole course with the only grass coming on the tees and the greens. At least that is a start. I was having a lot of trouble with dust and didn't want to go near anything that was not totally green. Not liking the dusty dirt roads, either, I resolved to stick to the paved highways.

I always fill my car with hitch-hikers. Or more aptly, people who are waiting at a public bus stop, and I ask if anyone wants a free ride today. Lots of hands go up. So it was always three or four natives driving through Africa with their big *mzungu* ('white man' in the Swahili language) chauffeur. I felt like it was my duty and that I was doing something good for the common man. Plus there is safety in numbers, as I do not want to be stuck alone out in the middle of nowhere.

One time we had room for one more, and a woodsman came in to fill the last spot. He had a nice big axe with him, and I asked if I could see it more closely. I held it up for all to see, and complimented him on its sturdiness. Then I said, "Mind if I keep it up here in front next to my feet for the duration of the trip?" He said he didn't mind, as the whole car busted up in laughter! You don't really want a native with an axe in the back seat. It is kind of like when the Oakland Raiders come to town. You've got to check-in your weapons at the door.

One of the ladies I gave a ride to had 38 brothers and sisters in total. I thought that was impossible, but she assured me it was true. One man had five wives, and they each had from between 6 and 11 kids. Only 3 were boys, and 35 were girls, and she could name them all. They ran out of girls names, so three sets of girls actually had the same name! The dad is a cattle and goat rancher. It was open to interpretation what 'flock' he was most proud of, the four-legged or the two-legged variety.

I just about never stop for broken down cars on the highway. Simply because of my lack of mechanical know how, but also because it's a bit dangerous. It might be a set-up to rob unsuspecting motorists, far away from any help. One time I saw some people who were waving desperately like they needed help. There were a lot of people, including a few women, in their car. I figured if people have women in their car then they are less apt to be terrorists, desperadoes or bandits. Because men and women together equals a little bit of common sense. With men alone, you think these could be robbers. These people were frantically waving and I pulled over, against the advice of my riders. Something told me I had to stop for just this one group.

We asked what we could help with, and the dad was immensely grateful. He said, "We have a flat tire and a spare to put on, but we don't have a jack to jack up the car." I said, "This is your lucky day." When I bought the car in Capetown it had two jacks in the trunk, and I had wondered why. So I went around the back, took out the extra jack and presented it to the man. I said, "We have two, so you can keep this one. This is a gift to you from the United States of America. Enjoy!" He looked at me almost dumbfounded, and was really thankful, which made me feel good. The Lord works in mysterious ways.

A Frisbee here, a jack there. In making small inroads of goodwill, it's not what you give, it's that you give, period. Even karate uniforms.

Yes, karate uniforms. As it happened, when I bought the car it also had a box of these in the trunk. Why, I had no idea. So I would go around dropping them off to people who had never heard of karate, and certainly had never practiced it. But to a little kid in an African village, getting one was the highlight of their lives. They could parade around in them, strutting their stuff. If as a result, there are villages in Namibia today with budding Bruce Lees, it is pretty much all my fault.

* * *

Traveling far from home has an insulating effect. It is almost as if you are living in a dream world, a very real world but still one unconnected to the capricious and sometimes harsh realities of your own life. In Namibia, a reminder of how harsh those realities can be crashed through the figurative window of far-off adventure and exploration.

My dad phoned me on my cell phone – I had taken a prepaid cell phone with me so that people back home could reach me. I was in the Kalahari Desert and knew right away when hearing his voice that something was wrong, since he wouldn't have rung me up unless he had pressing news that couldn't wait.

He confirmed my fear. He said he had some bad news, and broke it to me that my mom had passed away. She had succumbed to heart disease. I knew her time was precious, as she was eighty-one and in poor health. Before she passed away, I was able to put in a new driveway, trim the trees, paint the house, clear out the backyard and make their house look totally new, so she had a beautiful place for the last six months of her life.

Still, it wasn't any easier being so far away, out in the bush, and that I couldn't possibly get back to South Africa to take a plane to Amsterdam and back to California for the funeral. It would take over a week to make it back, so I decided it was best to write the obituary, and email it so it could be read right at the funeral.

* * *

In Memorium: Helen Theresa Blin

2 Feb 2002

I take this day to celebrate the richly successful life of my mother, Helen Theresa Blin. Born of solid Midwestern roots and values in Ashtebula, Ohio (just outside of Cleveland), she was the daughter of Hungarian immigrants. When she became of age, she took the brave and bold step to move across the country to California – no easy feat in those days! This adventurous gene (some might say the Gypsy in us) must have somehow been passed along to her offspring, as I heard about her passing while here in the Kalahari Desert of Namibia in southern Africa.

She met and married my father, K.C. Blin, and devotedly was in charge of raising a fine family of four children – which I am sure she would unequivocally say was her finest and proudest achievement of her lifetime. She would keep us kids enthralled with stories of her early adventures in California. Her favorites included the camaraderie of working as an executive secretary in the hotel industry in Beverly Hills. I love her for passing along this story-telling trait to me, as well – as it certainly has made my life that much richer!

I was blessed to get to spend the last six months of Helen Blin's life with her and my dad. Together we made household improvements, while enjoying the simple pleasures of our lush green yard in Tujunga.

Indeed, she spent one-half of her 81 years there. She loved the juicy fresh fruit off the trees, the joy of watching the squirrels frolic in the backyard grass, and got a real kick out of the birds fluttering playfully in the bird-bath.

In his book, "Don't Sweat the Small Stuff...", Dr. Richard Carlson reminds us to live every day as if it were our last. It might be: "When are we going to die? In fifty years, twenty, five, today? Last time I checked, no one had told me. I often wonder, when listening to the news, did the person who died in the auto accident on his way home from work remember to tell his family how much he loved them? Did he live well? Did he love well? Perhaps the only thing that is certain is that he still had things in his 'in basket' that weren't yet done.

"The truth is, none of us has any idea how long we have to live. Sadly however, we act as if we're going to live forever. We postpone the things that, deep down, we know we want to do – telling the people we love how much we care, spending time alone, visiting a good friend, taking that beautiful hike, writing a heartfelt letter, going fishing with our family, and on and on. We come up with elaborate rationales to justify our actions, and end up spending most of our time and energy doing things that aren't all that important."

One hundred years from now, we all will be gone from this planet. There will be all new people here at that time. What counts for us is what is happening right now. Live life to its fullest.

I woke up this morning thinking how lucky we are to have nice people like my mom and family and neighbors and friends in our lives. Thank you so much. We are truly blessed, and I wish for you all the happiness and joy that life can bring.

Love,   Christopher Scott Blin

* * *

It was at this juncture of the trip that I cruised northward through Namibia, only to run into that stern border guard who prevented me from entering Angola – precipitating my secret little swimming excursion across the Okavango River to Angola and back. That experience would stand as an exhilarating adventure, and there is a funny postscript to it.

Remember the guy on the beach who had 'forgotten' to inform me about the crocodiles known to habitate in those reeds, any one of which could have decided to make me into a blue-plate special when I was temporarily stuck down river? Well, I actually became good friends with him thereafter.

There may not have been many who would have forgiven, if not forgotten. But I do not like to hold grudges, and want to get to know the people I meet. Was he really trying to get me out of the way so he could get his hands on my car that was still parked on the beach? I doubt it. He just wanted something for guarding my car. But before he could put his hand out, I had an idea, and asked, "You want to help me out?" He said yes. "Then lets pick up all this trash on the beach."

The beach was littered with plastic because it is not bio-degradable. There was also a lot of broken glass that can be stepped on, and a lot of other trash. Together we cleaned the entire beach, which was about forty yards long. We filled three containers full of trash, then I paid him some money. He was over the moon because he earned something that day, and I felt good about leaving the beach in pretty good condition. We had left it better than when we found it. The old Scout in me was satisfied.

* * *

The Angolan civil war had spread, with some rebels taking refuge inside the Namibian border, and they were involved in hit and run attacks in the Caprivi Strip. That was where I next ventured, and it seemed to be a middle ground with war zones on either side. Fortunately, there was no shooting, but there was military activity all around. To get through that little strip, which is a three or four hour drive, you'd have to be in a military convoy. There were two each day, in the morning and the afternoon. I was told it was very risky because guerrillas like to lie in wait for people to kidnap or kill. Snipers fire from the side of the road. In fact, four rebels were killed just the day before near the very spot I was on. You are escorted in a line headed and ended by military trucks, with maybe forty cars in between.

Since missing the convoy that day, I had to stay there at night and then join the convoy the next morning. While waiting, I happened to meet a British couple who were also traveling around and had to wait for the convoy. I was running out of gasoline, and this was the first and only time in all my trips that there was no gasoline in the stations around the area. Everything was dry. I would drive to one, then another, and was looking at my gas gauge the entire time. What would happen if I totally ran out?

With the British couple, we got word that there was only one place that had gasoline around, 120 kilometers back from where we just came. That is 70 miles worth of back-tracking! They were in the same predicament that I was in. So we got a couple of gas cans, I left my car there at the military check-point area, jumped in their car, and we drove together. We filled up their gas tank and the extra gas cans, and came back to my car. With their nice company, it made a frustrating situation just a bit more palatable. Ironically, war zone or not, the Caprivi Strip was a very pleasant way to end a day – which had admittedly started out with its share of fiascoes.

I had found paradise when having a delightful meal at an inn called the Caprivi Cabins, overlooking the peaceful Zambezi River: high up on a balcony at the resort, swathed by shady trees, a light breeze and lots of sunshine. Hippos and crocodiles were down below in the river. The hippos, I am told, are supposedly 50 times more dangerous. They can chase canoes and chomp them in two. The previous Christmas season a tourist and his new bride got too close, and after their boat was destroyed, she was eaten alive. Imagine returning from your honeymoon a widower. Could anything be more tragic?

Ending the day, I was able to relax around a campfire with some natives at the village of Divundu. A man named Lawrence and his sister were reading aloud from my travel diaries, and to my surprise were quite good at speaking and reading English. The scenery reminded me a lot of the Panama Canal: quiet and peaceful, with lots of green jungle on each side of the river. But reality was always a step away.

The next day I was safely able to go through the Caprivi Strip in the military convoy. While driving, I was filming with my video camera from the driver's seat. Once in a while, from the military cars in the front and in the back, there would be a jeep going back and forth in the other lane, and these guys saw me filming. Clearly, they were not happy about it.

At the one rest stop, they said, "We need that film, we need that camera!" Oh no, big trouble. Did they believe I was a spy? A mercenary? This was not the time to mouth off, as they had guns, and I did not. With no hesitation, I handed them my camera. They calmly explained they would return it to me after the convoy ended, saying they didn't want the tape to fall into the hands of the guerrillas. At any military or sensitive area like a border or a dam or a power station, they don't want people taking pictures. It's the same world-wide. This was a highly sensitive military area, so they were watching me like a hawk. Later they had me rewind the film to the beginning, and then film over it – and they pointed to a mundane tree on the side of the road. So, when all was said and done, my everlasting image of the Caprivi Strip is a peaceful tree. And the memories of a river of (almost) no return.

* * *

Botswana, $1 = 5 Pula

Heading next to Victoria Falls, I found myself at the geographical nexus on a river where the four countries of Namibia, Zimbabwe, Zambia, and Botswana all come together. It is the African version of the Four Corners area. I was taking pictures of a ferry boat and saw there were trucks lined up on the side of the road, massive lorry types of trucks in convoys, probably two hundred in all. I asked someone what they were all waiting for, and was told by some South African truck drivers that they needed to be taken across the river on ferry boats. None seemed to be going anywhere fast, and they told me the wait could be up to four days! That would have driven me nuts, but they were used to it.

The trucks would carry a load of cereal grains or supplies up north, sell them for cash, then drive back and get more. They could have gone down around the river where there's a route by land, but they decided it made more economic sense this way. So here they sat, whiling away the time, as only two trucks at a time could get on these ferry boats. The drivers would just camp out and wait, buy some food, sleep in their trucks, and wait some more. It was as if time stood still.

Victoria Falls is one of the three biggest falls of the world, along with Niagara Falls and Iguacu Falls in Brazil. Typical American that I am, the oddity is that I would get to see Victoria and Iguacu, yet still haven't gotten to Niagara Falls. It's like they say about people who live in New York City being the only people in America who haven't been to the top of the Empire State Building.

Victoria Falls is considered a remarkable spectacle because it is the largest single sheet of water in the world – over 100 meters tall, and over one mile wide. One can view the falls face-on, and explorers have been doing so for centuries, the most famous perhaps being the Scotsman David Livingstone, of "Stanley and Livingstone" fame. He visited the falls in 1855 and renamed them after Queen Victoria – though they still are known to the locals as Mosi-oa-Tunya, or the "smoke that thunders".

The effect is truly mesmerizing. The falling water generates spray and mist that rises typically to over 400 meters, and is visible from up to thirty miles away. At full moon, a 'moonbow' can be seen in the spray instead of the daylight rainbow. During the wet season the falls spill over 19 million cubic feet of water each minute. I'm glad the sun was shining on my visit.

* * *

Zimbabwe, $1 = 60 Zim. Dollars (officially), 300 Zim. Dollars (cash on street)

Following the Zambezi River took me to Zimbabwe, the very name of which strikes dread in many people in the West, given the seemingly endless controversies in the one-time British colony of Rhodesia. Indeed, one may think of Zimbabwe as the polar opposite of South Africa. While both countries have similar histories with a relatively short period of majority rule, the flip side of South Africa's thriving nature is Zimbabwe's struggle to adapt to the realities and responsibilities of freedom. Not by coincidence, Zimbabwe's progress has been slowed by a general lack of respect for law and order – an instinct that begins at the very top, in the pseudo-dictatorship of President Robert Mugabe.

He has toyed with the country's status as a republic, and brought on untold human rights abuses. These include a law enacted that said any criticism of the President is grounds for treason. This law was used to put political opponents in jail in the run-up to the 2002 elections, when I was there. The election was a farce, with political cronies taking hours at a time in the voting booths. Long lines of voters never even made it into the polling places to cast a vote, and the ruling government remained in power.

These actions lead to a lack of confidence, and production fell off dreadfully. There were massive shortages in fuel and consumer goods, which also caused crippling inflation. More bad news came in the form of an AIDS epidemic. I encountered many blacks who were bitterly disappointed by the sham nature of the country's independence, and who were just straining to own some land and till the soil. They are a gentle and polite people, who are aware of the great promise of their traditions. The country was named after the great civilization of 2000 years ago, when it was known as Great Zimbabwe – the name deriving from "dzimba dzemabwe," meaning "houses of stone" in the Shona language.

There are still ruins of that medieval Bantu civilization, very similar in appearance and structure to the pyramids. These ruins may be metaphorical of the state of things in Zimbabwe today. As the first elected president in their history, Mugabe turned the country into a Marxist state without allowing much competition. Thus, what was once the bread basket of southern Africa – its farmers producing so much food that they would export it to the six neighboring countries – now lays dormant, engulfed in famine. The white farmers were not planting their land because of uncertainties of Mugabe's 'land reform' that would give white-owned farms to the black people.

I met a white farmer who told me the situation. He said that he and his father and brother all had farms next to each other, and the government confiscated one out of the three farms. The farm that was confiscated for land distribution happened to be the one that had the biggest house on it. And that farm went to cronies of the ruling government, not to native farmers. Land reform didn't benefit the peasants, but instead people who didn't know anything about farming who had the right political connections.

Still, against all odds, the natives somehow made the system work for them. I stayed as a guest in one of the huts of native Africans who lived in a small little village on a big farm, and were actually quite self-sufficient. They would work the fields and would get a stipend amount of money. The farm owner would sell them goods at a reduced rate so they would be able to have their own community and also have consumer goods. This was a company town with a white overlord, but there was a spirit of common cause here, and people seemed to be earning a living and being productive.

Even so, the famine continued to worsen, because most white farmers were not planting anything. One farmer told me why. Thieves would load up a crop of corn, for example, on the back of a truck. The farmers catch them at gun point and say they are under arrest, and take them down to the local police station. There, the police would hold the guys for a little bit and then let them go, saying this is a political situation, not a criminal one. This happened often enough that the white farmers just threw up their hands and said they're not going to plant anything because the police aren't going to enforce the law.

When the farmers are told by the government they are not welcome, they listen to other countries, such as the national governments of neighboring Mozambique or Zambia. In essence they say: if you're getting kicked off your land there, then come here. We will give you land at a reduced rate and we'll give you a tax free haven for the first ten years. No taxes, just do what you did over there. Show us how to do it, with the expertise that you have.

So this is what is bleeding Zimbabwe dry, and it is a national tragedy – a global one, really, given the resources that could be exported from the country. All Mugabe needs to do is consider the sorry example of Idi Amin in Uganda three decades earlier. After that country had become independent from the British, Amin took power and told all the white people to get out. Within a couple of years, he saw that there were a lot of Indian people there who earlier had come over from India as indentured servants, and that they were very good business people.

Amin could have learned a great deal, and benefited from the Indian people. But he took the approach of saying that they're as bad as the white guys, and they have got three months to get out. All the Indian people from Uganda had to leave, and they went to Kenya or Tanzania. When they did, the entire economy of Uganda careened downhill. You cannot take something away from somebody and give it to somebody else who is not prepared for it. The people who receive it have to be able to earn it for themselves.

Idi Amin's descent into madness was hastened by the ensuing civil war when he obsessed over killing all his political enemies. If Robert Mugabe heads in that direction, I grieve for the consequences.

* * *

Inflation is an absolute killer here. The official government exchange rate for the Zimbabwe dollar was 60 to the U.S. dollar. (Note: just six years later, in 2008 the rate had skyrocketed to over 10 billion to the U.S. dollar! They then had to chop off ten zeros and print new currency, just so people could buy things without using a suitcase to transport their cash.)

In 2002, if you went to an ATM machine you could get 60 to a dollar, the same as if you cashed a traveler's check or got money out of the bank on your credit card. However, if you went to the local businessman around the corner, you got a much better deal. I was getting my hair cut one day and the barber asked me if I would like to change some money. I asked how much is the rate? He said 300 to the dollar – the same currency that comes out of the ATM machine! Would you rather have 60 or 300? That is a no-brainer. It's not a five or even a ten percent increase; it's a 500 percent increase!

So I told every tourist that I knew who was going into Zimbabwe, "Don't bring your credit cards, don't bring your ATM cards, don't bring your traveler's checks. Bring cash – U.S. Dollars, South African Rand, or Euros – because you'll get a 500 percent better rate on the streets than you will at the banks at the official rate. And don't ever pay for anything on credit cards, just pay for things with cash."

Of course, there were times when people wanted to scam you. I found the usual exchange rate anywhere from 290 to 310. Once as I was driving, some guys on the street said they'd change money at 350. That perked up my ears – 350 instead of 300 – so I pulled over at a parking lot of a post office.

When I stopped, they asked, "How much do you want to change?"

"Fifty US dollars," I said.

I was still sitting in my car and rolled the window down a few inches to make the exchange, taking a fifty dollar bill from my wallet. They looked as if I'd pulled out a Rolex watch. "Let me see it," one of them asked, motioning that he wanted to examine it. This set off an alarm bell in my noggin. "You can't touch it," I said, figuring the first thing he'd do is run off with it and it's good-bye 50 dollars. "You can see it from there."

So I held it three feet away, inside the car. I waited for them to make their next move, which was to repeat the offer to exchange for 350 on the dollar. We did the math and it came to 17,500 Zimbabwe dollars.

I asked, "Do you have it?" and they eagerly replied, "Oh yes, here it is" – and one of them produced a wad of bills wrapped with a rubber band. Instantly, my mind peeled back in time to that high-stakes poker game in Bangkok, when I was played as a pigeon by that 'businessman' with a roll of bills that he refused to count in front of me. Apparently, con men world-wide have the same playbook.

"You've got to count it out," I insisted.

They wanted me to merely hand over the fifty, whereupon they would give me the roll of bills for me to count – by which time they would be long gone, scattering down some side street or alley. I had no doubt that stack of bills amounted to next to nothing of worthless bills. So I said, "Forget it, boys. It's not going to happen." Now they began to make excuses, something about the police are coming so they've got to go. And they split, before I could even see a cop. I had some business at the post office and went in, and upon returning to my car, guess who were waiting? With incredible persistence, they had come back to try another tack.

"We got some money for you," one said. I replied, "Hold on just a second," and opened the door, climbed in, shut the door behind me, and locked it. I rolled the window down a few inches again, and said what I had the first time around, "Let me see the money, and count it." One began to count out the wad of 17,500 Zimbabwe dollars, and I told them, "Okay, great. Give it to me, and I'll give you the $50 at the same time."

Not surprisingly, he hemmed and hawed. "No, no, we've got to wrap it up for you."

About out of patience, I said, "No you don't have to wrap it up for me." But he made a show of meticulously wrapping up the bills into a nice little roll. But instead of giving me the roll, he put it on top of my car, while he peered down at me. By now, I knew the scam: when he had put it on the top of my car, obviously he had someone else put another worthless roll of bills there, as well. So when he said, "Here you go, let's switch," he had already made a switch. I said to hold on a second.

I rolled up my window and backed out the car very calmly, and then drove off. But while driving away, I rolled down the window and yelled, "By the way, you guys, screw you" – and shot up a one finger salute for good measure.

Later that same day while in a cafeteria, some guy recognized me and said, "Hey, aren't you the guy who needed some change? You still have the 50 US dollars to change?" I looked at him – and it was one of the guys from the gang that couldn't count straight! I gave a look of disdain and said, "You're a brazen bastard. I can't believe that you tried to rip me off, and now you're coming back to ask me if I want to do it again? Get the hell out of here!" I did change money later that day with a guy at a shop. In a place of business like that, you are less apt to be conned because you can always come back to the scene of the transaction.

* * *

The Elephant Hills Golf Club is right near the Falls. I played nine holes that first afternoon, and was the last one on the course. Towards the end of the day, it's like playing golf at a zoo! There are no fences around the course, and all the beautiful animals come out of the surrounding jungle to eat the nice grass. I saw gazelles, wart hogs, impalas, even a waterbuck, which is the largest antelope in Africa – a huge elk-like creature with two big sharp antlers.

I felt like Doctor Doolittle, and was really tempted to 'talk to the animals' because these wonderful things are out there grazing on the grass and just loving it. They are completely nonthreatening and you walk around them to play your shot, with the urge to say, "Good day, mate" to each one. I would call that golf as nature intended it.

On the eighth hole as it was getting towards dusk, I hit my shot onto the fairway. While I walked to the ball, a group of antelopes there scampered off into the bushes on the adjacent fairway. Getting closer to my ball, I heard a great roar from out of the bush that caused the antelopes to hightail it out of there! I thought, uh-oh, I'm here alone and there is a lion or some other man-eater in that bush. Whatever it was, it had to have me in its sights. Was this how I was going to cash in my chips? As a lion's entree on a fairway at Victoria Falls?

First of all, I held my golf bag between me and that bush, as a makeshift barrier. Then, thinking that the best defense is a good offense, I put on a good show for the monster in the bush: stomping on the ground and yelling, "Damn, how bad I'm playing!" I came up to the ball, threw my clubs in mock anger onto the ground, took a massive whack at the ball and – turning it into the best shot of the day – it sailed right onto the green. I picked up my clubs and began to stomp off, cursing all the way to the green.

It was bad manners for a dignified golf course, but good strategy for dealing with whatever animal was in there – who by now was hopefully thinking that this strange white man was a mean ornery bastard and not to be messed with. I never heard it growl again, and never saw it, to my great relief. So there you have one big difference playing golf in the Third World – you share the course with wild animals, and I don't mean the kind with a thirty handicap. There are actually "Beware of Crocodiles" signs posted at the water hazards. If you're armed, you're safer. I really thought for a moment there that I'd have to defend myself with my pitching wedge. It was also one of the best safaris I had on my trip to Africa. Call it a golf safari.

The next day I played in the men's club tournament, and they took pictures of me sitting about ten feet from a crocodile, which had no intention of attacking anything. I wondered if perhaps that croc had been treated to a nine iron across the snout at some time or other, and was wary of being turned into the exterior of someone's nice new golf bag. Or else it just might have been a big golf fan. Playing golf 48 times on the trip through eastern Africa, I would see a course from the road and just stop and play. Back home it's expensive to play golf, but in Africa it is great value – sometimes even being around $10 for a full round.

* * *

While in Zimbabwe, I followed the Zambezi River and came upon a beautiful, rustic place called the Hippopotamus Lodge. It was for sale, and for a fleeting moment I seriously considered buying it, because the deal could be closed for less than $50,000. Break out the credit cards! The vista was absolutely breathtaking – a paradise in the middle of nowhere, right on a gleaming jungle river. The birds were migrating, flying down the river in V formation, about five feet above the water. I thought: I'll never see that again, and cursed myself for not having my video camera ready. Then, all of a sudden, another group of white birds swooped in and I got out my camera and started filming the thick flocks of birds soaring just over the river. The groups just seemed to keep coming.

Well, I came to my senses – a real hazard for a dreamer like me – and didn't buy the lodge. But I did come away with something: the memories of a canoe trip, when somebody there rented me one for exactly one dollar for the whole day. It was an old wooden dug-out canoe that an African tribesman had made, and they gave me an old wooden paddle, as well. I went for a ride on the river and was told – rather needlessly – to stay away from the hippos.

Being extremely wary, and determined to use that wooden paddle to fend off any intruding water creatures, I took the boat around what was called Hippo Island in the middle of the Zambezi River, circumnavigating the entire island. It took me about a day to do, including paddling over to the other side of the river which happened to be in Zambia. I saw some young kids tending cattle at the river, where the cattle were getting a drink. There were about six of these kids, and I gave some chewing gum to each. Their reaction was giddy glee, no different than if I'd given American kids new PlayStations.

Heading back down the river, I actually spotted a group of hippos, but was careful to stay about 75 yards away from them. Their snorting noises and air expulsions as they surfaced reminded me of a whale-watching trip. I made it back safely, just a nice canoe ride up and down the Zambezi. If the Africans wanted to think of me as a crazy *mzungu* who braved the hippos and crocs in a native dug-out and lived to tell about it, I wasn't going to object.

* * *

In Zimbabwe, one of my native car-mates was a man named Miles. As I dropped him off, along with his wife and two kids, his village turned out to be on a huge farm. It was so big that it contained about 25 huts and buildings in which all the native farm workers lived. Miles asked me where I was staying that night and I said that I would look for a hotel or something similar. "Nonsense," he said, "you stay with us at our house."

He put me up in a nice little hut, and just in the nick of time before the skies opened up and the rain came down in sheets. Luck had come through again. If I had pitched the tent anywhere in the area that night, I may have been swept away in the storm.

The next morning was bright and sunny and I discovered that I was the talk of the village – the big *mzungu* who had shown up from out of nowhere. They took me up and introduced me to the owner, a hale and friendly white man, Peter McKenzie, who told me about what's going on now in Zimbabwe with the farmers. He knew what he was talking about, too. His brother's farm had been confiscated by the government.

Later in the day, Miles asked if he could accompany me to Zambia, which is about a day's trip away, where he could buy some things and come back and sell them for a profit. I told him it was okay with me, but wondered how he would be able to pay for the items. He said he would ask Mr. Mackenzie for an advance on his salary. However, he was having a hard time summoning up the nerve to ask.

Knowing that buying and selling those goods from Zambia was his dream, I did him a solid favor. Later, while sitting around with Peter and Miles shooting the breeze, I said, "You know, Miles would like to come to Zambia with me, buy some things, and come back and sell them here. He is too proud to ask, but I bet he would like a modest loan to make it happen." And Peter gave the loan, saying that Miles was his finest worker, that his family and children were here, and adding, "I have a feeling that it's a good investment." – words that warmed my heart.

So Miles and I were to drive up to Zambia together, but before we left he was showing me around the worker's village. They had a well with a water pump that wasn't correctly working because a little linchpin holding the thing together was broken. They'd pump and pump, but only a little water came out. Later in the day at another area, I happened to look down on the ground and saw a foot-long piece of rebar – a metal scrap used for concrete work that helps strengthen the concrete. I picked it up and told Miles to take it back home and use it as a linchpin for the pump.

He did, and it worked like a charm. The water was flowing freely! All the episode really proved was that we were at the right place at the right time, finding that metal scrap. But because of it, maximum satisfaction was gained for the whole village – one more place had been left for the better.

Zimbabwe has a lot of challenges to overcome, to begin to prosper and evolve in the right direction. That will be an exciting time, and I hope all of the white and black farmers I met in Zimbabwe will be around to build the dreams they all share.

* * *

Zambia, $1 = 4120 Kwacha

I like to make friends with just about everyone. Part of it is the vibe I always try to emit, in accordance with the second of my rules: be gracious. But simply, they will be remembering you for a long time, so you might as well make the best of it. You might be the only American that they ever met, so they might think that all Americans must be just like you. So you try to put on your most humble, unassuming, try-to-be-nice face for all people. You can't walk around with your chest out and being braggadocios because people will think you're an arrogant person. I always act like a guest in someone's country, and I try to do the right thing.

One example: I stopped into a small village one hot day to buy a cold drink. The village literally came to a stand-still. The music stopped, and the people all stopped what they were doing to see what the big *mzungu* was going to do. So, watching everybody watching me, I wanted to give them their money's worth. I walked around in a funky little Mick Jagger-type of walk, just a little bit crazy, and it made everybody laugh. They were all looking at me the whole time, probably saying, "What's he doing now? Looks like he's ordering a Coke. Now he's pouring the

Coke. Now he's drinking the Coke." Sometimes I caught them gazing and I raised my glass to them, and their expression was, "Oh he's cool, he's toasting us." They will remember all that. The mundane becomes the memorable.

It's the same as my own memory of being in London in 1984 and seeing the singer Rod Stewart – not in concert, but on the streets of London in his jeep. He made an illegal U-turn, just turned around in the middle of the street. And just as he did it, he looked at me and my friends on the side of the road. Seeing us gawking at him, he put his finger to his mouth and said, "Shhh, don't tell anyone!" We just laughed ourselves silly. That was over twenty years ago, and I'm still telling that story. Just think what these African guys are probably going to be saying: "Remember when that big *mzungu* came into our village and drank a Coke, and then toasted us? Yeah, that was cool. When was that anyway? About 20 years ago, or so?" And when you think about it, how cool is that?

* * *

Subject: Mount Kilimanjaro Greetings!

1 Mar 2002

Jambo ('Greetings' in Swahili) from the slopes of Mt. Kilimanjaro here in Tanzania. Have spent 2 nights here while adjusting to some welcome cooler temperatures: the summit has snow on it year-round, while still being so close to the sweltering hot equator. Tanzania was formed by combining the former colonies of Tanganyika and Zanzibar. And its culture is a pleasant mix of both Islamic and Christian, as well as Arab and Black African. Some Muslim truck drivers really showed their hospitality and came to the rescue when I was stranded with 2 flat tires – due to some severe pot-holes on a dangerous stretch of road.

The Indian Ocean here at the big city of Dar Es Salaam ('Haven of Peace' in Swahili) is like swimming in a warm bath. Its coral shores can be tricky on the feet while entering. Saw some ancient Arab wooden sail boats that were packed 10 feet high with cargo, and loads of people on the top of that! Those brave souls were headed out to Zanzibar Island on an over-night trip. Like a major sea-faring accident just waiting to happen!

Further south, Zambia is the closest thing to a 'Police State' I have ever seen. There were 16 police check-points from Lusaka to the border. This really restricts the freedom of movement around the country. And they nit-pick on any obscure vehicle code violation in order to extract some bribes from drivers. Really had to do some fast talking song and dance routines to get out of a few of those unscathed.

Drove off the beaten path to the jungles of Zaire (Congo) for a day trip, through some native villages. When stopping at a village (in any country) a group of kids will follow you like the Pied Piper, and squeal with delight an seemingly minute little things!

Actually, being a Westerner in Africa is not for the faint hearted. You are the center of attention at all times, and must be on your humblest behavior. It is as if a famous rock star is seen on the streets of your town. If he does the slightest thing wrong, you know they will all be talking about it for years to come.

You are also seen as a major source of the local economy, so people flock to you like flies to... fly-paper. Hoping a little bit of anything will fall their way. I now know how a celebrity like Jay Leno feels when he says he has to have a stack of 5 dollar bills in his pocket at all times so he can tip anyone who helps him at just about anything – just so he's not seen as the cheap rich guy. Same here, but with a lot less decimal points. People get by on really small amounts here.

Have stayed as a guest of lovely families in village huts with thatched roofs, as well as homes of shop owners in cities. The people are always so hospitable, and their food is really good! Helped get a mechanical part that fixed a water pump at a village well. Boy, that is a hard job. The ladies have to pump the water, then carry it home in 5 gallon buckets on their heads!

Hope all is cool with you. Cheers, Christopher

* * *

Tanzania, $1 = 953 Shillings

The East African Community is comprised of the three former British colonies of Uganda, Tanzania, and Kenya. To go from one country to the other, the natives don't need passports, nor even have to stop and be checked, it seemed. I had to stop as I'm obviously a foreigner traveling in a private car, and had been used to paying around $5 to bring my car across a border, plus what ever it costs for visa paperwork. I was in for a rude awakening at the border going into Tanzania, as they stung me for as much money as they could get. There were road taxes, special insurances, you name it. They wanted $80 to cross the border, and that floored me, as I could live for weeks on that! But I had passengers in the car, and felt obligated to just pay it and move on. Without them in the car, I would have been tempted to turn around and try another route.

One dark night in Tanzania, I was driving around Dar Es Salaam with a few friends and we happened to make a wrong turn on a one way street. Just then some police waved us over, and they all had machine guns – an excessive show of force indeed for a routine traffic violation. They must really take their traffic laws seriously. They told us to get out of the car, and took us to sit in the squad car. I hoped that it was all a show, a scare tactic to get us to pay some money. It was working. The good news was that for all the guns, the cops were willing to take what

I pulled from my wallet – the equivalent of a single dollar. Talk about getting off cheap. I was really motivated by their 'little friends' named Uzi. You just don't argue with Mr. Uzi.

* * *

The showpiece of northern Tanzania is Mount Kilimanjaro. The tallest free-standing mountain rise in the world, Kilimanjaro features the highest apex in Africa at 19,340 feet – called Uhuru Peak. It is snow-capped twelve months a year, even though it is almost upon the equator. Yet the glaciers that have covered the top of the mountain for the past 11,700 years are eroding, adding fuel to the fire about global warming.

There are actually two big mountains right close to each other here, Mount Kilimanjaro and Mount Kenya. When the colonial Europeans were first divvying up Africa, Kenya was ruled by the British and Tanzania was ruled by the Germans. They had to put that border somewhere in between, and they drew a line from Lake Victoria to the coast. Everything north would be British and everything south would be German. Then someone said, wait a second, if we draw that straight line it looks like you're going to get two mountains on your side and we're not going to get a mountain. So they moved the line just a little bit over, so Mount Kilimanjaro was on the German side and Mount Kenya on the British side. Life was much more simple back then.

The first day at Kilimanjaro it was raining, so I waited a couple of days for clearer weather while exploring Kilimanjaro National Park. That first day, there was a guard who kept eying me suspiciously. I was the last one at the park and he didn't quite know what to make of me. Like those cops, he had a big machine gun with him. But unlike the cops, he was also drunk. Not a good mix – for me.

He obviously had a lot to drink throughout the day and he was telling me things with such bravado that I was fidgeting nervously because I didn't know what a drunk with a machine gun was likely to do. Anything might set him off and he could just start shooting. Fortunately, he took a liking to me and I was able to hang out there in an uneasy kind of peace. So, over two days, I had learned another vital lesson for survival in the Third World:

Be especially nice to the ones with machine guns.

* * *

Before leaving Tanzania, I was able to use my *eclat* as a big foreigner to wangle into the plush Royal Palms Hotel in Dar Es Salaam. It is five star international quality, just the kind of place I always love to visit. Accompanied by one of my native riders named Francis, his eyes just lit up when he saw the place, and I wanted to give him a memory he'd never forget. Anyone Western looking is treated royally. In the lobby everybody would ask, "How are you, sir?" and then say, "Have a very nice day, sir." All par for the course.

I was meeting with a Middle Eastern businessman who was interested in buying my car. He asked if I wanted to try the breakfast buffet. Eying the $15 price tag, I demurred, as that amount could feed a family of four here for a month – and certainly feed me for at least a week. "Nonsense," he insisted, "Come as a guest of my company." I said, "Can my 'driver' come too?" He answered, "Certainly."

And with that, we took Francis to the dining room for a buffet breakfast. He couldn't believe the unending variety of food! I told him, "Go fill up your plate with as much eggs, sausages, bacon, and potatoes as you want. Get an extra plate for the fresh fruit and yogurt. Don't forget the pancakes and French toast. And, Francis, when you're done... go back and get some more!" He was in hog heaven. Later we went swimming at the pool outside, and he had never seen water so clear and fresh. At one point, his eyes were welling up a bit.

He told me, "Christopher, I will never forget this day."

Again, it was nothing on my part. But for one man, it meant everything. That is why I, too, will never forget that day. Because in human terms, it meant everything for me, as well.

* * *

My last night in Dar Es Salaam, I piled seven of my friends and their children into the car and took them to an ice-cream shop on the mezzanine terrace of the Emirates Airline building. It is a gorgeous place with a modern marble counter-top and a big elaborate chandelier.

Upon arriving, I saw a sign that said, "Special: Cans of Diet Sprite for 100 Schillings." That is about ten cents a can. I assumed that ice-cream cones were probably around the same as cans of soda. So I bought cones for everybody, figuring the lot would come to less than a dollar.

Then a bit of a surprise came when we found out the cones were Western prices – a dollar each, or seven bucks in all. Quite a shock, since Peter pays five dollars for his room and meals with the family – per week! If you figure a room and board back home in the U.S. wouldn't be less than $250 a week, then a dollar spent here with the locals actually spends like fifty bucks back in the USA. Could it be I just spent the equivalent of $350 on ice cream? I would rather just have thrown the family the cash instead. They could use it a lot more than the Emirates Airlines.

But splurging it on the family was worth it, as they would never indulge themselves in such extravagances. And the memory would be as savory for them as the ice-cream.

Kenya, $1 = 78 Schillings

On the northern edge of Tanzania when crossing into Kenya, I was not going to let the same high priced shake-down happen again. I'd been told one must pay something like a $200 deposit with a customs broker because Kenya didn't want anyone to bring a car across, sell it and reap a big profit – none of which would go to the government coffers. They assured me the deposit would be returned upon leaving the country. Yea, right. Don't count on it.

By speaking with some of the locals, I found out the secret of getting over the border without paying those enormous fees – which are only applied to foreigners, not to the natives from the region. Some of the local shop keepers took me aside and said, "Why don't you just do what we do?" They told me to drive my car parallel to the border down a little "no man's land" zone between the two countries that led out of the sight of the border guards. Being night time, it was pretty dark and it could have been a red herring, just to get me alone to be robbed. But I was game, and did as they suggested. I parked by a little gas station, came back and presented my passport to the guards, and they stamped my visa. So when I went back to my car, I was good to go.

It was a brilliant plan, and it worked. And when I left Kenya later that month, I did the same thing. Bingo, right through again. Sometimes, the best laid plans of mice and men are plans that seem too simple. Which is why I always tell myself to keep it simple, stupid.

* * *

I cannot really say that I am all that religious, but I do count my blessings. Every night in bed I give thanks by saying to myself the 23rd

Psalm. This day at the border of Kenya, I jotted down all the sections of that famous prayer that seemed to fit that very day:

1. (The Lord is my shepherd, I shall not want.) I didn't need anything, just waited around until it all worked out with my entry visa.

2. (He makes me to lie down in green pastures.) I woke up in a green pasture, in my tent.

3. (He leads me beside the still waters. He restores my soul.) I swam in the river, with its still waters.

4. (He leads me down the path of righteousness for His name's sake.) I walked along the jungle paths to get to the river.

5. (Though I walk through the valley of the shadow of death, I shall fear no evil.) I had to walk across the border late at night alone in the shadows, but was not afraid.

6. (For the Lord is with me. Your rod and Your staff will comfort me.) The long staffs of the Masai warriors were numerous.

7. (You prepare a table for me in the presence of my enemies.) I had a great meal of goat and rice, and there was a man there who praised the Al Qaida terrorists.

8. (You anoint my head with oil.) I had to wipe the oil from the goat barbecue in my hair, as there were no napkins around.

9. (My cup runneth over.) I got a free refill of my cup of mango and avocado juice blend!

10. (Surely goodness and love will follow me all the days of my life.) The goodness and love of all the joyful kids I swam and played Frisbee with was abundant.

11. (And I will dwell in the house of the Lord forever. Amen!) It just
    keeps going and going...

* * *

After crossing into Kenya, I met up again with the same people at the
border. I actually stayed at their house as a guest the first night. One of
them was named Abdul Aziz and he was interested in going to Nairobi,
the capital city, which is about a half day away. So the next morning we
were off. Abdul knew where the best roadside food joints were, and we
had some nice meals there: goat, rice and gravy, and chapatis, which
are soft India-bread tortilla type of things, and you eat them with just
about anything. They can be made sweet for eating with your tea, or
you can have them plain with your rice and goat meat.

When we got to Nairobi, we saw the US Embassy site that was bombed
on August 7, 1998 by Al Qaida operatives, nearly simultaneously with
an identical bombing of the U.S. Embassy in Dar Es Salaam, Tanzania.
The blasts took a heavy toll: at least 192 were killed in Nairobi and
nearly 5,000 injured; 10 more died in Dar Es Salaam and 74 injured.
Knowing that the bombings were a preface to the terrible events of
September 11, 2001, standing at this antecedent of Ground Zero was
a reminder to stay vigilant and always be prepared.

Nairobi is a bustling city, as there are lots of people, lots of mini buses
called *matatus*, and no car exhaust emission standards. You can see cars
puffing away with a big cloud of black smoke behind them, and the
air can choke you. The old world still exists in the form of swarms of
people selling things on the street or at make shift market places on the
side of the road. The streets are absolutely packed and jammed.

My friend introduced me to a young lady named Pauline who was a
friend of his, and we all slept at her house that night. I had a leisurely
stroll around the block with Pauline, she showed me some of the sights,

135

and that night we had a nice meal at her house. Soon after, my eyelids began to get heavy and I was quite tired, so I excused myself and went to bed. The next morning, we got up and went on our way. I dropped Abdul off where he wanted to go and continued on my own journey.

About two weeks later, I was up in northern Kenya and discovered that one of my $100 traveler's checks was missing. With a stack of travelers checks, I'm quite officious about numbering them and knowing which ones have been used. This one wasn't the first one nor the last one, it was about three from the end. There was no way I would have taken out and spent a traveler's check from the middle of the pile. They were in a money belt worn around my waist, tucked in my pants, between my skin and clothing, so no one could touch them unless I specifically took them out.

Putting the pieces together, I deduced what had happened. When I had gone to sleep at Pauline's house, exhausted from the trip, they may have slipped a 'mickey' into my food or drink. When I was out cold, they harvested the check from my pouch, which was still wrapped around my middle. They took it off me as I was asleep, and then carefully put it back on. I was none the wiser. And if I had to guess, I would say that it wasn't the first time the people at that house had done something like that. They were too slick.

Fortunately, American Express replaced the check straight away, so I got my hundred dollars back. It could have been a lot worse, as I might have lost much more than a C-note – possibly even as much as my life. Be aware.

* * *

That first day in Nairobi, some other people weren't as lucky. The newspaper the next morning told of a massacre in the northern suburb of Keriobangi, leaving 21 people dead. A mob of people from the extremist Mungiki sect went into a different tribe's area, and the death squad jumped out of their cars and trucks and started chopping up people with machetes and axes. Imagine, you're sitting at your local pub or restaurant and you're not facing the door. You happen to be facing the other way having your drink, and all of a sudden someone rushes through the door and chops off your head with one fell swoop! That's what happened more than once, and in a short time there were twenty-one bodies, some with heads and limbs severed. Some of the heads could not immediately be found because people were kicking them down the street like soccer balls.

This is hatred that you do not see in the Western world. We think of a school massacre such as at Columbine when some kid goes wild with a gun and kills six of his schoolmates, and all of a sudden there are television crews on the scene reporting it constantly for the next six months. Then there's a one year anniversary of that terrible 'massacre.' In Kenya this very real massacre was news for only about a week in the local papers and television news; after that it was swept under the carpet and they went on to other things.

And yet incidents such as this happen with seeming regularity. People have become inured to them. It's just a sad fact of life that religious and tribal hatred is rarely dealt with. If you think racism is bad where you and I live in the Western world, it's nothing compared to what tribalism is in Africa. People hate people with seething passion just for being a member of another tribe. One can even make the case that some rulers encourage such strife so they can keep people from uniting in common cause against the controlling government. But because things are rarely done, all that people can do is merely hope they don't find themselves in the wrong place at the wrong time.

* * *

In Nairobi I was a guest of Dr. Charles Ugunda, and did some work at his medical center. He was doing gynecological work, and I helped with the organization of the office, as well as the expansion plans and marketing of the center. He also ran an orphanage for AIDS orphans and for other new-borns who's parents could not keep them. If they did not leave the kids there, they would surely kill them quietly on the way home, he said. The twelve young babies slept in two beds in one room, six to a bed. The babies were naked, and the heat was provided by a little heater. There were a couple of plastic rattles per bed, and the nurses gave them some cuddling once in awhile. They lie side by side on the beds, the sheets often soaked in urine, with some feces.

I looked to find a better way of doing things. For example, after changing the bed sheets the kids would quickly urinate on the fresh bed again, pretty much keeping them in an almost constant state of dampness. I put them in a bassinet of warm water in which they could urinate to their hearts' content before putting them back on the fresh bed. That kept the beds dry a bit longer. Just trying to help. Be gracious.

Dr. Ugunda's home was in a secure compound behind locked gates in a nice part of Nairobi, but in the evening gunshots would ring in the distance. People were shooting at each other, and it felt a bit like the place was under siege. I was also on the fringe of a crowd at the soccer stadium as they got tear gassed by the local police. So much for crowd control. When the sea of humans gets moving, all you can do is stay on your feet and keep going – for fear of being trampled underneath.

Only the army and police are allowed by law to carry weapons. If this is so, they seem to have quite itchy trigger fingers, if my ears heard right. One lady told me a story about her friends having a house on the outskirts of town, in a more rural setting. They got a knock at the door at about three o'clock in the morning, and it was a man who announced matter-of-factly, "We are robbers and we have guns, and we know you do not." Her friends were given five minutes to carry all their valuable possessions into the front room, unlock the front door, and retreat to the back of the house. If they did this, their lives would be spared. The bad guys got away with cash, silverware, and even a television.

I'm not a big gun guy, never having carried one for my protection anywhere in the world. But I do believe in the right to bear arms, as this right keeps all our houses safe at night. The bad guys do not know who has a gun and who does not. We sometimes take this right for granted. Be aware.

* * *

Gradually, I came to learn some of the Swahili language. Not a lot of it, but some essentials such as "*karibu*" (welcome), "*jambo*" (hello), "*hibarri?*" (How's it going?), "*missouri*" (fine), "*assanti*" (thank you), "assanti sana" (thank you very much), and even some of a more modern vernacular, such as "*matatu*" (mini-bus), and one other that I completely misconstrued – "*umevaa kinyasa*" (You're wearing shorts). Here's the explanation as to how I learned this phrase:

I was driving in Nairobi one hot day with the car windows down. It is hot in the tropics, and all the technology my car has is '2-60' air conditioning. That is, I generally roll down 2 windows and go 60 miles an hour. I stopped at a street light and some little kids who live on the streets, street urchins if you will, crowded around my car and they put their hands right on the window sill, looking in. All of a sudden one of the kids said, "*Umevaa kinyasa*." In my ears when he said it quickly, his dialect made it sound like, "You're a freaking ars-hole." (or even worse!) I thought, man, this little kid only knows one phrase in English and that's it!

I turned to my local friend who was sitting next to me and asked, "Did he just say what I thought he said?" And my friend replied, "He said, 'You're wearing shorts.'" Apparently, seeing a man wearing shorts in Africa is quite a big deal – a fashion faux pas, even! In most of Africa grown men don't show their legs, they wear long pants; shorts are reserved for young kids like the little boy himself. And when he saw that I was an adult wearing shorts, he might have chuckled to himself. I'm only glad it was a kid who uttered those words. If it had been a grown man, I might have punched the guy.

I can just imagine the headline: "Freaking Ars-hole Sparks International Incident!"

* * *

After finishing the assignment at the medical center, I took a gander at a map and saw that I'd gone halfway up Africa's eastern tier. 'Capetown to Cairo' had a nice ring to it, and I was not far from actually bisecting the entire continent. So I decided to put my Ford Laser into gear and continue on along that locus. First stop was a place called Isiolo in the northern half of Kenya. The paved road stops right there, and the rest is desert dirt road all the way up to Ethiopia. There is a military checkpoint there, and they don't allow anyone to go beyond unless they have a military escort because civilization sort of ends right there, as well. Me being me, I told the guards I want to drive through and make my way to the border, about 500 miles away.

Giving me the by-now all too usual 'Are you out of your mind?' look, they explained that there was no way I could make it in this little car, that even a four-wheel drive might break down in the desert. I wanted to try anyway, but they wouldn't budge. Not unless I was part of a government convoy. As we were going back and forth, I noticed that a man who was selling vegetables near the checkpoint had been listening in. He came over and introduced himself as Abdul Aduba, and said his tribe lived on the border of Kenya and Ethiopia. He offered to be my guide through the desert, and I readily agreed to give him a ride. When

I told the guards I'd be taking the man home and he'd be my guide, they gave in.

It was a bit of a daunting feeling when the gate came up and the horizon before me was nothing but an extended desert. The ride was no picnic, either. The dirt and gravel roads were very difficult to navigate. There would often be two tire tracks with a high ridge of loose dirt between them. Without high clearance, I would put two wheels on the ridge, and two wheels down in a track. This is like driving on a sideways angle. Not enjoyable. They were not kidding when they said these roads are tough on cars. We drove from 10 a.m. to 4 p.m., and got a full share of flat tires along the way. When the first tire blew, we changed it and kept going, then found a small town where it could get repaired. About a third of the way into the desert, two others blew and we only had one spare. With seven miles to go before the next little town, we somehow made it there on three tires. Luckily the Laser was a front-wheel drive, so with two good tires on the front, they pulled the back end – with one good tire and one not. It was slow and tedious, but better than sitting out there in the middle of a baking desert being a target for anyone who happened to come by.

Abdul kept me entertained by telling me about other intrepid visitors who had tried to make this drive. One of them, he said, was a Japanese man who was on his own, camping out in the desert, and he saw some people creeping up on the far side of his car. Realizing he was about to be robbed, or worse, he put to work his martial arts skills on them. Even though they had spears and machetes, he turned the tables on them, battering and holding them until authorities came. They were arrested and given three years in prison for trying to attack and kill him. A happy ending, indeed. Except I didn't know martial arts.

Abdul also said there were wandering nomads, or desert bushmen, who will try to rip off anything they can get their hands on – even the sheets people use to cover themselves with when they sleep in the desert. They are awakened, sheet-less and screaming, as the thief runs off into the dark. He knew that because it had once happened to him. And later that same night, he heard in the distance the cries of it happening to several other hapless campers, as well!

We limped those last seven miles on three tires into the little desert village of Nerille. I would have to hitch back to Isiolo to get new tires the next day. There would be no traffic until the morning, so we learned about the desert from the locals. We walked through a dry riverbed, and came upon four people who were huddled around something. As we came closer, I saw that it was a hole that had been dug about three feet in diameter and ten feet deep. At the very bottom of this small well, there was a little boy.

He was standing in several inches of water in the pit of the well, holding a cup with which he could scoop out the dirty, murky water into plastic jugs all around him. The boy, who was obviously down there because he was small and could fit into the hole, would fill each jug one by one and hand them up to the people outside the well. The jugs held three to five gallons, which are quite heavy to carry back home balanced on top of the head. This wasn't water I would normally even think about drinking, but in the desert where there is such little water, it was heaven sent. I drank along with everyone else.

After finding a room to sleep that evening, the next morning I went about the business of somehow hitchhiking back to where we started at Isiolo, buying two tires and a new rim, and hitching back to Nerille with them. I was sitting at a cafe and saw some dust rising just down the road. Then a car appeared, coming southward. I left my breakfast on the table, and ran out the door to flag down the car. At the wheel was a white American who was doing some sort of work on a government project. He graciously gave me a lift to Isiolo. I had to shop around to buy the tires and rim, and of course the prices were laughably high – there was that unwritten 'rich *mzungu*' sign around my neck – but I paid them just to get it done without a hassle. Now, I was faced with another problem. How was I going to get them back to Nerille?

Sometimes I really do believe there's some kind of hidden power looking over me. This was one of those times. At this service station where I bought the tires, a big truck was filling up with gas. "Got room in there for a guy going up north?" I inquired.

"Hop in," came the reply. As it turned out, it was the easiest ride I'd ever come up with. Indeed, I've had far tougher times on the road than hitchhiking through the African desert, carrying two tires. Go figure.

* * *

Before leaving Nerille, I got my new tires mounted at a local shop. When driving off, the car only got about a hundred yards down the road. Then it stopped dead. I looked under the hood and saw that some wires had been cut. Someone had clearly fooled with the wiring while I was away, apparently to sabotage the car and get me to pay for more engine work.

Hopping mad, I went back and demanded to see the tribal chief of the village. I was taken to a ramshackle little house with chickens and goats traipsing through in the yard, whereupon an old man of about seventy years heard me out and was helpful. By the way, he had the most beautiful young and sporty wife around. Clearly one of the spoils of being a tribal chief. With the wisdom of Solomon, he ruled on the spot a fair price to fix the wires. I could only surmise that this sort of thing happens quite regularly to naive outsiders, in order to get them back to the shop for more expensive work. In a way, that said something about development in the Third World. With a gimmick like that, those guys could have been valuable workers at any mechanic shop in America.

I headed north about twenty miles before my radiator overheated. The desert was really taking its toll. Stopping in Laisamis to get it fixed, it is a dusty missionary town with a Catholic church. Abdul remarked that he liked the Catholics because, he said, "They help anyone, it doesn't matter what religion you are." I thought that was nice coming from a Muslim. All the children of the town wanted to touch my car, as they were used to seeing huge four wheel drive trucks, and may never have seen a car so small as my tiny Ford Laser.

At this point, I was still set on making a complete bisection of the continent. But while fixing the radiator, we discovered several small holes that had to be fixed with outdated tools. They actually used hot coals to heat a soldering iron. It didn't quite cut it. Plus, the gas tank was now leaking, as well. No sense in continuing through the desert with all these leaks. So I decided instead to head back down to Capetown, from where I still had my airline ticket home.

While still in the desert, I spied a young boy who was a shepherd marshaling his goats and camels. This was the first time I'd seen camels in the desert, and there were about 10 of them. As I approached on the dirt road, the boy ran next to the car. I thought he was having fun, and waved while passing him. But he just kept running to keep up with me, for maybe a hundred yards. Not knowing if he wanted to tell me something, I stopped and he began pointing to his mouth, sign language for 'water.'

I had maybe a half gallon of water, and gave him a drink. I thought he would chug it right down in big gulps, but instead he took just one sip – another indication of how precious water is in the desert to the natives. They are conditioned to taking a sip and preserving the rest. "You can have some more," I said, and he drank more and said thank you. Continuing on, I became a little spooked at the thought of not having enough water to get through the desert this time. So that kid taught me a little something about survival. I'd be okay, though, since covering ground in the desert is a lot quicker by car than on a camel's back.

* * *

Back on civilized paved roads, heading south in Tanzania, I picked up another native rider, a man whom I had actually met earlier on the way up to Kenya. His name was Innocent, which was reflective of the wonderful names people have in Africa. Two of his relatives were named Lightness and Reward. We drove from Arusha in the north of Tanzania down to Dar Es Salaam, a half day's drive away. Innocent had a brother there whom he said might help sell my car, something I would have to do before heading back home to America.

After arriving in Dar Es Salaam, he took me to where his brother lived and we spent a weekend together. I'd promised Innocent that if his brother sold my car, I'd give them ten percent of what I got – which would be a handsome reward indeed. We drove around all weekend, trying out his brother's contacts, and I bought the lunches, dinners, and beers along the way. However, I never got a reasonable offer on the car, and told him I'd be leaving. I drove him to his brother's house, said goodbye, and waited for him to get out. But he continued to sit in the passenger seat.

Finally, he said, "I need some money. I did work for you."

I said, "The car never sold. We tried, but it was a waste of time."

"But I still need some money."

He didn't want to get out of the car until getting something, which certainly was the most passive attempt at being squeezed I'd had on the trip. I didn't know what to do, but luckily saw a police station right across the street. So while he sat there, I went into the station and said, "Can you get this guy out of my car?"

Two cops came out, looked over the situation and told the suddenly not-so Innocent, "Get out of this man's car." Which he did, whereupon I jumped in, and rolled the window down a few inches to listen. He gave the cops a sob story, and they weren't buying it.

And yet, the cops now told me to get out of the car. They wanted me to come into the station house so they could make a report. That usually means time wasting, foot dragging, and bribe paying will follow. I couldn't accept that, starting to get hot under the collar on an already blazing hot day under the African sun. "No," I stated, "I'm not getting out"

Looking a bit askance, one cop stated, "I'm a policeman, you have to do what I tell you."

I added, "And you also have a gun. If you want to, go ahead and shoot me now, but I'm not getting out because I think I'm in danger right now. If I get out, something bad is gong to happen to me." Now they were totally flabbergasted that somebody was talking to them that way. Seeing their discomfort, I laid it on thicker. "I want you to call the U.S. Embassy right now," I said, "because I think this is an international incident."

Having seen this tacky little local con escalate into something way beyond their purview, the cops huddled and talked for a minute or two, then one came back, looking somewhat apologetic. "We've decided," he said, "not to make a decision. You can go."

Silently congratulating myself on my acting, I thanked them and started up the engine. But as the cops walked off, Innocent snapped. He got right up to the window, stuck his fingers into the crack of open space, and started pulling on the window – trying to yank it right out! I yelled out to the vacating cops, but at that moment the window shattered into a million pieces! The cops turned on their heels, handcuffed and hauled Innocent off to the station, under arrest for destroying private property. However, all that meant was that I'd have to come into the station and file a report after all.

The cops said Innocent would spend the night in jail, and that I'd have to come back the next day to get restitution. Well, there wouldn't be much anyway, so I just walked away from the whole thing. I ended up getting the window repaired, and just got out before anything else could happen.

* * *

Driving south, about an hour from the country of Malawi and knowing the border would close at 6 p.m., I really leaned on the gas pedal to get there fast. But there was a young native in a T-shirt and no shoes walking alongside the road. On his big toe was a white bandage with a blood stain, and he was limping along, so I just had to stop to pick him up. He was extremely grateful. He spoke no English, so for the next 20 minutes we taught each other English and Swahili. After awhile, I wondered: this guy was going to walk this far? So I asked where his home was, and he motioned, pointing over his shoulder, "Back there."

Back there?! I halted the car with a screech of brakes. Remember the old adage: "A good deed never goes unpunished." I ended up giving him money to take public transportation back to where he lived, and said good-bye. This got me thinking as to why he did not speak up when we passed his house.

Lets say you are standing on the sidewalk one day, and a stretch limousine stops right in front of you. The door opens up and a rock star from Aerosmith asks you if you need a ride. You say, "Sure!" You get in and they pour you a drink from the wet bar. You are really enjoying a big cigar and the quadraphonic sounds reverberating off the fine leather upholstery. And when they ask you where you want to get off, you probably say, "Back there."

It's the same thing. This may have been the man's first time in a private car, and to him it was like Futureworld. He just wanted to keep riding, and would have ridden all the way to the Malawi border if he could have, just to enjoy this luxury. He never got to. Maybe next time.

The delay made me get to the border late, so I spent a night in a village near the border. The next morning was April Fool's Day, and while driving to the border I realized I'd have to leave Tanzania without being able to show any documentation that I'd entered the country legally. And my visa had expired, to boot. Fool, indeed. I had left myself open to having to cough up more big bribes to be let out of the country. Unless I could think fast.

The border crossing was on a river, with a bridge and an iron gate. How to get through without paperwork? There was no possibility of mixing in with the locals, as even they were checked thoroughly before that gate could be opened. The solution came about in a most peculiar and ironic way. On my way, there happened to be a policeman walking on the side of the road. He flagged me down and said he needed a ride to the border. As we were driving there, I was almost amused that there was a cop sitting right next to me and I'm technically an illegal visitor to the country. How in the world was I going to talk my way out of this?

As it turned out, my passenger was worth a thousand words. At the border, the guards saw him in the car, flung open the gate, and we drove right through! I dropped him off at his station, then went in to the immigration building to use the men's room. Upon coming out of the building, everyone just assumed I'd gotten my paperwork stamped.

But I was already through the gate, so who needs anything more? I went back to my car and calmly waved good-bye to my police friend before driving across the bridge to the Malawi side. Again, a little luck had gotten me through without the hassle of paying another blasted bribe. Who were the fools now?

* * *

Malawi, $1 = 70 Kwacha

Subject: Lake Malawi – Wowie!

7 Apr 2002

Greetings from the Great Lakes region of Africa. These lakes (which include Lake Victoria, Malawi, and Tanganyika) are like 600 kilometer-long inland seas, and you cannot see the land on the other side. Here on Lake Malawi, it is the closest thing to a tropical Caribbean-type resort with crystal clear water and palm trees. I was catamaran sailing among the islands, then body surfing in some strong waves – and it is all fresh water, no salty ocean!

You would think the people here would know they live in paradise. Yet other more pressing problems always seem to bring us back to reality. Malawi is one of the 10 poorest countries on earth. There are food shortages, with starvation a daily reality in the rural areas. Some villagers must eat grasses and leaves sometimes just to survive. Cholera, malaria, and AIDS are all problems. Makes my car problems with blown tires, or a bout with the flu seem quite minuscule. These challenges, coupled with government gross mismanagement of international aid have caused several donating nations to halt all aid until the government programs become more 'transparent' (less corrupt).

This is where all the used clothing ends up, which people donate after cleaning out their closets. There is a grand selection of T-shirts with English phrases with a misspelled word, or out of date styles and colors, or some other small defect on an otherwise useful article of clothing. I met missionaries Tom and Carla from Kentucky who quit their jobs back home and are building an air strip and a school. They wanted to do something constructive for mankind, while they were still young enough to have lasting memories of it all. We all share similar goals, deep down inside.

Always must keep a watchful eye out for treachery. I give rides to a lot of the locals. Once I caught a guy leaving my car with my video camera under his shirt! After a sound scolding, I let him go. I asked another what they would have done to him on a local level. Most likely they would douse him with petrol and set him on fire. Crispy critter, right then and there. Swift justice.

Cheers, Christopher

* * *

At Lake Malawi I gave a lift to a German couple, and we visited a resort on the fresh-water inland sea. Later we drove further south to Blantyre, a big commercial city in the heart of a country ravaged by poverty and a famine in the countryside. Tellingly, the West would only become aware of the country's scores of homeless children when the rock star Madonna would adopt one in 2006, apparently cutting through the red tape with an offer the Malawi authorities couldn't refuse.

It was in Malawi that I got sick for the first and only time on the trip. I came down with a case of the flu that was accompanied by diarrhea. While staying at a backpacker's hostel where Western businessmen also sometimes lodge, fortunately there was a Danish doctor who gave some medication, and I recovered in two days.

The next day, again able to keep food down, I went with friends to a food stand and we ate beef strips with the traditional African corn meal paste called *nsima* in Malawi. The same staple is popular all throughout Africa and called by various names such as, *ugali* or *sadza* up in Kenya, and *too-oh* toward the west in Nigeria. The natives of Africa eat this like we eat bread. They ground the corn mixed with water into something like pizza dough. They make a pot of some beef and vegetables on the side, and eat it with the dough with their hands, popping pieces of the dough spread with the stew into their mouths. It is rather bland, but the natives love it and eat it morning, noon, and night.

During the lunch, a crowd of people gathered around my car. I thought they might have been attracted by the 'For Sale' sign hung on the windshield. When returning to the car, one of the back tires was flat. There just happened to be a tire repairman around the corner. Just a coincidence? He took the tube out and inflated it. There was nothing at all as far as a hiss of escaping air. Then he walked it over to the water tank with me close at hand, and immersed it completely. Still no hiss. His assistant called out for a valve stem remover, and I helped by bringing one over. Just then there was a big hiss of air. Aha! The boss said he had found the leak.

Did he think I was that big a fool to fall for that? Obviously, he had simply punctured it right then and there, as my gaze was elsewhere for a couple of seconds. I cursed to let him know I was aware there was a hole, then let him finish the repair job. But I wasn't going to let him get away with it.

When he asked for his payment, we went to an Indian shopkeeper right next door who agreed to be a translator. This was in his shop, and he had closed his doors for his afternoon prayers. I then locked the door and told the crooked repairman that I knew what he and his accomplice had done. He could compensate me for wasting my time, or else face the wrath of the big *mzungu*. I asked to see what money he had in his pockets. He pulled out 40 kwacha, which is about fifty cents, and handed it to me, knowing he'd been caught. I took it, unlocked the door and walked out. On the porch, I tossed the money to a beggar. Be gracious.

Preventing that rip-off wasn't enough. I wanted to teach the crook a lesson, just enough to make him think. I grabbed his bicycle air pump – the life blood of his business. Taking it with me would have been his financial ruin. Deciding against that drastic step, I instead tossed it in a nearby thorn bush. Let him fish it out. Hopefully all those stickers would teach him a thing or two about his lack of ethics.

* * *

Mozambique, $1 = 23,800 Meticais

Further south in Mozambique, I met a native named Enoch, who could speak good English. He said he'd gotten ripped off, and I said, "Yeah, I can relate to that." I gave him a free ride down the length of the country to the capital city of Moputu. At a beach called Xai Xai (pronounced "shy shy") we took a swim, then afterward Enoch had what seemed to be a seizure. He crumpled to the sand and lie there shaking, and obviously in pain.

When he could speak, he said he had Malaria and that he'd need some medicine. He asked me to take him to a doctor he knew in an inner city area of Moputu. So we wound up at a slum of a house, which was once a mansion but now was dilapidated. I gave him the equivalent of two dollars for the medicine he needed, and as he went in I waited on the porch with some other locals. When some police started to walk down the street, everyone told me to take cover! I asked why, as the police are always good to me. They said these are bad cops who would want to shake me down for a bribe. They became more agitated, and began waving their arms and saying in broken English, "Get down! The police are coming!"

I hadn't the foggiest idea what they were blathering about, but I went along, as they were insistent. I ducked down behind the railing, and peeked through to see the uniformed cops pass by. Minutes later when Enoch came out, apparently having taken his medicine, he was in a big hurry. "Come with me!" he practically ordered, and we both ran to the car and jumped in. "Quick," he said, "let's go!"

"What's the rush?" I asked.

"This is an unlicensed doctor's office. They compete with the established system. The police are always hassling them." It sounded plausible enough, and honestly, the neighborhood was decidedly skeevy so I had no problem making tracks out of there. I thought little of it. We spent the next few days at the beach, dining on some heavenly sea food, and he even fixed me up with the cutest 18 year old named Miriam. She was the best salsa dancer around, in this delightfully Latin, Portuguese-speaking land.

At one point, my car was stopped at night by police. They began to search every scrap in the car and in the trunk looking for anything illegal. Then, finding nothing, they eyed Enoch and asked to see his identification. When he couldn't produce any, one cop told me, "This guy is here without ID and we're going to have to lock him up." Then came the kicker – "Unless you pay to keep him out."

When would this madness ever end? I was so sick of it that I again felt emboldened. "Listen, I don't know this guy," I said, "so I'm not giving him – or you – any money." It was another case of cops who had never heard this kind of lip before. I suppose they could have run me in and taken their chances. But it was clear they wouldn't, and after awhile, they just let everything drop. They never got any money, nor did they throw him in jail.

Later, I was talking with an ex-girlfriend of Enoch. And during the conversation, she said, "You know, Enoch's a great guy. It's too bad he has that heroin problem."

That hit me like a brick! The cops, I realized now, could indeed have busted me for being at that "doctor's" house – it was really a drug den, the heroin equivalent of a crack house. It dawned on me now that I had given Enoch money to get a fix! I can be so gullible sometimes. As soon as she told me, my feet were ready to run. "Well, I've got to go," I told her. "Tell Enoch good-bye." The worst part of leaving so quickly was having to say good-bye to Miriam. Yet there was no way I could hang out with the wrong crowd. I could only imagine getting mixed up in a drug raid! Suddenly the words "Midnight Express" kept ringing in my mind.

* * *

Swaziland, $1 = 10 Emalangeni   (stays pegged equal to the South African Rand)

The next day, going into Swaziland had a whole different feel for me. Because the Swazis are so used to white tourists coming in and out of South Africa, it was the first time I crossed a border in Africa without being accosted by a mob of people looking to milk the wallet of a big *mzungu*. It was a strange feeling. Almost as if I had forgotten to use my deodorant that day. They were staying away in droves. What a feeling!

By the time the trip was finished, I'd gone through ten tire changes. That is testament as to how bad the roads are. Most times I'd buy used tires, as was the case in Swaziland when tire number ten blew. Two days and a hundred miles after it had been put on, someone pointed out to me that the grooves on it were bogus. They had been carved into the rubber with a soldering iron. Looking closer, I was incredulous. A completely bald tire had little checkered grooves cut into it to make it look like tread – meaning that it was worse than a bald tire! Having been weakened by the soldering iron cuts, it was downright dangerous. Still, having paid for it, I hoped for the best, and used it as the spare. Be aware.

I almost got hit by a speeding car one morning in the Swazi capital city. My friend Noel and I crossed the street in a crowded market. The car's side mirror hit my hand, it was that close. My toes were almost run over. The idiot driver had no business going that fast with that many people around, and it made me really think twice about safety. Sometimes I just take it for granted, but now must be extra alert, as there is much more crime because South Africa next door is in such a state of change right now.

Subject: Swaziland Rantings

2 May 2002

I write this from South Africa, returning after surviving the 'wilds' of the African continent. Boy, it sure is good to get back to what amounts to Western civilization again! There is something about an infrastructure of cars, freeways, clean water you can drink from the tap, and even toilets that you can sit on. Ah!

Just passed through the tiny Kingdom of Swaziland on the way here. The Royal Family there has some weird traditions going on. The King is a young guy of 34 years, who gets a new wife once a year. He has 8 wives in 8 years. They tell me his dad before him had over 600 sons by countless wives. (They don't even mention how many daughters he had!) The yearly choosing of the King's wife is at the mandatory 'Reed Festival' where girls from the ages of 14-25 or so parade topless in front of everyone, with just a reed skirt on. Some say it is an honor. Others claim otherwise, and have sent their daughters to South Africa around that time.

Last year there was a controversy when one school girl of 16 was chosen as queen, but did not want it. (You see, once a queen, you cannot go back to your family again. The parents receive something like 5 cows as a dowry present.) The girl's parents and neighbors protested at the palace. They said she was forcibly taken and raped by the King. The Royal Family bought off the protesters with cows, yet the girl's father was mysteriously killed 3 months later. Someone had to pay for the Royals' loss of face.

The Royals of Swaziland are all over the place. You meet princes who own car repair shops, and all sorts of everyday businesses. The 'have-nots' (non-royals) are starting to get disenchanted with the Royals big spending, especially in these tough economic times. The money and power of the country seem to be kept all in the family. Storms are brewing.

Cheers, Christopher

* * *

South Africa, $1 = 10 Rand

Finally, I was back where starting from months earlier – and in one piece! I stayed at another backpacker's hostel, the 'Brown Sugar', in both Johannesburg and Durban. Built from converted mansions, they boast huge rooms with high wooden ceilings and immaculately manicured lawns and gardens. The bathrooms are as big as a normal bedroom! The bathtub, which I used twice a day, is long enough and wide enough to hold my 6 foot 5 inch body. That's pretty impressive.

As it happened, I was fortunate to be there. The first day in Durban, on the coast, my back got tweaked while playing a round of golf. I had a lot of pain in my hips, legs, and lower back. This kind of thing happens once every three or four years, and I just have to bear with it for a couple of days until it snaps back into place. Took the opportunity to do nothing at all except read novels, and the best part was reading in the big, hot bathtub. The water really helps with the pain, as it takes the weight off the vertebrae that is pinched. I also swam forty laps at a time in the pool – including breaststroke, backstroke, and butterfly. Yet walking out of the pool, it reverted back to pain. The whole incident lasted only two days, then it was back to normal again. Thank goodness!

* * *

After five months since first arriving in Capetown in January, I made return flight reservations to America, then went about selling the car by putting a 'For Sale' sign in the window. Within hours a black man named Elton came up to me and began talking himself up as the can-do kind of guy who could get the car sold as a middleman. He said he was a broker of merchandise, and that he knew people who would be very interested in buying. He asked what the price was. I said a thousand dollars. "Oh, no, no," he demurred, "I know those who will pay more – maybe even three thousand." I would believe it when seeing it.

As he told it, the people he knew were real wheelers and dealers. The scam sensor in my brain sounded a faint alarm, but with my natural curiosity to see something first, I went along. Elton took me to meet a man named Chirwari, who got in the car with us and explained that the two of them were both brokers and they knew wealthy merchants. If I was interested, we could cut out the middleman on a 'deal' and have enough money at the end to buy the car for triple the price. Far from convinced, I simply told them if that's true, just go get the money and come back with it. I would give them a cut and they could deliver the car.

"Oh, no, no," came the answer. Instead, they needed to show up in an impressive car (like mine?), as a taxi simply would not cut it. Besides, a white man in their car would bring more credibility for their 'deal'. I told them they had only half an hour before I would lose interest. So we wound our way to meet another black man and his wife, Lee and Nancy. They were jewel sellers, mainly tanzanites from Tanzania, which they said are semiprecious stones that look a little like white diamonds.

Lee and Nancy got in the back seat, and they had an envelope with some white stones in it. With my usual suspicion, I said, "How do we know these stones are good?" Lee thought a minute and replied, "Okay, we'll give you half, 8 of the 16 stones we have here. You take them down to the jewelry shop and they will appraise them."

The plot was thickening now, as we took the stones and headed to the jewelry store. Upon arrival, Chirwari got out and went inside. Elton and I sat in the car at the curb, and a distinguished looking older white man in a business suit came out. He introduced himself as Mr. Anderson, shook my hand and explained that they had some Swiss bankers in the shop doing some important business. He said he would take the jewels, appraise them, and come back out to the car in ten minutes.

Which he did, right on time, saying, "Yes, the stones are good. We can give you three thousand dollars for them." I was intrigued, if by some miracle it was legitimate. Mr. Anderson said his assistant would go to the bank for the cash. "Can you come back in half an hour?" he asked, to my assent. Then he sealed the envelope with the jewels and put his signature across it, saying, "These are the ones we want."

We were all sitting in the car, making idle chit chat, when a thought came to me. I told the pair, "Why don't we go get the rest of the stones? This guy would pay six thousand for them all!" We drove back to see Lee and Nancy, and planned to offer to buy these and the eight other stones. They wanted me to be the negotiator. Lee got in the car and said he would part with them all for two thousand dollars. I proposed half of that. We agreed on fifteen hundred – which instantly would leave us with a huge profit! It sounded good. Way too good. To be true, that is.

Right on cue, Lee said we could take the jewels over to get the rest appraised, if we would leave a deposit. Of course, that sounded perfectly reasonable – though I was a bit perplexed as to why he hadn't asked for a deposit on the first batch of stones. In the scam game, those first eight stones were the hook. The second eight were the sting. As soon as the word "deposit" was uttered, all eyes looked off into the heavens. Who could possibly know where to get a deposit? I'm sure they were all thinking: Ah... the big *mzungu*! He must have tons of money...

Although I didn't immediately let on, that was the end of the fun and games for me. The scam was now exposed. If I had paid any kind of deposit, all these guys would vanish into the woodwork with it. Now, my only thought was: how can I get these guys out of my car, and get the hell out of here?

After some quick thinking, I told Lee, "I know where we can get a deposit. We'll be back." I took my two guys on a ride to the nearest corner telephone booth. "Why don't you try to reach one of your contacts on the pay phone, while I try my cell phone," I said, figuring they would want to act as if they were involved in getting the money, at least for appearance sake. First, one got out and went to the phone booth. Then I told the other one, "I think your friend wants to talk to you." So he got out, too. I then locked the door. Whew! I rolled the window down a bit and said, "Hey you guys, I just got a call on my cell phone. I've got to go." The last thing they saw was the dust from my tires.

Finding my way to a restaurant for lunch, and while relaxing with a burger, I couldn't stop thinking about the 'deal'. What if it wasn't a scam? What if there was money to be made? After finishing, I drove back to the jewelry shop, intending to have a few words with Mr. Anderson. Upon walking in, I asked a nice black lady at the counter, "Is Mr. Anderson here?"

"Who?"

"Mr. Anderson. The distinguished white gentleman who was here before."

"No one works here by that name."

"Thank you very much," I said, and walked out, now knowing beyond a doubt that I'd just saved a lot of money and pain.

Eventually my car sold for nine hundred dollars to a guy from Congo who knew it was a good deal. It was a little sad to part with the wheels that had taken me through thick and thin, and muck and mire. That plucky little car and I had been through a lot together. Even upon completing an unforgettable journey through Africa and winging my way home, I knew this journey would be stamped 'Part One.' I would be writing my own 'Back to Africa' script soon enough.

CHAPTER FIVE

Not quite ready to end this exploration, I took a circuitous route back to America – revisiting some favorite haunts in western Europe and then getting a first taste of that continent's eastern developing area, down through the Balkans. After leaving South Africa, I flew north to Amsterdam, always a pleasurable destination for the weary man. Having recharged my batteries – no detail necessary – I felt adventurous enough to make my means of travel simple: my own two feet and an upraised thumb.

As stated previously, although hitch-hiking may be frowned upon in the more 'civilized' parts of the world, I have found it to be safe and often the fastest way to go. Good judgment will be your best guide. Look at people, see if you can relate with them or if they are a threat. Obviously, if sensing a threat, politely decline a lift offer. A possible threat might be if someone is 'dodgy' looking, such as if he's acting nervous or maybe just a tad too over-anxious. Or someone who is physically bigger. Other tips: try not to enter if there are several people in a car, who could overpower. Make sure that it's going to be with people who genuinely want to share a ride and have some good company (and there is no shortage of them). Don't just sit there like a lump, either. Make conversation. Always try to tell a story about travels that is enjoyable to them.

The first destination was Germany, where I'd studied and made so many good friends on my first trip abroad. It felt like a homecoming – though I did not repeat the experience of hopping another box car train. This time stuck to the back roads, staying in Bavaria. The World Cup soccer tournament was on TV, which was being held in Japan, and you know how the Europeans love their soccer. The entire local town seemed to be in a tavern hoisting beer and watching the Germany-U.S.A. quarter-final game. I had to get in the spirit of the friendly rivalry. Being in Africa since early January, I wasn't able to get to a Super Bowl party, so why not create a Super Bowl party right now? We had hot dogs, chili, chips, betting pools, and all the comforts of home. So what if a round football replaced the pointed football? A party's a party.

* * *

Subject: Top Differences Between Europe and Africa

21 Jun 2002

Greetings from Bavaria, in Germany!

Well, 5 months of African adventure have come to an end, and now it is time to visit some friends in Europe who I have not seen since studying in Germany way back when... Sure is good to be able to send emails at a quick speed. Maybe now I can reply to all those letters. Ah... civilization! But it comes with the 'sticker shock' you get when you start to pay regular 'Western' prices again. Seems like everything is 2-3 times higher in price than just last week. Must plan just a bit more now.

We made it to the longest day of the year, June 21, the Summer Solstice! That is saying a lot since it stays daylight here in Europe until 10 at night (even longer farther up north in Scandinavia). Before flying up from Africa, it was getting dark around 5 p.m. as winter was setting in. Writing this from the little town of Donauwörth on the banks of the Danube river, which was first settled when the year was 900 and something. They just celebrated tho town's 1000th birthday back in 1977. Talk about history! It is the kind of peaceful place where they not only don't lock their houses or car doors, my friends here have been known to leave for a swim at the lake with the house doors wide open – and think nothing of it!

I have been staying with Florian, a friend from studies here years ago, and can still hang with the language without butchering it too severely. He is now a doctor with a fine family complete with his wife, 2 great kids, and all the trimmings of rabbits, turtles, guinea pigs, etc. His doctoring skills came in handy with some acupuncture treatments for my back. It really works! We have been playing a lot of golf, as well as tennis on clay courts, which is a real treat for me as we don't have many clay courts where I come from.

Have been visiting ancient castles with moats and drawbridges, as well as churches dating from the year 1100 or so that are around 70 yards long and over 5 stories high! Absolutely ornate with marble and frescoes by the masters of that era. Makes me wonder in awe who the people were who built these things so long ago.

The leafy green forests, green grassy meadows, and fresh water lakes are everywhere, and the peaceful flowing Danube river runs all the way to the Black Sea (near Russia) from here. It has a bike path along its banks, and is very tempting, as I have been biking all over the place. Have to get around somehow, as I sold my car in Capetown 2 days before flying away.

Getting back to fond memories of Africa, at least now I don't have to worry about a baboon picking up my golf ball on the fairway and running off with it! Desert dogs don't bark at night warning of an imminent hyena lurking nearby. Don't have to be x-rayed (for swallowed gems) after leaving a diamond mine. Ah...

Looks like Yugoslavia may be next on the agenda. Auf Wiedersehen! Christopher

* * *

The autobahn trail led southward, through Austria, Slovenia and Croatia. Most remarkable about the route are the wonderful majestic mountains of Austria. Then came the feeling of crossing over behind the old Iron Curtain into lands that were left behind by progress for a generation of communist totalitarianism. This, of course, was not long after the bloody civil wars that made the region a living nightmare during the break-up of the former Yugoslavia in 1991. That outrage cost thousands of people their lives. In the wake of this terrible tragedy, one could see village after village all around the region that were no more than ghost towns, abandoned and never re-populated when their residents moved back to their safer historical homelands. There were still bullet holes in the houses, and burned out buildings not yet repaired. One can sense that inhumanity worked to turn the clock back, and that civilization itself had taken a monstrous hit. A peaceful reintegration of much of the countryside was not fully completed until 1998 under UN supervision.

Still, the people were starting to get their lives back in order again. I did my part, shopping at markets that tend to sprout up in town squares. In return for the presence of a Westerner in an area so ravaged and so 'undesirable' for travel, I was invited to people's homes for meals. And what meals! There were mouth-watering plates of lamb, freshly roasted on the spit and carved on the table. The meals are as tasty as anywhere on the planet.

I also did my part to join in the work force: one day, after grabbing a ride aboard a flower truck, instead of getting off right away, I helped the guy unload flowers all day. In a scenario like that, I will always try to earn my keep. Not incidentally, this will give my resume a rather exotic touch, now saying something like: "Also worked in Yugoslavia."

* * *

Austria, $1 = 1.1 Euro

28 Jun 2002

I spent a night in my tent under a freeway overpass on the road to Slovenia. At first I felt frustrated, out in the middle of nowhere. But you must always look on the bright side!

Being far enough away from the road, say 30 feet, and down on a lower level where no cars can see, I got to air-out the tent, after it got wet the night before. This was the driest place around! Rain out in the open, yet nice dry sand underneath to sleep on. Quite okay.

There are a lot of people who see the USA as thinking we are the world's policeman. Like Sasha for example. Riding with him, he said he is afraid of George W. Bush's stand on terrorism. Speaking all in German, I explained that most people love to live in peace. Even the poor people of Africa survive and grow. But someone who wants to kill me because my life is successful, AND kill himself (because his is not?) at the same time, is not the kind of person who should be talked with. Only knows and expects violence. Perhaps his anger is misplaced. If we do not like our government, we vote the bums out and let someone else run the show. If the terrorist wants a new ruler, he has to kill the king, then he becomes the king.

I also told Sasha that I studied in Germany in 1983, and the Germans had worse fears about Ronald Reagan. And 20 years later, the Cold War has ended and there is one less threat to the world. Do the right thing, and we can talk 20 years from now.

The warrior with the best weapons is the winner. That is why we obey the police – they have guns to enforce the laws. Let Germany lead the coalition if they get attacked next. Someone has to do it, or else it is like letting the inmates run the asylum.

* * *

Croatia, $1 = 7.2 Kuna

Further south in Croatia, where the citizenry calls itself 'Republika Hrvatska' in their native tongue, I also got to vision yet another dream landscape. Adjacent to the highway carved into the mountainside, down below are the crystal clear waters of the Adriatic Sea and the most absolutely beautiful scenery of literally thousands of islands dotting the coastline. This must be where Thousand Island salad dressing got its name. On the first night there, I traveled through Zadar and found myself in another coastal town called Split, located on a small peninsula on the eastern shores of the Adriatic. Split is one of the sunniest places in Europe, with miles of vegetation of the evergreen Mediterranean type. There is great cultural activity during summers, when the prestigious Split Music Festival is held.

The town, built in 300 AD, was designed and ruled by the Roman emperor. On his order, massive walls were erected encircling his nine acre palace. Some of them were 700 feet long and 70 feet high, even though at the the time not a single person actually lived in Split. Talk about paranoia. The walls are still there, thick and unyielding. Long after the emperor was gone and settlers began to move in, the present day city grew to include both inside and outside the walls. The city center is maybe a half mile square, and people actually live in ancient buildings 1700 years later that are still foursquare and secure. Perhaps unique, in that the natives live in a former Roman palace!

The walled city interior is marked by old-fashioned cobblestone streets, cafes, theaters and shops. The night I was there, they had one of the Music Festival concerts, which included a dazzling light show. The concert was sort of background music as I wandered up onto one of the castle-like wide ancient walls to walk along. Maybe a hundred yards from the concert, I could still hear the music and see the lights. It felt all very peaceful and bucolic and I lay my head back to rest and take it all in. When opening my eyes, there were three guys sitting there with me – perhaps in their early twenties. One of them said something to me in Croatian, so I said, "I'm sorry, I don't understand what you're saying."

His friend, in broken English, spoke up, saying, "What he's trying to tell you is that everything will be safe for you if you pay him some money." Sizing up the situation, I was in the wrong place at the wrong time, as nice and nonthreatening as that place at first had appeared to be. In fact, I resented that my night of peaceful meditation and exploration was being soiled by some junior league Croatian punks. I had to do something because up on top of that wall, no one could really see me. Considering the options, the only thing to do was bluff.

I put my hand in my pocket, my fingers around a canister of pepper spray. Then I said to them, "You know guys, it looks like we might have a disagreement here, and I think we should settle it right. Lets fight right now."

Looking a little stunned, the guy who was translating had an animated conversation with the others. All of them eyed my hand, clearly believing I had a gun or knife in that pocket waiting to say hello to them. After a few moments, the guy said, "I guess you can go," and I calmly turned and headed back down to the concert. The key to getting away was holding my tough-guy pose, making it look convincing, although I don't know how I did it with my knees knocking as they were.

But again, at the risk of sounding redundant, you must stand up for yourself against local thugs. And you must try to avoid situations where you might run up against a gang and you're all alone. All I know is that I would have fought them if they'd forced me to. I would have pepper sprayed the biggest guy and tried to get one more shot off at another, and then beat the stuffing out of who was left. But I'll take the peaceful way out any day. I was more than content not having to try my hand at being a super action hero. Be aware.

* * *

Heading further south along the coast of Croatia, I came through Bosnia and Herzegovina, one of the other breakaway Yugoslavian republics, which is still actually divided into two parts: the Federation of Bosnia and Herzegovina and the (Serbian) Republika Srpska, and still administered by a representative chosen by the UN Security Council. There seems no end to the labyrinthine process of giving people in the region the right to self-government. But given the alternative, which was total destruction, they're willing to wait while they get their lives back together.

A labyrinth is a good metaphor for the geography of the Balkan countries. Bosnia has a very small coastline – just about a mile long, that holds a sea port for ocean shipping. You pass right into it, and out of it right back into Croatia again. Farther south you go through Serbia Montenegro on the way into Kosovo. This area, too, is in a state of flux. The people of Kosovo are ethnic Albanians, unlike the rest of their nominal 'country' (Serbia), the Serbs. In the 1990s Serbian strong man Slobodan Milosevic tried to 'ethnically cleanse' the country of them. It almost worked. Great hordes of them, three quarters of the population, became refugees and fled to Albania.

During the subsequent U.S.-NATO bombing runs of Serbia, Milosevic had a change of heart and let them back to their homes. Incredibly, nearly all of them came back, and were still doing so when I was there. Now, international governments are working to restore their villages and cities, which are rife with bullet holes and bombed out buildings. There is so much construction, it is like a boom town. The Serbs lost the war, and the Kosovars won overall with big help from outside. They are in a defacto state of independence right now.

Going into Kosovo I was riding with a Slovenian man in a flashy BMW car, so I knew he was a real operator of some kind. When we got to the border, he got out and began talking with the border guard. They were at it awhile, and it struck me that they were doing some negotiating – which of course, meant how much the guard could shake the guy down for. They made some sort of deal and when they broke their colloquy, the guard went and got a screwdriver and the two men walked to the back of the car. The trunk was opened and the guard leaned in and started unscrewing the car's stereo speakers, as well as taking a turntable in which was stored dozens of compact disks. In exchange, the guard handed the driver what couldn't have been more than a few dollars.

These were very expensive electronics items, worth hundreds of dollars in the West. Meaning that on the Kosovo black market the price was through the roof. So I was flabbergasted that the guy had given it all away for a fraction of what it was worth. As we drove away, I asked him, "Why did you do that?" He smiled.

"The reason," he said, "is that I'm going to come back this way tomorrow night on my way back up to Slovenia. I'm a businessman and I'm going to pick up three or four Kosovar workers. They're going to come to Slovenia with me and work for very cheap salaries. They're undocumented and I'm going to pay them under the table. And you know what? This border guard is not even going to ask me a thing about it. He's going to let me go straight through. All I do is just mention his name and everything is going to be fine." He paused. "That's how business is done here."

* * *

The capital city of Kosovo is Prizren. There, I met a young guy named Bek who ran his own little burger stand. I told him a few of my stories and drank beers with him and his family. When his dad found out I was American, he began to get emotional. With tears welling up in his eyes, he stood up and gave a ten minute speech of thanks to the U.S. and NATO for bombing the Serbians and letting the Kosovars come back to their houses where they had spent generations. He even had me film his speech on video tape. It was very touching seeing him with tears in his eyes. Seems not everyone around the world wants to cut down the 'big guy' USA. Recalling the Kosovars extol and express gratitude for America makes me get emotional myself, as I did that day. It also provides context and confirmation that, even if America makes mistakes, it is still the world's last best hope to help people's lives.

Later that night, I pitched my tent across the street from Bek's burger place. It was a school yard closed for summer vacation, and it was a nice grassy area. I was stretching out, dozing off, when all of sudden there was a slash of bright light. It looked to be a big spotlight shining right into the tent. Pulling aside the tent flap, there was a man in a police uniform striding briskly to the tent with his flashlight. It turned out to be a German policeman, of all things. Kosovo is divided into sectors under the control of the United Nations, there to keep the Serbs from making any more trouble. Obviously I was in the German sector, and the cop eyed me closely.

Fortunately, I could speak German with him. "What are you doing here?" he asked me in his native tongue, looking rather confused at the sight of a tall white man in these environs. The thought occurred to me that he may believe I was some kind of unforeseen enemy. I replied, "I'm a tourist," unaware of the fact that 'tourist' might sound more than a little like 'terrorist.' He seemed to know what I meant, but that didn't keep him from looking shocked nonetheless.

"We've never had a tourist here before, you're the first one," he said. "Why would you come to Kosovo in the middle of all this?" I may well have been the only person from the West to have visited Kosovo not wearing a uniform. Not even considering what a rarity this journey was, to me it was just a place I wanted to see. "I'm just passing through on the way to Albania tomorrow," I chirped with a surreal ingenuousness. It was said with such conviction, apparently, that he accepted it and wished me a good night.

* * *

Albania, $1 = 140 Leke

Albanian Language (phonetically, as it sounds to me):

thank you = fali minderi

hello = toong

how are you? = sie ennay?

good = mir

please = you loot em

The German cop wasn't the only interested party who noticed the big, out of place Westerner. The next day I arrived at the border, and one of the Albanian guards wasted no time in demanding ten dollars from me, as a "tax" to come into the country. Here we go again, I thought. Doesn't this kind of petty extortion ever end?

Once more, I wasn't going to accept it out of hand. "Where does it say there's an entry tax?" I asked. He didn't show me any documentation, so I knew this "tax" was going into his pocket. "I don't have any money," I told him.

"Let me see your wallet," he countered. I opened my wallet and showed him just the few small bills in it. This was by design, as another golden rule of travel is that when you cross a border, never have a lot of cash with you, because soon enough it won't be with you. Wanting to just move on, I first offered to pay him by credit card. He said he couldn't take it. I knew that. Next I offered to pay him in travelers checks. He couldn't take that, either. Knew that, too. There was nothing left to do but wait it out, another stalemate brewing. Would this one take hours? As it turned out, it didn't. It took all of about ten minutes before the guy realized he couldn't get blood from a stone, or speakers from a car, and simply let me go ten minutes late. Another lesson learned. Just by waiting sometimes you can get by.

After hopping into a mini-bus at the Albanian border, I rode a grueling six hour martini-shaker into the capital city with 10 other people – and what a bumpy ride it was! Those were the worst roads I have ever ridden on, and this includes those in Africa. This was a main road into the country, not secondary back roads. And every mile was covered with potholes and degenerated into stretches of dirt, completely unpaved. This was another example of the infrastructure of these war-weary, battered nations not being able to sit back, catch their breath and go about the business of sinking some money into public projects like road and bridge building. But how can that happen when everybody is always expecting the shooting to start all over again? Indeed, that war is on the brain here and never far from your consciousness, is once again made clear by one look up into the high ground. There, in the endless Albanian hills, are thousands – tens of thousands – of dormant machine gun bunkers. They look like little cement igloos with hole-like windows to stick guns out of.

The bunkers are empty now, but no one is in any hurry to get rid of them, or to shutter the windows that face in the direction of Yugoslavia. This is another symbolic remnant of man's stupidity, in this case not of the Yugoslavian civil wars, but of the 20th Century's longest conflict: the Cold War. When Albania lived behind the Iron Curtain, the communist rulers rarely let anybody in or out of the country. They were deathly afraid even of Yugoslavia, even though both were communist countries. That's how paranoid and isolated they were. A cold chill runs down the spine at the thought of how many people who tried to sneak across the border wound up being gunned down from those bunkers in the hills.

I struck up a conversation on the bus ride with an older gentleman. He didn't speak English and I spoke no Albanian, but we used hand signals and pictures to talk at great length about taxes, how much a house cost, what electricity cost, and so on. He got by in his simple life on around $120 a month for his family and his five grand kids, and made ends meet probably a lot easier than the typical American. Whenever hearing one of those stories about someone living to 120 years old in the Balkans, I am not surprised. It's not the easy life that makes you live longer; it's the hard life, lived with a sense of vigor and purpose.

* * *

I grew to be quite comfortable with the eastern Europeans, finding no problem whatsoever getting rides or lodging. Because public transportation is so much cheaper there than in western Europe, I would ride the buses whenever convenient and end up holding court in the back of the bus, laughing and joking with the locals. One day the sky opened up in a downpour, and while waiting it out in a train station I struck up a conversation with a friendly face. By the end of our talk, he said, "You're coming home with me as a guest of my family." That is typical of the reception you can get all over the world.

Earlier, a lady had asked me, "Aren't you afraid, being so far away from home?" I jokingly replied, "Ma'am, having just spent five months in Africa, at this point I ain't askeerd o' nuthin!" Maybe too dumb to be scared? But life has a way of fooling you, taunting you when you least expect it. I had, by instinct, learned to keep my guard up. Then when you relax that guard just a bit, when you tempt fate like that, something really scary actually does come up. The funny thing is, everyone said to watch my step in Albania. Watch out for the Albanian mafia, I was told. Even the Kosovars, who are their blood cousins, say to be weary. The military is all over the place, they have itchy trigger fingers, they shoot first and ask questions later. Anything can happen there.

Well, I must have forgotten all those warnings. In the main central park of the capital city Tirane, after a wonderful day of swimming in the lake and an evening meal with friends at a cafe, I was walking along the farthest part of the park near the fence. Suddenly a male voice barked the equivalent of "Who goes there?" in Albanian, and I answered as usual something like, "Hello, do you speak English?" The next sound was the 'lock and load' click click of an army machine gun! And his voice got more and more agitated!

I froze, put my hands in the air, then fell to the ground. I kept saying "English, English!" but he was an army guard on the other side of the fence who spoke no English at all. And he was mad. He clicked that machine gun bolt three or four times, each time shouting something unintelligible. I was petrified. When would those bullets start to fly?

I finally crawled like a lizard in the grass back to the road. After checking my pants, I ran back to the cafe. Someone there spoke English, and he came and sorted it out with the three or four soldiers who came to see what was going on. I gathered my composure, and learned to stay clear of the fence that had a military base on the other side of it.

* * *

Serbia, $1 = 60 Dinar

9 Jul 2002

Have been pretty lucky while hitching in Europe; sometimes getting rides in just 5 minutes! It really compares to fishing. You just gotta throw in yer line! It pays better than fishing, as a long trip simply costs a lot more than a fish. And you get to meet a lot of fun people.

But it is unpredictable. So I have devised a little system (like always!) to measure the results. Keep 'despair' and 'pain' to a minimum. If it is too hot or rainy (pain), simply go do something else! Possibly toss the Frisbee, eat, or simply explore some interesting place. The despair part comes from being dropped off in a place with no hope of getting an easy ride. And with no one to talk to. You question 'why' you got yourself into this unfavorable position. This only happened once or twice the whole time, like today for example.

Half way to Palanka, a police guy dropped me at a turn-off on the open highway. At least there were some shepards herding their flock of sheep nearby, but then they left and it started getting dark. I do not want to hitch in the dark. Panic could have easily set in. Came close. Then a car picked me up before I knew it. Whew!

Always think of the most positive thing that can be done at any point in time. Then just do it.

* * *

Macedonia, $1 = 61 Dinar

When the calendar turned to July, I was on the road in Macedonia. The very name makes centuries of history come alive, which is why one can almost sense the ghosts of Alexander the Great and the ancient Roman and Byzantine emperors who regarded Macedonia as a cultural and trade gateway. Few areas have been coveted by as many countries and empires, and it took until 1991 for Macedonia to at long last declare its independence from the splintering Yugoslavia.

While there I actually swam some rapids with some Norwegian fellow tourists, and the lakes were clear for lots of swimming. And then I usually get a group dynamic going with the town folk – with a little help from my trusty Frisbee. The kids around the world are great Frisbee throwers. It always seems to bring out a big crowd of eager locals. I might even go a step further and call the Frisbee a tool of international goodwill! Just like sports in general. It just happens to be the easiest sporting equipment to take along on a trip.

While hitching for a ride first thing one morning, I bought bread for my goose liver pate spread, and gave half of it to a family who's kids were playing with toys on the front lawn. We started throwing the Frisbee while waiting for cars to come by. The kids were giggling and squealing, just having a ball chasing it all over the place. Well, one errant throw happened to sail right through an open window of the house next door! The old lady there came out with soap suds on her hands saying something like how dare I disturb her chores. She was ranting and raving, and remember, I speak no Macedonian whatsoever. She had two kids in her house who could have easily retrieved it for us. But nooooo! She was not going to return it. The grouch!

Not knowing the words for please or sorry, my body language of humble forward shoulders and praying hands said it all. After 10 minutes of pleading, still no joy. So taking matters into my own hands, I jumped through the window to get it! It was a work of gymnastic art to get in there, as it was just a bit higher than an easy ground floor window. She had hidden it by then, so I grabbed a hammer that was just lying there as collateral for a trade, and went back outside to the yard.

The grouch would not come out to talk terms, so I flagged down a local town policeman that just happened to be passing by. The oldest kid was quite animated while explaining the whole scenario. In no time at all we had negotiated for release of the Frisbee hostage. Simply traded the hammer for the Frisbee. It was more embarrassing for her, as she has to live there forever with those neighbor kids. A ride picked me up at that very moment, and I was on my way to the next adventure. What good timing!

* * *

Bulgaria, $1 = 2 Leva

Bulgaria is a very interesting place. For one thing, it is the only place in the world where you nod your head up and down for 'no' and shake it left to right for 'yes.' More importantly, Bulgaria is becoming a thriving independent country once again – granted a bit late, given that this was the crown jewel of Slavic Europe during much of the Middle Ages, exerting considerable literary and cultural influence over the Eastern Orthodox Slavic world. Now, after years of growing pains following the fall of the Iron Curtain, it is an active member of NATO and plans to join the European Union soon. It is also a burgeoning arts and culture center, with Westerners streaming in for film and music festivals with regularity. One wonders what tourists think when they see people nodding 'no' and shaking 'yes', and perhaps how many guys have had their faces slapped because of it.

One can certainly eat hearty in Bulgaria, with plenty of the native cuisine to go around. As in Kosovo, being an American surely had its benefits. People were so eager to meet and speak with me that they would stop me on the street. Upon learning that she found an American, one lady kept heaping cucumbers and tomatoes on me. I said, "Ma'am, I can't take all these from you." She demurred, "No, no, you're a friend." So I was there making a pig of myself, devouring complimentary cucumbers, tomatoes, apricots, ice cream bars, you name it.

Great camaraderie can be found with truck drivers at the ferry crossing from Bulgaria to Romania. I tried the cold cucumber and milk soup, and it was heaven in a bowl, especially with salt, pepper, oil, and yogurt mixed in. It's cold, like vichyssoise, and actually quite good! And the french fries came with white goat cheese crumbled on top. A cholesterol cocktail, to be sure, but a whole lot more satisfying than any deep-fried mystery meat at the Bucharest Burger King.

How do you make conversation when you don't speak the native tongue? Again, to use a golfing axiom: you use every club in your bag. Use anything that works. This is not as much of a problem as you may think. You would be surprised at how far a few words can take you. For instance, all you really needed to know in Bulgarian are (now, these are how I would pronounce them phonetically):

thank you = blago derian
hello = z'dra vay
please = molya
how are you? = kak si?
yes = da
no = nay
excuse me = venya way
water = woda
train = vlack

Or, in Romanian:

thank you = mol zu mesk
please = tear roque
excuse me = scooz aye
hello and good bye = areeva dairy
how are you? = chay esta? or chay fatch?
good = puna
yes = da
no = nu
cheers = nor oak

The rest can be accomplished with the prudent use of hand signals, drawings, or just plain body language. Words are overrated. I believe that most of our communication is from the soul.

Food in fact, would become a synonym for my Balkan run. All the Slavic countries seem to share an implicit bond, through their taste buds. This is all to the good. After all, religious and cultural divides seem to disappear when diverse people eat together. A whole lamb roasting on a spit, for example, can shelve a lot of arguments. Which may be why it is quite a common sight when traveling through these Slavic towns. Add some thick pita breads, sausages and cucumber sauces and you get *chevapis* that melt in the mouth. After a few of those, a fast-food burger will seem like a crime against nature.

Speaking German really helps in these lands where not everyone knows English. Also, lets hear it for the modern European Muslims who are not fanatics and dress in style (including excellent mini skirts and flowing hair with head scarfs optional). And I keep having to explain the 'no topless beaches' in America: with us it is reserved for really special occasions, otherwise it becomes another boring everyday thing. And who wants that?

* * *

Romania, $1 = 32,000 Lei

Going to Romania is like sampling a smorgasbord of attractions – gypsies, Count Dracula's digs in Transylvania, the Blue Danube, the Black Sea, the Carpathian Mountains, the historic capital city of Bucharest. But Romania had been a virtual prison-state until being released from four decades of the yoke of communism in 1989. Under the unspeakable brutality of the dictator Nicolae Ceausescu, no one could speak their mind for 40 years for fear of a myriad of secret undercover spies and government informants. Even your neighbors and family could not be trusted. The revolution culminated with Ceausescu and his wife summarily executed on their country's national television station. No going back.

It is improving now, however one cannot help but think of it as an 'old world' country. Its very name, a derivative of the word for 'Roman', recalls its ancient role as a principality of the Roman empire. In fact, they still speak a Romance language in which about a third of the words are similar to Italian. This is unique, since it is geographically surrounded by Slavic languages and even Cyrillic alphabets. Old world architecture dominates the cities, and even in the hinterlands a strong echo of the past lives in the somewhat bizarre lifestyle of the gypsies.

The gypsies, in fact, are technically known as the Roma People, and most Roma speak Romani – an Indo-Aryan language. They still can be seen, as they were portrayed decades ago in Hollywood movies, living in colonies in the woods and, yes, even living in abandoned stores practicing their obscure customs. Perhaps it was because of the gypsies' legendary reputation for bilking people out of money, that I ran into more pressure to protect my wallet in Romania than in any other country.

My first day in Bucharest, someone offered to help me find a bus ride to the Black Sea beach. After he steered me to the bus station, I paid the price of the bus fare, told him thank you very much, and offered him a tip. He wanted double the price of the fare, as a kind of finder's fee – or more accurately, a keeper's fee. I was a little annoyed but wasn't averse, as he had taken the time to help me out.

"Here, I'll give you a nice tip," I told him, "but I'm not going to give you double the price of a hundred mile ride." In his mind, that was a fair price – if he could get it, that is. And when he didn't, he began getting in my face. Here again was petty extortion simply because I was targetable as a Westerner. I'd been through the drill too often to back down. Do that, and there will be a crowd lining up to fleece you for whatever you have left.

"You know," I said, "I'm starting to not like your attitude. How would you like a punch in the nose to go along with it, right here in front of the bus?" Funny how his knowledge of English improved so quickly. And he backed away, whereupon I climbed into the bus and took a seat. Having considered his next move, my erstwhile aide-de-camp slithered his way onto the bus and fronted up to me. Not knowing what he'd do next, I stared back and waited. Then, in the blink of an eye, the next thing I knew he was scrambling off the bus – with my baseball hat in his hand.

This was the first time since grade school someone had swiped a cap from my head. Evidently genuine American made lids are some kind of status symbol. For me, they keep the bright sun under control. Which is why I would have normally run after the guy, but hadn't seen anyone move so fast since Carl Lewis at the '84 Olympics. So I grieved the loss of a San Diego Padres cap, and wrote it off as a tip for Mr. Speedy.

Another incident was with a group of supposed Turkish tourists. I say 'supposed' because I'm sure they were actually Romanian gypsies, but said they were Turkish to throw off the scent for anyone with a healthy suspicion of gypsies. Which happens to be most people – including most Romanians.

Subject: Dracula's Greetings from Transylvania

20 Jul 2002

Yes, there really is a Transylvania, a mountainous region right here in Romania. And Dracula was an actual person: Vlad Dracu, also known as Vlad the Impaler. He drove the Turks south of the Danube River in 1478, and united the regions of Romania, Transylvania, and Moldova into one country. His blood and guts reputation ('Draconian') stems from the way he would do away with the captured enemy. Not with a wooden stake through the heart. It was a bit lower. And up from the other side. Kind of gives a whole new meaning to the phrase, "Sit on it, Potsie." With thousands of people left skewered like roasted chickens, it really drives home a point (pun intended). His rule was so strict that if people saw a bag of money on the road, they would leave it there out of fear of brutal retribution to the whole area.

While sitting on the Black Sea beach one night around 10 p.m., four guys who said they were tourists from Turkey came over and were friendly. We shared a few beers, then they took me for a walk down the beach to a few discos. They kept going for over an hour. They also wanted to go swimming, but I declined. (That surely would have been the end of my wallet and clothing.) I turned back, and they followed. We even danced together with groups of girls at the discos. After finally shaking them around 4 a.m., a short while later two of them magically reappeared, asking for money for cigarettes. I was more firm, saying, "Go away." Well... after a few punches were traded with my 'friends', the cowards ran off. I chased after them, but let them go. It could have been worse, as they had an empty wine bottle right there on the ground that they could have used as a weapon. And they would have, but I saw it and threw it into the sea. A bop on the head with that bottle could have been disastrous.

The next day I realized that those guys had tried to drug me. I remember feeling a tiny 'splash' while holding my beer, but thought it was a bug or something flying into it. They were walking me down the beach waiting for me to drop! Good thing that I am such a big guy that the drug was not strong enough for me. Probably needed two. My equilibrium was a little out of whack for the next two days, but nothing serious.

Plans are now in the works for printing a shirt that reads, "I was drugged and left for dead in Romania, and all I got was this lousy T-shirt!"

All the best, Christopher

* * *

Yes, the gypsies and I collided a few times. Once, while standing near a bus stop, I knew my destination but didn't know if I was supposed to take the bus on this or the other side of the street. It didn't take long for someone to wander over trying to 'help' me. In this case, it was an older rather corpulent gypsy lady. As she tried to converse with me, but getting nowhere because we didn't understand what each other was saying, two more gypsy women in that familiar wraparound, tablecloth-style garb joined us. A minute later, there appeared five in total.

It surely was the oddest 'gang' to ever be surrounded by. Not one of them seemed to be under seventy, but the oldest rule of the rip-off is that there's safety in numbers. I didn't know what any of the hags were saying, but knew what they were after. "Hold on, hold on. *Uno momento*," I cried out, with my hands up and palms out in a universal sign to slow down. I then carefully and dramatically zipped close the zipper of my back pockets and added, "Now, we can speak."

I laughed during the exchange, not really believing I was in any danger from this band of Geritol gypsies. And in turn, they laughed as well – fully aware of the reputation gypsies have lived with seemingly forever. The word in the Slavic countries is that if you get a crowd of gypsies around you, they're gonna pick your pockets. Even the sweet little old ladies are not beyond reproach. Let them distract you, as they obviously were trying to do with their group effort, and your wallet will be gone and left floating, empty, in the Blue Danube.

Not being big on stereotypes, I set out to learn more about the gypsies, as real people. While darker skinned, they are actually of the Caucasian race. Originally they came from the Middle East – the name itself is a bastardization of the word 'Egypt' – and went through Europe in nomadic bands as mercenaries. Wherever they went they were persecuted, with their language and music banned. Some later even faced involuntary sterilization and the Nazi concentration camps. This was the product of fear and paranoia, an overreaction to customs and beliefs.

Nowhere among their customs is thievery, and yet that is their legacy, unfairly. Even I indulged in the stereotype with my little joke. The unfortunate reality no matter where you are is that those who are 'different' – in this case a bit more boisterous and attention seeking – become convenient scapegoats for society's ills. In self-preservation, making themselves different from everybody else, they exist on a separate plane. The gypsies have a separate society within a society. But with that comes resentment and an 'us against them' mentality. When you build up walls instead of breaking them down, assimilation becomes difficult, if not impossible.

Accordingly, when I asked Romanians about the gypsies, some would say, oh yes, they're nice people, they contribute to society, they're good in music, folklore, culture. Then others say, hey, don't trust them, they were born to steal, and so on. And it hit me that we all hear the same things about different groups that want to boisterously stand out right here in America. There's a lesson there. Different customs are fine, even beneficial to a goal-oriented society. But a separate society is sheer folly – and could lead to mistrust and even danger.

* * *

There were other incidents. One starry night in Iasi (pronounced, believe it or not, as 'Yash'), Romania I pitched my tent in a public park, between some bushes so it was more or less out of the way. At about 2 a.m. something started rattling the tent pole. A bit startled, I looked outside and saw two guys who appeared drunk and had stumbled upon my little oasis. "Who are you?" I asked in English. Their answer was incoherent, so I jumped out of the tent so that they would see a big guy in case they had any ideas about mugging me. As it happened, we were across the street from the local police station which was closed at night, but it gave me an idea.

"I am with the California Police Department (the what?)," I said, surprising even myself with how convincing it sounded. I went on gliding the lily, "Staying in my tent is part of a training mission with your police."

Preposterous as it was, not to mention my acting talent, they seemed to buy it and walked away, as I went back to sleep. Man, I thought, that was easy. But then about 20 minutes later, while rolling over on my other side, I actually startled someone immediately *outside the tent* – who himself let out a bit of a muffled shriek! It was the same two jokers. They were ready to cut the tent open and try to steal something. Or worse, attack me as I slept. That made me blow sky high. That they had a knife meant nothing to me. I didn't appreciate being threatened like that. "That's it!" I exclaimed, "That's enough, I'm coming out!" I shot out of the tent, brandishing a Swiss Army knife and my trusty pepper spray.

That was the first time I had ever taken out the knife for my own protection. It was also the first time ever being disturbed in my tent. I must have looked pretty wild eyed, because when the cold steel of the knife was visible, the dynamic duo scattered like cockroaches into the night. However, they still might come back, so I jumped into the cover of a wooded area. Staying there in a bush, I sought to keep them away if they were still around, by yelling, "Come on out, you guys, I'm ready for you!" They didn't come back, but I did see them in the distance outside of the park and in the lighted street. They were yelling something back, taunting me, but they wanted no part of an altercation. And after fifteen minutes I went back to the tent, moved it to another area of the park, and went to sleep – keeping one eye open.

* * *

Hungary, $1 = 243 Forints

At the Hungarian border, I got a taste (though not literally) of eastern 'values' when we went through customs. Two travel partners and myself all had bottles of vodka we had bought in Eastern Europe where it's really cheap. The rule then was that you are allowed to bring one bottle of liquor out, which I did. But the other two guys brought out 56 bottles! They had bottles stashed everywhere, under their car seats, in their luggage, hidden in the trunk, everyplace. I said to myself, "Smugglers!" Their intention was to re-sell the bottles in the West for a pretty penny, lots of pretty pennies.

Somehow they were able to get through with no problem. On the other hand, I was questioned by the agents for not having some little stamp on my paperwork. So then, of course, they wanted money from me, and we went through the usual rigamarole. Again. It was becoming almost routine. Same result, as we were onward in record time.

* * *

Poland, $1 = 4 Zlotys

Traveling north, I was able to have a look at the country that has arguably come the farthest in economic progress of all the former Soviet satellites. Poland now lives in peace and independence after centuries of being invaded, partitioned and moved around like a pawn in a chess game played by outsiders from Napoleon to Stalin. This is more than fitting for a nation that wrote Europe's first modern codified constitution, and the second in the world after the Constitution of the United States. Now it is a democratic republic, something many people old enough to have lived through the horrors of World War II might never have thought possible.

Thus, one can understand why the Poles are enjoying their lives. The historic southern city of Krakow is situated on the Vistula River with a beautiful old-world square where hundreds of people happily mingle about. Looking around, a sign on a cafe said "karaoke," which made me muse that the Japanese have exported their sing-alongs everywhere. It would seem perfectly suitable right here – heck, it even sounds a bit like 'Krakow'.

Melding into a happy atmosphere with people singing both Polish and international songs, it never fails to amaze me how many songs that hit the charts in America make their way to the farthest corners of the planet. Jukeboxes and radio waves are always dominated by these songs, from Madonna to the Backstreet Boys, despite the fact that few can understand the words. Those singers, and their accountants, probably have no idea how much in royalties the artists miss out on when their songs are played in the middle of the jungle, the desert, or right here in a Krakow karaoke bar.

Eager as ever to fit in with the local crowd, I saw an opportunity to indulge in one of my favorite pastimes: singing for an audience (admittedly, for those having to hear me sing, it's likely more punishment than pastime). I wasted no time bounding up on the stage, grabbing the microphone and belting out a loud and sincere rendition of the old Frank Sinatra ditty, "My Way." This is always an oldie but goodie because that's how I try to live life, in my own way. There was no TV monitor to read the words and follow along, the words were just on a piece of paper, and it's up to the singer to keep up with the music. The audience seemed to love it, and gave a strong ovation. They asked how I pronounced all those English words so well. I said, "I'm an American; it comes easy for me!"

* * *

While the Poles cherish their new found freedom, they have not forgotten the awful scars of their history. They recognize that one does not move into the future without learning from the past. Rather than razing the sickening concentration camps that Hitler had strewn around Poland, the Poles took the far more difficult task of preserving these death houses as shrines to those who were murdered in them. Indeed, I made it a point to visit the most infamous of the Nazi extermination camps – Auschwitz. The very name of it brings shudders to the spine.

Located 37 miles west of Krakow, Auschwitz housed three separate camps and forty to fifty sub-camps. It is a huge place, around forty square kilometers, though it still seems unimaginable that anywhere from one to three million people died within these parameters, with the number still being debated by scholars. Considering that at least ninety percent of the dead here were Jews, you realize that about a third of all Holocaust victims were murdered right here where you stand.

It has been said that voices cry out in the wind at Auschwitz. I can attest to that. Walking around the barren grounds, there is an acrid, ineffable irony in the very first thing you see – the sign at the entrance to Auschwitz reading: "Arbeit macht frei," or "Work shall make you free." The lie of hope that would never be fulfilled. Then, winding around fences still laden with rusting bared wire, you must literally force your gaze into the prosaic brick buildings that were the crematoria. Here, the voices ring out, and if you listen hard enough you realize they are the voices of the children who had teddy bears ripped from their arms as they were lead to the ovens.

I heard of individual stories of cruelty. There was a separate sub-camp at Auschwitz that was kept totally separated and was allowed basic comforts. Here people could write letters to their family and friends, glowing letters about the comforts and easy life here. This was meant to pacify future train loads of arrivals. Then they were later circulated out and taken off to the horrors of the regular camp.

Some prisoners were assigned to work-details at the gas chamber and knew the grizzly truth. One of these workers actually saw one of his old neighbors, a lady, and tried to warn her that it was a death camp. When she hysterically began telling others, the Nazis took her and tortured her until she revealed who had told her that. Then they came for him, strapped him to a trolley, and wheeled him to the crematorium ovens. They burned him alive, very slowly, his feet first. And all the people he worked with were forced to watch. The point was made clear.

There are simply no words to describe the depth of feeling and emotion that run through the mind on this tour. Going from one awful venue to another, the groups of visitors shuffle along almost in a trance, saying hardly a word, all lost in private thought. While paying my homage, I was enveloped by a feeling of complete and utter frustration. What would I have done if trapped back then? Would I have been in a position to do something to save myself and others? Makes you really see the need for a 'right to bear arms.' Without that, only the government and the crooks would have firearms to protect themselves. Be aware.

I have a tendency to tie myself in knots trying to figure out how people can be so inhuman to each other. Standing inside Auschwitz, I felt we might never have the answer. It's beyond any and all of us. We are all part of mankind yet we continually find ways to destroy what we feel threatened by, and erect fabricated justifications for it. Still, I was made better as a human being by coming to Auschwitz. I had to see, and feel, the darkness that can exist in the human soul in order to keep committed to finding and working for the bright, noble instincts we humans also have within us. That, I understood, is why the Poles kept the camps intact. Because while an effort was made to destroy the human spirit, it did not perish along with the victims. It remained alive, it wouldn't be crushed.

That lesson became more clear, and was a moral imperative for me in the days following the visit to Auschwitz. It was, and is, a personal call to arms – not armaments, but arms that build and heal and teach. Indeed, it is the very reason why I continue onward to the very corners of the world.

* * *

Lithuania, $1 = 3.43 Litu

Heading up to the Baltics, I went through the former Soviet republics of Lithuania, Latvia and Estonia – in decreasing stages of transportation. It was a rainy day so I decided to splurge with a first class train ticket. Even a man of the soil like me could use some tender loving care, not to mention a comfortable bathroom once in awhile. After getting off the train, I rode on a truck driven by a man who had a liquor store delivery route. In no time, we were making deliveries together, lugging cases of booze from his truck.

When we finished his route later that day, I took a five kilometer walk to the border where Lithuanian, Poland and Russia are interconnected, at the Russian enclave of Kaliningrad. The stroll came about because there was no bus scheduled along the road. Eventually a tractor came along and I thumbed a ride with the driver. So, over the course of three countries, transportation had gone from a first class train to a truck to a tractor. If pushing on, the next step probably would have been an oxcart.

* * *

Belarus, $1 = 1800 Rubles

On the road from Lithuania to the border of Belarus, another former Soviet republic, I met a guy who gave me a ride. He at first passed me on the highway, then actually turned his car around and came back for me. I guess he was keen on having me as a rider and hearing my stories. He was going into Belarus to buy some cheap gasoline, at half the price as he would regularly pay in Lithuania. At the border the guard wanted me to have an entry visa already, in order to get in. This time I had a different idea: lets just do a trade instead. Since I like to collect native coins, we agreed to swap my American coins for his Belorussian currency. I got my souvenir, he got hard Western cash.

Speaking of such matters, while Lithuania, Latvia and Estonia are all now in the European Union, using Euros as their currency, back then Latvia had a particularly strong currency. Around the world there are so many different weak currencies with lots of zeroes at the end, that it becomes ludicrous. Something that costs thousands of the local currency translates to very little in US dollars. These currencies are barely worth the paper they are printed on. The exchange rate of the Latvian lati, however, worked out to half of the dollar. That meant actually buying things using small coins, instead of shelling out something like 100,000 yen, lei, or rubles. That was easier, and a relief. Imagine, a government that did not rob its citizens' savings with high inflation rates.

* * *

Latvia, $1 = 0.59 Lati

The Latvian population is about one-third Russian people, yet there is such a strong aversion to the country that held them enslaved for so long that they even have a "Museum of the Soviet Occupation." And anyone speaking Russian in public might be told sternly that, "We do not speak Russian here, we speak Latvian" and that if they persist, then they should "go back to Russia." Seems close to the very same imprecation hurled at protesters in America during the Cold War! Small world, indeed.

One would be hard pressed to find traces of the Russian occupation in the daily lives of the Latvians today. The cold, dark, gray shroud of a subdued and repressed people had been long lifted by the time I arrived at the shores of the Baltic Sea. Contrary to my assumption that all the seas of the world would be equal in salt content, the Baltic can actually be labeled 'low in sodium'. Where we swam, you could probably even drink it if you really needed to.

I was fortunate to meet a Russian businessman who was kite surfing on the sea and invited me to join him. That day may have been the most fun I had on my journey through Eastern Europe – not so much the surfing, as much as afterward when he introduced me to four quite bodacious Russian girls who were sunning themselves topless on the beach! Usually I had found, if girls are topless they might dawn a towel if a stranger comes over to engage in a conversation. These girls thought nothing of it at all. Needless to say, neither did I. Never mind cucumber and milk soup, this was even more heavenly. I did everything in my power to keep my hands to myself. Later, we all went out to dinner and had a great time. By then it was all hands on deck.

* * *

On the road in Latvia, I accidentally left my hat in the car with a family when they dropped me off. By the time I realized it, the car was long gone and I figured I would never see it again. Minutes later, they came back looking for me so they could return it. That is special. The guy was named Auseklis, and he then invited me to stay over at his house. The next morning his wife made breakfast, and he let me use his office to send e-mails over the Internet. It was like being the guest of honor.

I might add parenthetically that Auseklis had three lovely daughters, 17, 18 and 20 years old. What's more, in presenting them to me, it seemed like he was asking, which one do you want? Okay, maybe that was my overactive imagination kicking in. Although I'm sure the girls would have loved to come to America, and he wouldn't mind for them to get hitched to an American guy. Maybe I missed the boat by not choosing Door Number One, Two, or Three that day in Latvia. Be gracious, just the same.

* * *

Estonia, $1 = 15.5 Krooni

On the way up through Estonia, a couple of guys, Ukrainian and Russian, not only gave me a lift but also took me out to dinner and showed me the time of a lifetime. They were spending money hand over fist at the restaurant. One of them brought out a wad of bills thick enough to choke a Moscow mule, and they kept peeling off bills to pay for beers, cigarettes, burgers, potatoes with white sauce, desserts, the whole nine yards. I was thinking, how can these guys afford all this? I assumed they must have been with the Russian Mafia, tentacles of which are known to exist all through Eastern Europe. And so I was leery. Would they want me to repay them in some way for their generosity – or else?

But they never did ask for anything. They simply took my business card, I took their address and that was it. Just outgoing guys who wanted to show how proud they were being good friends to a traveler from the West. Although, I must admit I felt a bit of relief when bidding them goodbye, without knowing exactly what 'business' they were in. Sometimes the less you know, the healthier you'll stay.

* * *

Finland, $1 = 1 Euro

First or Third World, it is a small world. I took the ferry across the Baltic Sea into Finland and met up with a girl named Laura Sirvio who I knew from 19 years earlier in California. Just looked her up in the local Helsinki phone book, and she was still there! She showed me around and we rekindled old times. When it was time to go, I wanted to hitch north to Sweden past the Arctic Circle. Laura smiled and noted that I hadn't changed a bit in all these years. We drove to the outskirts of Helsinki where she stopped alongside the highway and waited with me until I caught a ride. When a car came by, she gave me a kiss and a hug, and I was off.

What Laura didn't tell me until later was that she had a bad feeling about these two guys in the car. There was something strange about them. They were not Finns, but more likely were from Eastern Europe, probably from Estonia judging by their accents. They were quite nice to me. We were having a great time on the road, laughing and joking. After 45 minutes they stopped to get gasoline, whereupon we went inside for a cup of coffee. We walked into the cafe and one of the guys excused himself to go to the bathroom. Then the other guy said he too had to make a pit stop.

Well, something about this sounded an alarm with me. I had been on the road and met enough people – more than enough – to know when something smelled funny. So I would go to the bathroom too. The second guy stopped in his tracks and told me to stay and have a seat, get some coffee, and they'd be right back. That sounded even fishier to me. And just then, he casually started walking in the direction of the front door. When he got close, he shifted into high gear, racing out the door! Of course, by then I was also running, following him out. And outside I saw that the car wasn't where it had been parked! It was down on the far side of the station, with the first guy gunning the engine!

Clearly, they were trying to rob me, to take everything I owned that was in my backpack in the back seat. With no time to think, I just acted like Batman. While the guy jumped in through an open passenger side door, I jumped headlong on the hood of the car and grabbed on to the only thing possible, the wiper blades. Lying on the hood as they're about to take off, I begin yelling at the top of my lungs every epithet possible. I can only imagine what would have happened if they had peeled out, swerving from side to side on the highway to shake me off. Chuck Norris, here we go!

Mercifully, those nightmare scenes in my head did not pan out. Instead of moving the car, they just looked at me and insisted, "Oh, no, no, we are just getting some gas at this front pump." Yea, right. They were figuratively spinning their wheels, trying to talk their way out of it. Before climbing down from the hood I yelled, "Open the door!" They did, and I instantaneously got my stuff out. Knowing better than to try and pacify me, they sped off without another word. If I had five more seconds with them, there would have been a melee. I was so furious, my whole body was shaking.

To this day, that was the only time I ever had a bad experience hitch hiking, and it teaches a lesson: always keep an eye out for the attitude of people, and don't let your property out of sight for a moment. Be pleasant and civil, but maintain a healthy dose of reality. You are the prey for those who would prey on you, so use common sense. If you think you're about to be suckered, odds are you are right. Be aware.

* * *

Norway, $1 = 7 Krone

I met a great gang of friends at a pizza restaurant in Narvic, Norway 200 kilometers north of the Arctic Circle. We hit it off really well and proceeded to a house party, then afterward to a nice disco that one of them owned. Because of the exchange rate, a pint of beer was the equivalent of seventeen dollars! Fortunately, it is good to have friends who are the owners. At 3 a.m. after all the discos close, we filmed the midnight sun. Stepping outside, it was just like a late afternoon before dusk. We were even playing Frisbee in the streets on the way home.

But now, after months on the road, I was ready to go back to the States. In fact, given the high prices of things in Scandinavia, it wouldn't have lasted much longer anyway. At a gas station in Norway, a burger alone cost ten dollars. I asked, "What do you get with it?" and was told "salad." That almost sounded reasonable: a side salad comes with it, right? Guess again. The "salad" was the lettuce and tomato on the burger! Uh, no thanks. I'll have a nice natural apple instead. The world is full of choices. By the end of August, I was on a plane bound for California.

Grateful Kosovars, relaxing after retuning from refugee status.

Buying the household water in Biu, Nigeria.

CHAPTER SIX

Back home for about two years working in the corporate world with a technology start-up, it just seemed that every couple years I'd take off for another international adventure. This wasn't by design, but perhaps some kind of inner alarm clock was set to go off when my curiosity and wanderlust began to roil. Perhaps even subconsciously anticipating the alarm, I had begun working with Rotary International, a hundred year-old organization of socially minded businessmen that today has a presence in 186 countries around the world, and a rank and file membership of over two and a half million. Its mission is similar to that of organizations like the Lions and Kiwanis Clubs: businessmen align in the noble cause of helping those in need.

The projects can be small or large, and in the case of the former, the idea is that development starts from the bottom up. This lays a foundation for progress to spread by taking a foothold among the communities. Rotary figured out that it is far more effective to feed this sort of progress when you give something away. Give people the nuts and bolts of their own future. There are local projects and international projects as well, some of which saw me with hammer and nails building houses across the border in Tijuana, or running a donation drive picking up Christmas toys for other poor kids in Mexico. District-wide projects sent several thousand wheelchairs to Malawi in Africa, and Rotary's central theme internationally is trying to rid the world of polio. This is their on-going cause of choice.

I pitched a project that would donate computers for a hospital computer center in Nigeria, having met and corresponded with the director of the hospital already. This hospital, not untypical for the Third World, was rather ramshackle and could use some modernizing. We put together a team to write the grant, and received one, along with matching grants for a two phase project to put the computers in and teach the staff how to use them. So for me, again, it was the best of both worlds: business and humanitarianism.

With the Nigeria project, a dozen computers would be shipped in total, and I would take some along on the plane trip – not quite strapping them to my back, but not far from it. Fortunately a few were laptops, but lugging all of them to and from the baggage areas was my responsibility. The grant money was hardly a motivating force; it was nearly trivial, covering air fare and expenses in Nigeria. Even then, I would end up giving some of it to the hospital on my own in the form of loans that never really were expected to be repaid. I wouldn't make a dime from the whole project, nor did I care. This was a chance to put my 'be gracious' creed to use, to help people in the Third World. And to see more of Africa, which had such a profound effect on me two years before.

For most people, this sort of project might have been earmarked as a two week journey. Get the computers delivered, install them, teach the natives a little about how to use them, then get back to the regular job. I wound up spending five months overseas, branching out after the job was done to go exploring other African territory, seeing what else might be done for people as the situation arose. That's just me being me, and I hope to never change.

* * *

Abuja, Nigeria $1 = 133 Naira

The flight to Nigeria was via London, and fifteen hours later I got off the plane in the capital city Abuja, was met by the hospital director, Ari Biu, and we spent the night at a local hotel. Ari lived near the hospital about eight hours away in the town of Biu (rhymes with view). Yes, he took his surname from the town; literally the name translates to "Ari from Biu."

This kind of construction is common here. Last names are nebulous so it's difficult to figure out who's who. Ari's wife, for example, calls herself Mary Ari. She took his given name as her last name, and his kids do the same. Then, too, whenever you are introduced to someone, they're often identified as the person's "brother." Sometimes, the brother would look twenty years younger. When asking about that later, I found that they might not really be brothers after all, that it could be a cousin or some distant relation. For brevity's sake, though, they just go with brother. Which explains the derivation of why many African Americans call each other by the same word. It came from Africa itself.

In just the few minutes from getting off the plane with the computers until getting to the hotel room, the heat and humidity were so suffocating that it was impossible to sleep, even though the room had a functioning air conditioner. In the morning I got my hair cut off to a buzz-cut, a small step toward survival under the hot African sun. It cost fifty cents. Good thing I waited, or else it would have been at least ten bucks back in the USA.

We then went to cash traveler's checks at banks in the city, and the scene was close to bedlam. The first bank must have had 200 people in it, and most were waiting patiently in lines that did not even seem to move. There is no way I could have handled that. The second bank could cash my checks, and the guy who took me through it all (it took an hour) must have gone to ten different areas for signatures, approvals, etc. I was nervous about letting the checks out of sight, so I followed him everywhere. What a spectacle, this big white man hovering over everybody at the bank.

In the end he had me sit in a lounge room, and said he would bring me the cash, which he did. It was 26,600 naira in N200 bills, and that is a huge stack of cash that could almost fill a shoe box. After counting it, I asked for the largest N500 denominations instead. Another guy took a big stack, and went to get it consolidated. After another ten minutes of waiting, I nervously said, "Say, that guy works for you, right?" Everyone busted up in laughter, then assured me he was okay. He came back shortly. Whew!

I had two great breakfasts of eggs and toast that first day at the cafe around the corner from the hotel. One was at night, as the chicken they were serving was way too oily so I passed on it all together. Go with what seems good for the system. The lady who was the chef cooked one full meal, brought it out to me, then *started* the next meal. Ari had dropped hints before to her, but she cannot grasp the concept of cooking them all together at the same time. His look said it all: welcome to Africa, buddy.

* * *

The eight hour drive from Abuja to Biu was eventful, to say the least. We went to the transportation depot to catch what we were told was a taxi – the only one that went to Biu. It only leaves when it is full of the required seven passengers, and we were the first two. We might be waiting up to two days, they said. That many people in an older model Japanese-size station wagon? I could not bear the thought, so we bought all seven seats. The computers we were donating to the hospital took up most of the room.

Our driver was named Hassan. His twin brother was Hussein, as in Saddam. Looking back, that should have been an omen because the ride seemed more like a botched suicide attempt. He drove at speeds up to 140 kilometers per hour and used his horn incessantly. I could swear he actually sped up around corners and when entering small crowded villages. Chickens were scattering, goats bawling, and thick smoke from exhaust pipes spewed everywhere.

There were 48 police checkpoints on the initial day's drive. Each one with military men with AK47 machine guns. Some waved us through, others asked for a tip for themselves. One evidently recognized me (?) and asked if I brought along that Bible that was promised last time. Maybe we all look alike, after all.

23 Feb 2004

Waiting in an auto park to get a lift out of town can be frustrating. The car will leave when it is full, we all know that. But there may be 2 or 3 cars going to the same place, each sitting there half full and waiting for more passengers. A small car might be N500 per person (say, $4), a medium car N400 per person, and a big bus N350. I asked them why they did not fill up one car, send it on its way, then fill up another car. It was like I was talking to a brick wall. Hellooo! Can anyone hear me? Apparently not.

I took my first bus today, as it looked like it was almost full. Wrong. Waited 45 minutes for it to fill. (The other small car went after only 15 minutes wait. Wrong choice.) But I got the front seat, which is what I wanted. More space there, less claustrophobic. A small car gets 4 in the back seat, plus 2 and the driver in front. All cars are packed like this.

The goal is to never pay until the driver starts the engine to drive off. I want to reserve the right to jump ship. They hound you to pay early, but I usually hold firm and calmly say no. I want to be in control of my destiny if they take too long to fill, and bolt to another. One time, they said they are ready to go, and they actually started the engine. I paid my fair, then they turned off the engine and said that they needed one more person. Tricky bastards.

They lied to me, and also to my friend who escorted me from the hospital – and he was from their tribe! I asked for a small sealed plastic pint bag of 'pure water' which you can buy for 5 naira (4 cents), to make up for it. The driver bought one, and everyone was happy. He turned out to be quite nice. The kids selling the small pint water bags call out, "Peyote, peyote." And that sounds to me like they are selling the narcotic drug of the same name. But it is just their accents for what they are saying, "Pure water, pure water."

Back on the bus ride, an older man let me have the front seat when it was filling up – or else I would not have joined them. No way was I sitting in the claustrophobic back seats. When the old guy left the bus after his ride, I paid for his motorcycle ride from the bus to his house. Felt good to return a favor. The kids on the motos asked if I was Indiana Jones! Not the first time I have been asked that, but it was the first time out deep in the heart of Africa.

* * *

Arriving at the Maitaimako Medical Centre, I was provided a nice room. During my stay Ari looked after me well. He lived with his wife Mary and their five kids aged 19 to 28 in a little store-front home about a mile from the hospital. He also had two young kids Paul (10) and Sarah (11) who stay with them as foster children while going to school for the next six or seven years. They have taken in nine kids like this the past twenty years. The kids go back to their real families every Christmas and Easter vacation. They get no money for the kids, but the household chores get done all the time so it is a win-win situation.

This whole northern part of Nigeria is seventy percent Muslim, and they totally dominate the government. The Muslim prayers heard over the loud speakers each morning at 5 a.m. in the dark take some getting used to. Yet Ari switched to become a Christian decades ago. He is even related to the Emir (king) of his tribe here, who remains a staunch Muslim. Talk about rocking the boat! Why give it all up? He says actions speak louder than rote prayers and trips to Mecca that ensure heaven.

When he describes his non-violent reactions to being shut out by the ruling majority, he is almost Gandhi-like in his tones. He is the kind of gentleman who will send a thank you note when being denied a building permit. The town's people rise up on his side when the injustice is found out. Things get done. He works major projects hand to mouth. As Ari was fond of saying, the Lord provides. And, bless her, so did Mary.

A bicycle was available for riding to the house every day for meals. Mary cooked for the whole brood, plus one – the visiting American. This was some of the most satisfying food I have ever eaten: spaghetti, potatoes, or rice, topped by unbelievably tasty meat stews teeming with hearty vegetables. They would also have the daily corn meal dish, called *too-oh* in the local Hausa language, which is the staple throughout all of Africa. I remember it being called *ugali* in the Swahili language, and *paap* down in South Africa. We would all sit on the mat out in the courtyard patio and pass the pots around to each other.

The family took me on a trip to the central market one day. The place was bustling with shoppers plucking foods out of woven baskets – foods that included dried baboons and dried monkeys. Kind of like taking a knife and fork to Cheetah or Bonzo. I still do not know to this day if it was for dried souvenirs, or if people put it in a pot and cooked it up for soups.

One other delicacy from this northern dry desert area is fried grasshoppers. Folks would eat them quick fried, in the same way we would eat french fries. You would see ladies at the market holding bowls two foot wide and a foot deep filled with these crispy grasshoppers, with no lack of takers. Doing the 'when in Rome' thing, I asked for a few and the price came to ten cents for a little bag of them. Figuring the experience of grasshopper munching was worth a dime, I got my 'fries' and they showed me how to eat them. You have to break off the thorax, which is a 'twist-off' process not unlike eating shrimp. It wasn't half bad, and I had fried grasshoppers several times as snacks throughout the stay.

After two weeks in Biu I went door to door at businesses getting recruits for the first meeting of our new local Rotary Club. We got twenty or so people at the meeting, and it was a good cross section of the community, both Christians and Muslims. I didn't want the club to be a bastion of exclusion, having seen the consequences that religious barriers had on Ari, who in addition to everything else he did was also a preacher. Yet his Christian beliefs had left him somewhat outside the community establishment. What a shame, wasting the talents of a good man. Indeed, he left himself open to become a target for nefarious people, and this would play out in full in the months ahead.

* * *

There is endless heat and dust in Biu. Dust is blown everywhere by winds. The pollution in the air – the smog I see and taste – comes from the winds that blow from December to March down from the Sahara Desert. Every year there is at least three months of this. Mostly the winds are at night or early in the morning. Day time is hot and I move to the shade when talking with someone on the street. They notice my taking cover, something they would not bother to do themselves, and laugh. I wore short pants for comfort, which was only reasonable given the brutal heat, yet I was the only adult in this city of 70,000 people who did so. It is not their tradition to show leg skin, but a white man can get away with it. It would be like an African coming to America wearing a long robe. No one else would, but for him it would be okay.

This dust hits early in the morning. The winds swirl the dust, and I felt it coming through the cracks in the window sill. It reminded me of the big wild fires in San Diego in October 2003 that burned over 2000 homes. That made for three days of not being able to breathe right. This dust is not as over-powering, but it is still irritating. I felt as if someone was right next to me smoking a cigarette all day, which made me faintly nauseous.

Sometimes I went to the public library, and there was a fine layer of dust on the furniture. It was dark inside, and I had to move closer to the open window to read. There were only about six shelves of books, each maybe twenty feet long. Not many. It was a dingy area to read, with a few chairs and a table. The inside of our hospital was even worse looking: walls and not much more, cobwebs, no dusting. It would probably be futile, as more dust keeps on mounting.

I couldn't do anything about the dust, but could do something about the condition of the hospital compound. We all pitched in and helped collect all the trash from the church and hospital grounds and raked it all up into little piles. This was no small task. Plastic shopping bags just flow in the breezes and stick in the trees and the bushes, so we had about ten people picking up trash. When it was done, they started to burn the trash right there on the side of the road. Being conditioned to the law in America against such burning, I turned to them and said, "Are you sure this is okay, that we won't get in trouble for doing this?" To a man, they all laughed at the big white guy. They had no concept whatsoever about air pollution. When they get rid of trash, they burn it. End of story.

One last time, I specifically asked, "What about burning plastic? Isn't that bad for the environment?" You should have heard them guffaw at that one. Nobody in Africa thinks as much as we do in the Western world about such things. That's good and bad. The bad is that the air quality can be simply dreadful, the product of the climate and no environmental laws. The good news is they just get things done without complications. Even so, maybe I had a bit of an effect. Ari told me that just me being there made everybody want to join in and pick up the garbage that normally goes nowhere. "You got something done here I never could," he said. If just a little thing like picking up garbage can do that, the possibilities for real progress are truly endless.

The only doctor in the hospital was a man named Dr. Wilfred Ugwoeruchukwu. Bet you can't guess why we simply call him Dr. Wilfred. He was a young guy in the Nigerian National Service Corps. They are called 'Corpers' for short. This is an organization in Nigeria similar in concept to the American Peace Corps. However, it is just within the country, not international. College graduates will join up and be assigned to different areas of the country to lend their expertise for one year. Then they'll be given jobs when they return home. It is like an apprenticeship or an internship, and may be a replacement to military service. Dr. Wilfred is an articulate young guy, always doing something good, and I don't hesitate for a minute predicting that he'll be a future leader of Nigeria some day.

If I was an inspiration, my contribution was nothing compared to Dr. Wilfred, who would always be doing some little bit to help the hospital. For example, he would help me fix the rim on a basketball court when we were playing ball with the kids. Late one night, I even found him fixing the lights in the dark, standing up on a table out in the middle of the courtyard. It mattered not at all to him that he was getting paid very little. In fact, the hospital owed him some money and couldn't pay. So they gave him one of the laptop computers I brought, as his pay. In the larger picture, there are many such selfless people giving of themselves in the Third World who will be paid very little for their good work. Those are the unsung heroes.

* * *

Ari told me a story he says is true. Seems an elderly native man from the countryside was ill, and unconscious. When he awoke, he was in a big modern hospital. There were white nurses and doctors all around him. They asked him his name and he looked up at them and replied, "Back when I was on earth they called me Joe, but here you may call me what you wish!"

Ari said that he felt a similar way when he was in California. He had spent a few years studying in Ohio, and knew America had nicer amenities than his country. But the modern buildings and organization and fine weather in California were awesome to him. He was describing heaven to his family over the phone. I remember first meeting him in San Diego the year before. We had lunch at a very nice modern area of town (University Town Center), and it really is a treat to a new comer. When you live there all the time, you get used to it. I can appreciate it a lot more after roughing it for awhile overseas.

Imagine: there is one phone in the whole city of Biu. It is at the Internet cafe, and that one doesn't work all the time. The service is so bad that it would take me six tries to get a FAX to go through. Electricity in the city shuts off about five times each day. It can last for twenty minutes, or up to several hours each time. Whenever Ari e-mailed us in the States when setting up the grant, he would have his son go three hours away to the state capital to do it each time. It says a lot about modern progress that even with only one phone in the town, an Internet cafe is a must. The service was sometimes slow as molasses, but people would be there to use the computer for even ten minutes at a time. The cafe was only two months old, yet it was already becoming the 'in' place in town.

If you went back in time to America a hundred years ago, the same kind of novelty and excitement must have greeted the telephone coming to the prairie. While most Westerners probably don't realize it when shopping on the computer, the Internet is the means of progress in the Third World today every bit as much as the telegraph and the telephone were back when America was a developing nation.

* * *

Biu is a town of 70,000 people, including one white man – me. When I would ride down the road on my bike, they would wave and call out, "*Sanu!*" their word for hello. You really do feel like a celebrity, almost as if Schwarzenegger or Madonna had come to one's home town. Everybody knows that you're there, and they all want to say hello. People would occasionally ask to take a photo with me. One lady came up to me and shook my hand. As she walked away we could hear her saying, "I touched the white man! I touched the white man!" If you're an American and you feel a little down, just go to a small village in Africa for a couple of weeks. You will come back under the impression you're a superstar.

I say hi to everyone who makes eye contact with me, and sometimes people would just stare and say nothing. This wasn't rudeness or being standoffish, it was just curiosity on their part, maybe even a case of being 'star-struck.' Often people yelled out, "*Batouree!*" as I walked or drove by. They were saying good naturedly, "Hey, white man!" in the Hausa language. I would always wave or acknowledge them, sometimes playfully correcting them by saying, "That's *Baban Batouree!*" – or more accurately... "BIG white man!" They always chuckled at that.

On the other hand, among the natives themselves, it is different. In a dog-eat-dog world such as theirs, a peer is a rival, an obstacle. I was in the market one day and saw a group of maybe twenty men gathered around and looking inward forming a tight circle. I wanted to see what was going on, maybe it was a new item for sale. A friend grabbed me by the arm and said, "Don't go near that." He explained that it was more than likely that there was some kind of argument brewing between two guys, and the rest of the crowd formed around them to egg them on to fight. I ventured that this sort of thing stopped for me after elementary school, that grown men don't act that way.

He laughed. "Maybe in America," he said, "Here, it goes on all the time." That's how they settle their arguments. They never got out of the elementary school attitude. It's survival of the fittest on a very basic level, which can make Africa a very scary place. Confrontation is part of the loam of the land. You can imagine how difficult it is for women to break out of the housewife mold. If you want to be a woman shopkeeper, you have got to be tough. Same for anyone who wants to come out of the closet: open homosexuality is a uniquely Western practice.

Sometimes I rode my bike to the Biu Dam, about seven miles from the center of town. There is no bus service, and ordinary people have no cash for a ride that far so very few people from Biu ever go there. A shame, too, because it is a welcome break from the heat. One time there with Ari's sons, I swam out into the deep water maybe fifty yards. This horrified the kids, who yelled to me, "Christopher, come back!" After assuring them that I was a good swimmer, they still were petrified the whole time I was in the water. They later said they were amazed, that they assumed I would surely die. They are deathly afraid of the water and had never seen anyone swim out that far. This seems to be true of many people who are from desert areas and not accustomed to large bodies of water.

When my students had completed their classes at the hospital computer center, we had a graduation picnic and a trip to the same dam. Sixteen of the students rode in the back of a pick-up truck to get there. When we arrived, eight of them would not get in the water. They wouldn't even roll up their long pants to the knee, not even to dip their toes in it. I was learning first-hand, in small ways, how hard it is for fears and innate customs to change in Africa.

While Hollywood scenes of voodoo rites and shrunken heads may be out of date, there is still a lot of superstition around. For example, I went on a hike with friends to a little swimming hole one really hot and dusty day. We hiked an hour, and when we came upon it, the people with me said, "No, no, we must not stay here, we must go on to the next one." So we hiked extra to get to a second watering hole which wasn't as good as the first. I asked why we bypassed the better one. A guy said, "Have you ever heard of the Bermuda Triangle? Strange things happen there. It is very similar to that first place. We don't go there because people get sucked under and never come out." Hard as I tried to convince them that there was probably an explanation, they refused to budge. Just let it go sometimes. Be gracious.

* * *

My first trip out of Biu was to the city of Yola, six hours away by bad roads in Nigeria's Adawama State. The mission for this brief trip was to get a letter of sponsorship from the Yola Rotary Club for the second phase of the grant. It involved no money, just a letter saying we would work together. We had originally used the Gombe Club, but they had ceased to be in good standing with Rotary International because of membership numbers.

But the first order of the day was the golf course I had spied on the way into town. Playing golf in Yola was a dusty affair. The course was in the desert with no grass at all, and the greens were made of hard black sand. Thus, they actually call them 'browns' instead of greens. The dust was shocking, and tramping along in loose dirt really kicked it up. I was filthy, head to toe. On the way home I shared Cokes with my golfing partner who gave me a ride. My lips were so parched, they cracked. At the hotel I washed and changed into a business suit, and couldn't believe how much dirt came out. It took a while to cool down before changing. More soft drinks helped.

My hosts were introduced before the meeting. Mr. Thomas "T.T." Madi is a past president of Yola Rotary Club. He was good natured and a laugh a minute. He told us that a good speech should be like a lady's mini skirt: long enough to cover the subject matter, and short enough to be interesting! He is a Deputy Permanent Secretary at the Ministry of Land and Survey. The current President was Colonel Ignatius Iyawa (retired), who was more serious and a bit hard nosed. Yet he would later stay with me for an hour in the motor depot while I waited for a bus to fill up for my ride back to Biu. Did his duty.

At the opening of the Rotary meeting they sang songs like "My Grandfather's Clock" and "Viva La Rotary," and were quite enthusiastic. The last song was "The More We Get Together, The Happier We'll Be." My dad taught me that one as a lad, and now here I was singing it on the other side of the world. I presented our San Diego Rotary banner, gave a short speech, and promised at least one computer for them.

The first item on the agenda for the Yola meeting was one husky fellow who was a bit upset about not getting a proper letter of introduction from the club while going to visit a respected minister. Not good timing for me to make even the simplest of requests. I decided to enjoy the festivities, and wait until the next morning for my business request.

The Colonel had been asked about this sponsor letter before, and there was always a lot of foot-dragging. So the next morning at his office I casually mentioned that the new Biu Rotary Club has already had several informal meetings (so what if it was only my host director and me – very informal!). But since this project has had such a fine history with Yola, a senior status club, we would be honored to continue on Phase 2 with Yola.

By implying he had some competition, I averted what might be on his mind. He may have wanted a bigger slice of any grant monies, just for his signature. He ended up getting my sample letter typed up with no changes. We promised him two computers for his help – one now with me, and the other when a colleague arrives later. The printing of the typed letter on club letterhead took a full extra day. No surprise on that. But at least all was set to go on Phase 2. All in all, it was a very productive trip.

* * *

Baga, Borno State, Nigeria

8 Mar 2004

Just a brief note about 'thrill rides'. Seems most people in America go to Disneyland or a park like that, and go on a roller coaster to get their bit of a thrill. I come to Africa to get mine. When going anywhere in Africa, there are lots of guys on motorcycles who will give you a 'drop' anywhere you want to go. Usually around 20 naira (say, 20 cents), but it could be upwards of N150 ($1) for an out of the way place.

This weekend at the town of Baga there were three of us on one bike, going in soft sand. In the dark, getting hit in the face by low hanging branches, we never really knew when we would wipe out. Got stuck in the sand briefly twice, but we made it. And to top it off, when the driver made it to the town, he sped up for the last 100 yards right through the crowded marketplace – while sounding his horn for everyone to get out of the way! They must be used to it, as nobody even complained or looked twice as they scattered.

Once there, we had beers at a pub that had a TV and showed two movies. One was the Nigerian version of Cinderella, and it was quite good. The other was a humorous look at a Nigerian villager who goes to London – and all the mistakes he makes in the process. I told everyone that I am going through the same thing over here! But he was a bit crazier. If I see something different, I just roll with it. Don't fight the locals, go with it. One pub had a theater seating area (wooden benches) for the big English League soccer game of the week televised live, or pretty close to it. That is a big hit with the guys, for 20 naira (20 cents) a seat. Big beers are 150 naira.

* * *

On a trip to the state capital of Maiduguri, we had gone in one of my students' cars, so we did not have the hassle of public transportation. I stayed in the car when my friends got out to do some shopping. Being a bit burned out from the drive, I remained alone in the car, set the passenger seat down and took a bit of a snooze. Minutes later two Muslim schoolgirls were walking by, looked into the car and saw this big white creature lying there. Never having seen such a sight before, they gave out a deafening scream! This suddenly woke me up. Seeing my look of bewilderment, they evidently realized I wasn't some sort of white zombie or skeleton, or at least not a dangerous one. Another victory for truth and enlightenment in the Third World.

We went on this trip to Maiduguri to attend a Rotary Club meeting. When we arrived, I knew the Rotary Club met at the prestigious Lake Chad Hotel on Friday nights. Checking there that afternoon, the staff said they used to meet there, but they had not seen them for months so they may have moved. They gave me several leads and we drove to each, with no success. The reason we drove around instead of phoning, is that the cost of phoning is a lot more than gas. It costs less to phone the USA (at an Internet cafe) than it does to make a local call, believe it or not.

We were told the Rotary President was Dr. Anthony Uba, and were given the address of his practice. We arrived there at 6 p.m. and met Dr. Anthony – a jolly, likable, rotund man. He said yes, of course there would be a meeting tonight at 7 o'clock at the Lake Chad Hotel, and see you there. An hour later we retraced our steps back at the hotel, where the staff were surprised to see us again. Bizarrely, they said there was nothing prepared for a meeting. This was strange indeed. Could there be a second Lake Chad Hotel? No, this was the only one. We waited there alone in the lobby fifteen minutes and were about to give up and leave.

We were actually walking out the front door when all of a sudden, in strolls Dr. Anthony and an entourage of about eight to ten others! He was sorry for the inconvenience, he said, but you know how traffic can be sometimes. The staff quickly set up a room, and the group had a fully-attended, official Rotary meeting. They put on a good showing for this visiting Rotarian from overseas, and I gave a speech about our project in Biu, and why we had come this far. We had a delightful dinner together afterward.

That was when it hit me that there really hadn't been a meeting scheduled at all – until Dr. Anthony heard me inquire about it. He didn't want to leave me high and dry, so he rounded up a group after I left his office, and went to get them all. He is really a nice man, always with a smile and a hearty laugh. Another wonderful friend and business ally to have made in Africa, I believed. And for my part, I never let on that I knew of the quickly arranged meeting!

Dr. Anthony even let me stay as a guest at his house, one that reflected his status and influence – as well as his potential to become a possible target for kidnappers. It was a tidy compound with barbed wire around the top of big concrete walls, and an armed guard at the heavy metal door. Could things really be that dangerous in Nigeria for people with a modicum of wealth? Did it mean nothing to some people that this was such a good man with a commitment to help his country progress?

I thought about these conundrums a lot while staying at the house, which was lovely and, blessedly, air conditioned – at least when the electricity was working. And when the power grid went down, even a nice place like Dr. Anthony's guest bedroom became a mosquito magnet. They come buzzing around your head like dive bombers and you have to battle them. To combat this I actually got out my nice clean nylon tent and set it up on the double bed, then got inside and zipped it shut! This was at 3 a.m. in total darkness. When his kids saw this the next morning, they thought it was about the funniest thing they'd ever seen. "Christopher was sleeping in his tent on the bed!" they squealed. That's me, always happy to provide some entertainment.

* * *

Ari and I took a bus to his home town of Garkida, about three hours away from Biu, to attend the funeral of one of his old neighbors who had lived to 103 years old. While we were at the service, he began passing me around to all the people there. It was show and tell, and I was the show. He may as well have said, "This is my *batouree*." I didn't mind, because meeting all these people was wonderful.

On the return trip home he suddenly turned to me and said, "See this turn in the road? Well, about three weeks ago I was held up on this road, right here." He related how bandits had stopped the car in broad daylight, ordered everybody out and to lie face down on the hot pavement. They then were told to take everything out of their pockets while being warned, "If you hold back even one kobo (a hundred kobos being equal to one naira, meaning it was like a penny) we will kill you." He said robberies like that happen usually at night. That is the reason why they have so many police checkpoints on the roads.

I did some quick mental math. "That happened three weeks ago?" I asked him. He nodded and I added, "And I've been here for two weeks." He nodded again. "And it didn't occur to you to tell me about that before I boarded a plane and flew out here?"

He looked a tad sheepishly at me. "Well," he said, "I was going to, but my wife told me if I did, you're not going to fly out here!" She may have had a point there. For the rest of the ride, I continued to sneak a peek out the back window, looking for the appearance of the Nigerian version of Mad Max. And I did that every time traveling back on that road.

Oddly enough, on another presumably safer road I found myself acting the part of Mad Max. That happened when going out with another guy from the hospital on a motorcycle to collect debts that people owed to the hospital. Even more funny was that the other guy, whose real name was Sidi, was nicknamed '*Dogo.*' This translates to 'giant' in the Hausa language – and he was three inches shorter than me! Africa is no different than anywhere else when it comes to collecting debts, even for two *dogos*. Not a single person paid up as much as a kobo. And had we pressed it, the two road warriors may have been left for road kill.

The Director's sons Soulimon, Genaka, and Tambaya would regularly join me to play Frisbee at a local school yard. We chose a cement volleyball court (no net on it) to get away from the dusty soccer field dirt. Right off the bat there were at least 300 kids surrounding the court five people deep, watching every throw. I gave them all my trick throws: behind the back, through the legs, over head. They responded with oohs and ahhs. They retrieved errant throws, and got to see first hand how hard it can be to do. They laughed at their friends when one made a lousy throw. I stayed in the shade of a big tree at one corner of the court – no sense in getting too sweaty. Let the kids get anything out in the sun, just to keep the fans active. At the end I always said, "*Na go day*" (thank you) and "*San jima*" (good bye) with a bow.

Roughing it really wasn't all that rough in Biu. I had a sink, tub and toilet in the bathroom attached to my room. Problem was, there was no running water in the whole city. You actually buy water from guys who walk around on the street pushing carts with five gallon plastic containers of water. It cost seven and a half naira per five gallon jug. I would buy twenty gallons for me and twenty for the other people living in the hospital. So it cost a dollar to get a supply of water for the week. I had a heavy plastic 30-gallon trash can with lid in the bathroom for storage.

To flush, I took a big scoop of water from the trash can and put it in the toilet bowl. To wash myself in the morning I'd put some water in a bucket, use an electric heating iron to heat it up, and douse myself in the tub. Any Westerner who can't manage to do that is probably so soft and so pampered that they wouldn't survive a one-day drought. Indeed, for rural Africans, these would be considered luxury conditions. All it really takes is a supply of fresh water.

* * *

At the initial introduction to my computer course we had 10 men and only one woman, which was Ari's wife Mary. I told them that I would not teach at all unless we got at least two women in each of the classes. They scrambled around the whole weekend to get wives, nurses, ladies who worked in the janitorial department, when they realized I was serious. They succeeded in getting five ladies in the morning class, and two in the afternoon class. The total registered were 15 in the morning and 13 in the afternoon, with two hours for each class: 10 to 12 noon, and 3 to 5pm. That gave three hours of break time in between, and they could stay there and practice during the break.

With the electricity going down so often, I made a rule that we will do book work when the electricity goes off, and all hands on the keyboard when power is on. They got 5 or 10 minutes each, and then switched around. They all learned M/S Word word-processing, as well as things like saving files, cut and paste, click and drag. Really basic stuff. We had some college kids who were way above everyone else, so they helped the others. Some had trouble with double clicking on the mouse. The *Solitaire* card game is excellent for this dexterity practice. We had two monitors (computer screens), so that was all the computing power we could use. The ladies found the touch-typing courses easy to pick up, and they helped the rest with it. A major goal was for everyone to have a resume at the end of the class (or a CV, curriculum vitae, as they say there). This project would give everyone something tangible to take with them for their professional lives.

We also did a lot of repair work at the hospital. The place was in a serious state of neglect and disrepair because of a lack of funds. We fixed all the doors, all the frames, prepped them for painting, picked up and burned the trash, just about everything.

Work was still going on when the computer classes graduated. The event called for a celebration. We arranged for a barbecue the next day and, as a present to them, I bought the goat that was to be the dinner. We brought it from the market, put it under a tree and gave it some water. "Don't feed the goat because its gonna be dead tomorrow, anyway." I was told. But we were all nice to it, just the same.

At 7 a.m. the next morning, I got up early for the occasion of the goat being slaughtered. This would be a local ritual that should be on film, so I began recording it with my video camera. A butcher had come and tied its legs together, then pushed it over. Only then did the goat start to wail with loud "baaaas," realizing the humans weren't so nice after all. Then the butcher stepped on its face and slit its throat. Blood splattered against the adjacent wall like a scene out of an Al Pacino film. It drained into the dirt until there was no further movement, and the ground had quenched its thirst. As the butcher cut the goat into pieces I began to go green, weaving back and forth and getting very light headed. I had to sit down. My Western stomach was not prepared for native customs that happen all around the world, everyday. We just do not see it right in front of us.

Later that afternoon we had a picnic under a big mango tree for 21 people. Mary and the other ladies in the compound spent hours cooking up a goat stew over an open fire. We ate the goat, which tasted quite good, along with rice, tomatoes and peanuts. After we had digested all that food, we went on an outing to the Biu Dam.

* * *

On another trip to Maiduguri, I got it in my head to make a quick side trip to Cameroon, the former French colony that shares Nigeria's eastern border. I had a few days to myself while waiting for some money to come into my bank account from overseas – which routinely took about a week. So I would do some sightseeing up at Lake Chad, the big lake that borders Chad, Nigeria, Niger and Cameroon.

Starting out on this small trip, I met several people on the way named Abu Bakkar. It was a huge coincidence when it first happened. Then it kept happening! But it seems that this is just a first name, like Billy Bob, and not a first and last, as I had thought. It took awhile to put it all together. While playing Frisbee with kids at a rest stop on our journey, they simply loved it! I started throwing with one boy, then a crowd gathered. Pretty soon everyone in the village seemed to get a throw or two. It was something the whole village will be talking about for years, I am sure. A big event, like when a traveling carnival comes to town. Our driver had stopped for his daily prayers, so I just did my thing for everyone else.

When getting to Gamboru Ngala town at the border of Cameroon, I hired a moto driver to take me from the bus depot right to the border. No one seemed to be stopping, but he stopped at the immigration place just for me. Thanks a lot. There they wanted to know if I had a visa for entry into Cameroon. I had been told I could get one for 200 naira at the border ($1.50). They said no, that was the fee to get a visa stamped and validated upon crossing. This led to an ordeal that was frustrating at best, and worrisome at worst.

The officers wanted to show that they take their border regulations seriously, and questioned me at length. I showed them my Rotary papers, and the project we were working on in Biu. Wrong answer. Seems when classified as a tourist, working at anything even without pay could be a no-no. The questioning soon was called an 'interrogation', and I asked them to please not use that word, as it had an ominous ring to it. This was getting serious so I said if they didn't want me to cross the border, I'd just go back to Biu straight away. Seems it was too late for that.

All I could think of was a worse case scenario of me being in a jail cell for 30 days or so waiting for someone to bribe my way out of it all, and then trying to explain it all to fellow Rotarians. The guards said it would be fine after a few more people question me. I took the opportunity to go outside and play Frisbee with some school kids, just to relieve the tension. The officers were nice to me, yet I still felt like that goat we slaughtered for the barbecue. We were all nice to it right up until the time the butcher stepped on its head, then slit its throat. Really nice.

They hinted that it was too dark to travel safely at night, and I jumped at the opportunity. I said, "Why don't I just pitch my tent here on your nice cool patio?" They agreed. There was no way I was going to spend a night in their holding cells, so I beat them to the punch with my suggestion. The tent was set up on the patio where the night shift people also have a snooze, as there is a cool breeze blowing at night. We all even went out on the town together that evening for beers and *suya*: barbecue beef on a stick with onions, tomatoes, and chili pepper.

I crossed over to Cameroon on my own later in the night, but it was just for a similar snack, then returned to the tent for sleep.

The morning came with more Frisbee with my officer friends, and the kids came back for more, as well. I was driven back to Maiduguri Immigration Headquarters for more 'interrogation' – again, making me wince each time they used the word. But everyone again was all smiles, for over an hour. Finally, the guy on the other side of the desk, Mr. Ali, asked me, "Now that we have been so nice to you, would you like to do something nice for the department?"

So that was it: 2000 naira ($15), cash in hand. His hand. I paid it after showing that it was the last thing in my wallet. He then wanted to introduce me to the top guy, Mr. Betso. I said there is no more money to pay off anyone else! He said it is okay, that it is all taken care of already. When meeting Mr. Betso, he was all smiles, "Says here, you are a Rotary man." When I agreed, he shook my hand and said he is a Rotarian as well! We even knew mutual acquaintances back in Yola. He went on to write me a nice letter of introduction to the Immigration guys up at Lake Chad, and even offered me an official ride there. They then hosted me there for the next three days! Mr. Betso even refunded me the 2000 naira that Ali had pocketed. As the boss, I'm sure he would get it back quickly. Everything seemed to work out well in the end.

* * *

Greetings from Lake Chad!

15 Mar 2004

Travelers coming into port here on the Nigerian side told of their two day boat journey from Chad. This was once a huge lake, but the water level has receded so much lately that lots of reeds, swamps, and small islands dot the coast. The hippos have eluded me so far, but the mosquitoes have more than made up for them.

Earlier I crossed into Cameroon, then sampled some of the local French language and customs of the area. Nigeria is the only English speaking land around, while the other French speaking neighbors all share a common currency (Central African Franc) throughout the region. Everywhere is semi-desert terrain, with lots of dust in the air. Sometimes it even blocks out the sun to a grayish ball in the sky. Camels cross the road to nibble on the tall thorn trees that bring some green to the brownish landscape.

I got to travel here while waiting in Maiduguri, the capital of Borno State, for some banking transactions to come through. Everything takes longer than expected, so one must be prepared for it. There always seems to be a snafu (situation normal, all fouled up) whenever in a developing country. You know it is coming, you just don't know when.

A lot of it must be things lost in translation. Some people simply do not understand what is said, even though they nod in agreement that all is clear. Breakfast at a hotel earlier was a classic. The gal explained that it consisted of eggs, potatoes, coffee, and Peak milk (a brand of condensed milk in a can). We had ample confusion on this last item as I thought she said everything from pink milk to pig milk! I said just bring me a cup of tea and a 5 gallon bucket of warm water for my morning splash bath. Half an hour later my bath water arrives, but no tea yet. The guy says he'll get it. Shortly afterward, a full breakfast arrives. But hey, with it at least I got a cup... of coffee! So be it.

Nigeria was in the news back on February 24. It was in the neighboring state of 'Plateau' where 73 people were hacked to death with axes, and their bodies burned along with three churches. Did that make it on the international news? Anyway, yes there are some tensions in this northern rural desert part of Nigeria where Muslims make up 70% of the population. Prayers over loud speakers every morning at 5 a.m. in the dark take some getting used to. Good thing there are no axes close to my bedroom.

Cheers, Christopher

* * *

The long-anticipated money transfer finally arrived at the bank in Maiduguri, and I picked it up on the return from Lake Chad. With a big load of change in my pocket, I went back to Biu for the last few days there, and ended up giving $500 of it to help furnish the computer center with a cement floor and some new paneling. We hired contractors to put in that cement floor, and all rolled up our sleeves and started working along side them. All the scrap metal that had once littered the hospital grounds, the last remaining trash that could not be burned, was put into the floor to help strengthen it. That killed two birds with one stone. Dr. Wilfred said I changed a lot of peoples' ideas about white men, as I wasn't afraid to get out and get dirty with all the workers. I said it happens a lot back home, so why not here?

I was sifting some sand for the cement and lugging it in wheelbarrows when I tripped and briefly scraped my knee on the ground. It really wasn't that big of a deal, but evidently word got around. Two days later I was again working with the group and saw a couple of guys approaching on a motorcycle, and then they stopped right in front of me. "We heard there was an accident here," one of them said, "and that you were injured."

"You mean this?" I said, pointing to my knee. "Yeah, I scraped my knee. Really, I'm fine. Thanks for asking."

"Oh well, nice to know that you're okay," he said, and they drove off.

It was such a curious exchange that I asked someone, "Say, who were those guys?"

"I don't know," he said, "but they heard that *baban batouree* was injured, and came to see that you were okay."

"Man," I said, "it's going to be tough leaving this place."

I didn't leave, however, before getting a major scare – again conforming to some strange law which states that something crazy seems to happen just before leaving someplace. I was raking up the back area of the hospital grounds, where they could plant a garden after clearing out tons of trash, rocks, and lizards. If they could just have found a way to sell rocks and lizards in Biu, these people would all be millionaires. While raking, my hand grabbed what I thought was a regular clump of trash to be burned. Then I noticed that in it was a syringe, and it was now stuck in my hand. After pulling it out of my pinkie finger and washing thoroughly with soap and water, a doctor gave me a tetanus shot. All the while, I couldn't help but think of the growing AIDS epidemic in Africa. I was a bit worried, but kept on going. Luckily, nothing came of it.

A bigger fly in the ointment, though, arose when I was starting to bike over to lunch one day and someone handed me a note that had been written by Ari. It read: "Christopher, stay in your room. The state security department is looking for you." What in the world is that all about? Putting two and two together, it probably had to do with the escapade at the Cameroon border. The growling returned to my gut. Something was afoot – but what? Why did Ari feel he needed to warn me to stay off the street? I just figured Ari was overreacting, and that he would explain everything when we next met. Hardly one to stay inside cowering in fear for no good reason, I went to find Ari. My last days in Biu I went about my work as usual, but kept an eye out for anything strange.

On the way back from a project, there was a frantic scene in front of a schoolyard with people panicking and running about. It turned out that a little girl had gotten hit by a car on her way out of school, and she was lying there with people around her. I wanted to do something but couldn't, as I was in a hired car that was moving along, and it broke my heart to see people in this town crying and looking helpless.

Later, I couldn't get it off my mind, and told Dr. Wilfred about it. He explained that many people who get hit by cars in Nigeria die not of the injuries, per se, but of shock because they lie there and people don't know what to do. He said it would have been easy to help with basic mouth to mouth resuscitation and first aid, but people don't know how to do that, and nothing gets done. What a pity, and a waste. Just a little bit of basic knowledge could save lives. For days afterward I felt terrible guilt – not being able to have done something.

My penultimate day in Biu I tried to recover a computer that had been taken for repairs by another Corper guy, but not returned. By hook or by crook I was going to find out where it was. By going to his place of work, his school, and the military barracks where he lived, eventually I found him and he said it was still in pieces. Seemed he was dragging his feet while hinting for some kind of another payment. I was so exasperated, and with me leaving, it is doubtful the computer was ever returned. That left me with a bitter aftertaste. After all the hard work, I would leave a bit disillusioned for not having made as much progress as desired. But that was just a little taste of bitterness and disillusionment, a mere appetizer for the main course to come.

* * *

As it happened, bigger rip-off artists in far higher places than the National Service Corps were lying in wait for my last day in Biu to arrive. That became obvious when I was packing my belongings up and was informed that a Nigerian state security official, identified as "Mr. Lawrence," wanted to see me. It must have had something to do with Ari's note. But at the same time, I really didn't care to become entangled in whatever was going on. All I wanted was to be on my way and not be thrust into another scenario where corrupt 'security' people would try to squeeze me again. I had a belly full of that nonsense. Meeting Ari, I told him, "I don't want to see anybody who can possibly throw me in jail, and ruin my stay. I just want to clear out."

"No, no, you have to smooth things out with this guy," he said, looking worried. "You can go, but we here have to stay and face the consequences."

Consequences? Of what? I still didn't know, but whatever it was, I couldn't just leave my friends hanging. A deal was struck: I would meet with Mr. Lawrence if Ari was also there with me, and if we didn't do it at the police station. So the session would be at Mr. Lawrence's house, which was on the outskirts of town.

We went there, and sat around twiddling our thumbs for half an hour before Mr. Lawrence came in. When he arrived, he got on his high horse and started pontificating about a white man daring to come in and trying to circumvent the laws of his country, that a white man should be respectful and follow the laws of Nigeria, and on and on. I still had no idea what he was referring to in making these accusations, and was none too pleased having to sit there and be lectured to by this pompous ass – until he finally got to the nub. He said he had heard about something "that happened at the border with Cameroon."

Cameroon! That had been straightened out weeks ago! Evidently, now he's saying it wasn't. It all began to make sense to me now. Clearly, the walls have ears in Nigeria and word gets around at the speed of lightning. People had found out about our Rotary project, and a plot went into effect at warp speed. It actually could be a much bigger scam than just the tiny 2000 naira bribe that was returned to me.

That little mole hill had been made into a mountain. They would use it as a lever to pry money not out of me, but out of the Rotary project itself. That ensuing phase of the project might be worth $10,000. That was just too big a pot of gold for a lot of people not to get their hands on. Mr. Lawrence was the point man. He was there to shake the tree and wait for the money to tumble out of it. He even brought up my search for the computer – which happened only the day before – accusing me of further violations of the law by going onto a military installation without permission. Entirely bogus. Talk about loading up the plate!

The aim was for me to be duly petrified, as I was sitting in front of this big security man with a gun. Well, I don't play that role – for anyone. So when he had finished his harangue, I asked if I could speak. And then I got on my high horse, too. "You know," I began, "you are working hard to do good things for your community, and I'm here with Rotary to do good things, as well. We are going to stand up and be forthright, and we're not going to stand for people who want to lie to you, a respected security officer! We will find them and expose them! They are in big trouble now. Lying to a security officer has got to be a serious offense."

I was measured, calm, not threatening in any way, but Mr. Lawrence knew I was deadly serious. He could have continued the tough-guy stance, but my different approach had caught him off guard. We could have had another impasse, like I was starting to get used to. Instead, we came to an agreement: I wrote a letter explaining what had happened at the border and at the military installation. Just to make sure he knew the stakes involved, at the end of the one-page letter was a little reminder. "It was a pleasure to be of service here," I wrote, "If I'm happy upon leaving, I will of course recommend that the second phase go ahead as planned. If not happy, it will be an entirely different situation."

It also seemed to defuse the tinderbox, and allowed me to leave Biu without further hassle. Again, I hoped this Cameroon thing was put to rest, that Ari was off the hook, and that I would be able to return to Biu for Phase 2 without any hard feelings. Even though Mr. Lawrence and his avarice would still be there, it would be a small price to pay to come back and finish the job we had started, hopefully with fewer bumps and bruises.

I left Biu as something of a hero at the hospital for standing up to a man who struck fear into the locals. Taking no bows, I was merely happy to have known such wonderful, selfless people trying to do good for their town. Dr. Wilfred hosted me in the big city of Lagos, as he had earlier finished his National Service Corps work. He had a passport, but had never traveled outside of Nigeria in his life. He was receptive when I said, why not come along with me on my plan to travel to the neighboring countries of Benin, Togo, and Ghana.

* * *

8 Apr 2004

Greetings from Ghana!

Having just completed the assignment with the hospital computing center in the deserts of Nigeria, I am taking a couple of weeks on the tropical beaches of Africa just to get back to normalcy.

All the students back in Nigeria have completed their computer course work, and we have the beginnings of two new Rotary Clubs in Biu and Garkida. I was even privileged to go out into small tribal villages on the 'National Day of Vaccinations,' to assist fellow Rotarians in their quest to eradicate polio. It can be a challenge in rural areas, where religious leaders fear some sort of Western plot. The volunteers do a good job of informing the moms, and the kids generally get their three drops of oral vaccine.

Back here in Ghana, it seems a bit cleaner and a lot less hectic. The locals speak English which is a break for me, as I butchered the French language in the tiny countries of Benin and Togo on the way here, while visiting local Rotary Clubs at selected stops.

Below is an open copy of a letter with a clever angle to it sent out earlier to leading international philanthropists. Still waiting for a positive response, as of press time. Chin up!

All the best, Christopher

* * *

To: Bill and Melinda Gates Foundation

Seattle, Washington

USA

Dear Foundation Director,

I am a Rotary International member from San Diego, California stationed over here in western Africa for several months. My mission is to deliver 12 computers to the Biu Maitaimako Medical Centre, and to teach the locals enough computer skills so that they may *continue to run the fledgling hospital computer communications center after my departure.*

Several items have sprung up since my arrival here. Firstly, when teaching the introduction to Microsoft Word, I was asked why their town name "Biu" (rhymes with view) was prominently displayed in the tool-bar at the top of the page. They thought I had customized it just for them! I explained that it stood for Bold, Italics, and Underline (BIU). They loved having their name associated with such a fine product.

I explained that Microsoft respects copyright rules all over the world, and I asked if they had ever received any royalties over the past, say, 20 years for the use of their town name. They said they had not yet received even one Kobo (ie: penny).

As you can see by the accompanying letter I wrote back home to my fellow Rotarians, the basic infrastructure here is dismal. This town of 70,000 people once had limited phone service. Four years ago (1999) a communications tower blew and that was it for a large chunk of this whole northeast state of Borno (pop. 4 million). An Internet cafe opened 2 months ago to allow communications without having to drive 3 hours to the state capital of Maiduguri. Combine this with daily power outages, and you can get the picture of what these people live with.

In order to make this hospital computer center a going concern, I would like to be so bold as to ask you for a grant from your foundation. Rough estimates might be in the neighborhood of $1 million for communications for the whole state, $1 million for a state electricity utility overhaul, and $1 million for completion of the 'Bill and Melinda Gates' wing of the Biu Maitaimako Medical Centre. More details can be supplied upon further request.

As you can tell by the post mark, there really is a town called Biu, Borno State, Republic of Nigeria. I enclose herewith a few letters my students supplied for this assignment. As English is their second or third language, please excuse any grammar mistakes. Their reasoning ability is actually quite good.

I look forward to a response by mail, email, or phone when I am back in San Diego. Thank you for your consideration.

Sincerely,   Christopher Blin

* * *

Benin and Togo, $1 = 540 Cifa

Benin and Togo are two former colonies where they speak French as the national language, whereas in Nigeria and Ghana they officially use English. Actually, their primary languages are those of each local tribe, but these western languages serve as a common denominator where differing tribes can communicate together. For example, Nigeria has three different regional languages: Hausa, Yoruba, and Igbo. They also have over 40 local tribal languages! All in an area just over the size of Texas.

Dr. Wilfred, who lived right close to the border at Lagos, wanted to cross over to Benin for his first international visit. He only had a limited time, and had to get back to the practice after lunch. Yet while I crossed over easily, the Benin border guards wanted to shake down Dr. Wilfred for as much as they could. They recognized a novice, and could almost smell blood. I tried giving him a crash course in being firm: 'just say no!' It took awhile and he ended up paying an extra 400 naira ($3). He was quite perturbed by the whole thing, as he is a respected medical professional and not used to such treatment. And incredibly, when he was coming back over the border after lunch, the Nigerian guards wanted extra money for him to get back in, as well!

Looking slightly shell-shocked, he went back to Lagos while I jumped in a taxi heading for Benin's main city, Cotonou. Upon arrival, I met up with a couple of Americans working in the Peace Corps. There was a Peace Corps mission house in the city where their people could sleep, and they pointed me to a hostel around the corner. I did hang around with the Corps guys though, eating fish and chips and trading stories with them.

Some of the Peace Corps people had come down from Niger, where they were working as teachers. They had learned a good deal of the native African language there, and I was amazed when they recognized the accent of a man selling watches at the beach, and started conversing in his local language. He was amazed, too. "How do you speak my language?" he asked, incredulous that white Westerners could master the complexities. It was all in their training, and is really excellent goodwill.

As for me, I got by with a few French words and phrases, the kind useful in any language when traveling. I started with the numbers one to ten. The other two absolutely necessary phrases are: "Where is?" and "How much?" Then just figure out the rest as you go! Benin was a gastronomical paradise, starting with the soft French bread and rolls. The Nigerians subsist on typical British style bland bread, and lets face it, the Brits were never well known for their chefs. I quickly became addicted to the French rolls, packing them with cheese, egg, avocado, spaghetti, beans, you name it. And it was heavenly!

* * *

Ghana, $1 = 8800 Cidi

In Ghana, after visiting the capital city of Accra, I ended up north at the Akosombo Dam which was built in the 1960s. It seems to be a small dam, but all the water behind it forms the huge man-made Lake Volta that floods the entire middle section of the country. It also produces a large flow of hydro-electricity that supplies the whole country and is also sold to neighboring nations for needed export earnings. I met some fishermen and asked them how much it would be to ride their canoes around on the lake. They looked at me, puzzled, never having heard such a request before. When I said, "How about a dollar?" they said fine. So while the big boats were hauling tourists for ten times that much, I paddled wherever it was possible to go. Giving rides to tourists might be a nice little side business for them. I even gave them some marketing ideas so they could get to share in lucrative tourist revenue and make an improvement in their own personal economic situations.

While in Akosombo I met with some South Africans at a ritzy hotel who were doing some telecommunications work there. They had an ingenious system that allowed people to communicate over the Internet in remote areas, and big mining companies had recently installed their products. Having just come from setting up a computer center in remote Nigeria, it occurred to me that this system would be quite helpful during Phase 2 of my project. We spoke informally about them putting the system in at the hospital in Biu, and they seemed quite interested. Their usual price for such work was around $10,000, but there was some flexibility for humanitarian non-profit entities such as hospitals. The upshot was that if they could do this, it would create healthy competition for the lone Internet provider in Biu – no small step in economic progress. We exchanged contact information, and I would be in touch after running the idea by the Rotary Club.

The coast of Ghana features beautiful white sandy beaches with clear blue waters and inviting waves for surfing. At a local beach hotel the prices seemed a bit 'touristy' for my tastes, so I found a family that had a big yard and asked if I could pitch my tent and give them some money. They were fine with it and I ended up staying two nights there, and played Frisbee with the kids during the day on the beach. I would buy a bag of mangoes, cut them up and give them to everybody. Sitting in the shade under a mango tree on the second day, about a dozen kids all crowded around me, wanting to know more about the world. I sat there thinking in jest: I'm like Jesus with the twelve apostles. They were looking to me as some sort of saint. If they only knew...

One or two kids spoke English and they translated the native language for me. As we were all conversing and laughing, out of the corner of my eye I saw a cute little girl sitting off to the side. I could see that she was a burn victim, as she had a scar of melted skin from ear to neck to chest. She just sat there quietly and sweetly, and I made sure to smile at her the way I did with all the other kids. Her name was Brigitte, and she wanted to fit in just like everyone else – which she was.

One of my little helpers pointed out her burn scar, innocently saying, "Look, look." Memories of that terrible event must have come back to poor Brigitte, and she began to cry. Seeing how sad she looked, I had the older girl translate what I told her: "God loves you more than everyone else because God saved you when it happened." Perhaps no one had ever reassured her that way. It made her feel loved and special, then through her tears, she gave me a hug. That little freeze frame of love and emotion may be one of the most everlasting moments of my life, and is one that helps crystallize why I go to these places. Be gracious.

* * *

A month later I was visiting old friends in Germany before heading home to America, and was feeling quite good after having 'survived' another rewarding trip to the Third World. Then out of nowhere, I got the shock of my life. While reading e-mails, one had been sent by a young American woman who had worked on the Nigeria grant. I nearly fell off my chair when reading that, "after what had happened back in Biu," I was no longer a part of the project! Staring at the screen for a few long minutes, re-reading every word to make sure my eyes weren't playing tricks, the words didn't change. I was shattered. Thinking of no explanation, I quickly banged out a reply, but there was no more word the rest of the day. Gradually, however, the outlines of this shocking turn began to harden.

Back in Biu, apparently Mr. Lawrence and others had strong-armed Ari, putting pressure on him to distance himself from me. This is something that would never have happened without a hand being forced. Ari was like a relative, I had played sports with his children as though they were my own. This was like a knife in the back. The root of the case was, predictably, the bogus 'incursion' onto the military installation and the Cameroon border incident. The molehill was now indeed a mountain. It all began to make sense now: the whole thing had melded into a meticulous scam to fleece Rotary out of a slice of the $10,000 grant monies. And job one was to remove me from any part of the project, lest they be denied their cuts. In so doing, the only person coming to Biu with Rotary cash would be a 24 year-old girl from San Diego. Easy prey.

It was stunning in its breadth and viciousness. Being attacked was a personal matter, and I had no intention of my work and character being slandered. When returning home I submitted my final project report on the matter of the Computer Center at the Maitaimako Medical Centre in Biu, Borno State, Republic of Nigeria. In the report I defended Ari from a strictly business standpoint. Having been treated very nicely, I wrote, "By the time I left, these people were like my family; we shared everything together. The hospital Director Ari Biu was always smiling and jolly, and often shared stories full of wisdom. His wife Mary's cooking was unbelievably good, and something I will remember for quite awhile."

I also listed the goals accomplished, including: teaching two computer courses for 28 students who finished with a Curriculum Vitae of their personal work histories; setting up the foundations of Rotary Clubs in Biu and Garkida; donating 12 computers (six of which were presently unaccounted for, possibly being repaired); donating $568 for manual construction of the computer center; buying an $88 Uninterrupted Power Supply (UPS); giving Ari a loan of $160 and a second loan of $80 for the clinic (neither loan was repaid).

However, my assessment of the down-side was blunt: "Now that the positives have been stated, it is necessary to examine some underlying concerns of this project. With no monies coming in from hospital operations, the center was out of money. Electricity bills were several months in arrears, and a minimum payment was made so as to avoid a shut-off. One must ask if it is the job of Rotary to throw good money after bad and bail out an entity that is surviving on unpaid loans."

The security problem was then addressed: "The local security forces in Biu (under the direction of 'Mr. Lawrence') found out about possible grant monies and put pressure on the hospital Director Ari. They brought up mundane incidents in order to have some leverage to intimidate, and made it clear that they would require a percentage of any new monies in order for these to 'go away.' Safety is a concern for any Rotary member who goes back to Biu. This northern region is an area where there was a massacre on February 24, 2004. Seventy three men, women, and children were hacked to death with axes, and three churches were burned to the ground. After I left, in June 2004 there were another 400 people who perished in the same manner. This is a dangerous place, even more so for anyone without knowledge of the people there. It is a powder keg waiting to explode."

It continued: "This project has brought a new computer center to Biu, complete with new computers and an uninterrupted power supply. Before any other phase is undertaken, it is strongly recommended that answers are found regarding where all the missing computers have gone, and if the hospital's license has been renewed. The security issue must also be addressed. Any other monies expended could find a large percentage going into the pockets of the local security forces under an increasingly bolder 'Mr. Lawrence'."

Then I dropped the axe: "It is strongly recommended that this grant should be concluded now, and the proposed Phase 2 be terminated."

It hurt me to write those words, as they were not written out of personal pique or spite. Being honest, the security corruption that allowed for this situation to develop was catastrophic. It would be insane to go back and continue, with more grant monies at stake. Rotary appreciated my candor and believed that I had been manipulated. However, they begrudgingly continued with Phase 2 -- although under a more watchful eye.

Nigeria can take steps to shake off its Third World reigns, just as I believe every undeveloped African nation can prosper, given the right direction. However, it will take a concerted effort on the part of the locals to just say no to corrupt forces such as those in Biu. I can even hope that some there saw my example in standing up to those forces as a path for their own actions.

A postscript to the Nigerian adventure was that on New Year's Day at the end of that year, Ari phoned me in California to wish me a happy new year. His tone was that of letting bygones be bygones. It was difficult as I had been wounded, even shattered, by what had gone down. I remembered the times I had gone to bat for Ari, and to my regret, and probably his, he did not return the favor. That will sting for a long, long time.

When the years have put some distance between me and those difficult months in Nigeria, the bitterness will fade and eventually fall away from the important memories that will endure. A small bulwark of progress was created in Africa. I will always take pride in the fact that, before it became a fulcrum of corruption, a hospital in Biu received new technology. Twenty-eight people became computer savvy, and those people would impart their knowledge to other people, and so on in an unbroken chain.

And when progress happens and Nigeria is on the road to the First World, the wounds will not hurt so much. Because, in the end, that is all that matters.

* * *

20 Dec 2004

Season's Greetings to all!

I pass along the story below that was sent to me, as it gives an idea of how Africa was earlier this year. Enjoy...

All the best for a merry Christmas season. Cheers, Christopher

* * *

A professor is sent to darkest Africa to live with a primitive tribe. He spends years with them, studying and teaching them. One day, the wife of the tribe's chief gives birth to a white child.

The members of the tribe are shocked, and the chief pulls the professor aside and says, "Look here! You're the only white man we've ever seen and this woman gave birth to a white child. It doesn't take a genius to figure out what happened!"

The professor replied, "No, Chief. You're mistaken. What you have here is a natural occurrence... what we in the civilized world call: an albino! Look at that field over there. All of the sheep are white except for one black one. Nature does this on occasion."

The chief was silent for a moment, then said, "Tell you what. You don't say anything more about the sheep and I won't say anything more about the baby."

A bird's-eye view of the Lines of Nasca (Peru)

CHAPTER SEVEN

Once more, after a two year tenure living the conventional life in California, the road beckoned. But where?

The answer came as I heard there was a Rotary conference scheduled to be held in Cuenca, Ecuador just after the new year of 2006. It was called a project fair, in which five South American countries were seeking funding for their local humanitarian projects. There would be visiting Americans there, as well as Europeans. There was a mid-December deadline to pay an $80 fee for the conference, but by the time I found out about it the deadline had already passed. So I didn't even bother with pre-registering, and simply went down on my own.

Ecuador, $1 = $1   (The U.S. Dollar is the national currency of Ecuador)

When my flight landed on January 13 in Guayaquil, the grandest city in Ecuador after the capital of Quito, it was close to midnight and I didn't really know the lay of the land. Being tired and just wanting a place for the night, I took a taxi straight to a modern $40 a night hotel. The next day, I found out the real prices at the more modest budget hotels are around $8 a night, and continued to pay that the rest of my stay.

Next came a three hour bus trip up the mountains to the picturesque old colonial town of Cuenca, where the conference was to be held. Things then began to fall into place. I went over to the host hotel and registered for the conference. It was $40, which was half the price tag of paying back stateside. This is another golden rule of travel. Try not to pay for things at home before you leave. Just go there and pay what the locals do! It is almost always a better value.

A funny thing happened at the first formal dinner of the Rotary Conference at Cuenca. I was sitting at a table consisting of only Spanish speakers, and the guy next to me interpreted when I needed help. The waiter came by with two wine bottles, each with a cloth napkin around them. He seemed to be asking everyone what I thought was "Red or white?" This would be very common to see at home. The first six people went with red. Now, I usually prefer white wine, as red can sometimes give me a bit of a headache even when not over indulging. But seeing that everyone was taking the red, I said, "Why not? *Rojo* (red) it is!"

A good choice, I'd say – as the waiter poured from the second bottle, red as well! There was no choice! I would have created a bit of a stir if I had said "*Blanco*" (white). They may have had to go get a separate bottle just for one difficult *gringo*! "Be aware, and be gracious" is my motto, and it worked to a tee here. They had a good reason to go with red, and following the pack can be rewarding. I had a great laugh – all to myself at this special occasion.

At the conference itself, there was an expo area where all the clubs from the five participating countries (Ecuador, Peru, Bolivia, Colombia, and Venezuela) promote their projects to the Westerners in attendance. This way they can solicit funding for the projects from abroad. Since at 6 foot 5 inches, and the most easily recognized white guy around, I was popular – to say the least.

They did not quite pull me to their booths, but were close to it. It was a bit much for me, but most of the booths were visited in the two days. They all seemed like really good projects and I honestly could not tell how I would make up my mind which ones to invest in. The English-speakers had a real advantage, as did the pretty girls (I'm only human).

At the closing formal dinner I sat next to an American Peace Corps guy named Jeff, and was also introduced to a local cutie named Olinka. She happened to dance with a countryman for most of the night, but I told Jeff that it is not who you start with, it's who you finish with. Later, she and I were the best swing dancers of all, and when she found out how good I was she never left my side.

Four days after arriving in Ecuador I was reminded to diversify my cash and credit cards into different places. Some in a money belt, some in a sock, and even a little bit in my wallet. Some crime reports on the local TV news reminded that if a robbery happens, it is important to be cool. Lose a little bit at a time, especially if a gun is involved. No sense in dying a hero in a strange land. Friends took me car shopping in their car down a dirt road where people wait and sell their own cars. This is a prime place for a robbery, so I planned to pay for it with a deposit and go to the bank for the rest with the sellers in the car. I would stand out like a sitting duck if walking down that dirt road alone flashing a big wad of cash. Be aware.

Separately, a kid came up to me and said he was American too, and was robbed of everything he had at knife-point. He wanted cash to get back on his feet. He said he was born in Eureka, California, "not far from San Francisco." He got a lot of his story straight, but when I asked him if he was close to Oregon he said no, as that is way up by Alaska. Later I told him I know where Oregon is – and it is right next to Eureka, but good luck (and good bye). He was a typical hustler, and every one tries something different. Just keep on asking questions.

The typical Ecuadorian meal (as is true of much of Latin America) might consist of beef or chicken, with sides of rice and beans. But here they also have hominy corn (like grits) at just about every meal. They soak corn overnight so it looks like a wet popcorn kernel that has sprouted. It is called *motay*, and they can even scramble it with eggs. Popcorn is also served just about everywhere as a starter to the main meal. There is also a bowl full of *aji* (pronounced 'ah-hee') salsa on every table that has lots of shredded onions in a tomato sauce. They think of it as spicy, but it is in no way comparable to a Mexican hot sauce. It is mild by comparison.

We also shot billiards with a game called *In order*, which is played like 9 ball, but using all balls 1-15. You get the point value of the ball you hit in. Minus 3 points for scratches. Minus 3 points and the ball value if you sink it and scratch the cue ball on the same shot. We played with the Rotary gentlemen after their meeting and it lasted until one in the morning.

* * *

Greetings from the Andes Mountains

1 Feb 2006

Greetings from 8,000 feet high in the Andes mountains of Ecuador in the town of Cuenca (pop. 350,000). The weather is quite sunny and mild, with no snow at any time year-round, they say, even though this is higher than mile-high Denver.

Went to a local soccer game the other day and saw the home team play against a Colombian team from Cali. Besides a pre-game fireworks display on the field, people in the stands were shooting off rockets into the air. With these swishing by your head it is quite scary, and dangerous. I pulled my jacket over the back of my head just for some protection. Some rockets hit the corrugated iron roof of the stands and caromed down onto people, with sparks flying everywhere.

Others were aimed for people on the field, just to make them 'dance.' It was like dodging a rocket shot at you in a war zone. Scary. A fan out in the cheap seats lit a flair and held it high. A flair is bright red and about a foot of flame in diameter. Very hot. Just an accident waiting to happen. I would hate to be the guy sitting in front of it. All sections of the stands are caged – as is the field itself – with barbed wire along the top. Quite fitting. The game ended in a 1-1 tie in the rain, close to midnight.

Bought myself a shiny red Chevrolet that is good on the gas mileage and can get me around in style. Headed now to the south of the country, then on to Peru in a few day's time. Visiting contacts from a Rotary International conference, and checking out which projects are best to pursue. Spanish language is coming back to me nicely.

All the best, Christopher

* * *

In Cuenca they were having a children's festival which included daily parades through the streets. Each morning people shot off cannons to wake everybody up. It happened the entire week and I thought we were under attack. I met some U.S. missionaries, Steve and Bobbi Clark, who are actually building an aircraft to fly out to remote parts of the jungle to aid with their missionary work.

Steve and Bobbi invited me to their house for a great lunch of beef brisket with avocado salad. Steve also surprised me by giving me a cell phone, as someone had donated two of the phones to the church, and all I had to do was pop in a ten dollar phone card to travel in style.

Although cellular service in Ecuador can frequently give the wrong answer to the question, "Can you hear me now?"

One of the more fascinating outings was going on a picnic with their team that was baptizing people in a local river. It was like going back in time several hundred years when missionaries were ever-present all over the country. But then modern-day reality set in when everybody began playing Equi-Volley, a local form of volleyball that is unique to their country. It is played with an exceptionally high 10 foot net, and they use an all-purpose soccer ball. Must improvise when necessary.

I decided to buy a car in Cuenca to get through the rest of the journey, and would later sell it at the end of the trip. When buying cars in the Third World, I have usually had good luck due to shopping around and comparing. This one needed a couple new hoses, and was good to go. We got the car title transferred very legally and quickly using a notary public, and I was in business.

With the new found freedom the car provided, I could now go to road-side cafes at my whim. Here would be sumptuous dishes of rice, beans and beef, all for the good-valued price of only a dollar. Just like the Africans, when these folks saw a big white tourist they were friendly, and I would do my usual thing of laughing and joking and getting to know them. I love to find out about their families and the work they do. They seemed intrigued by this, as the ordinary natives never seem to get to engage in these kinds of friendly conversations with Westerners – usually only seeing tourists if they work at or close to the tourist hotels. I was different, and gave them an up-close personal one-on-one encounter. And in exchange their restaurants are the best values in town, far away from the tourist traps. It is a win-win situation.

It is not unusual to see a whole pig being roasted on a spit as you drive by a restaurant or even at open-air little cafes. They just carve off the portion you want as you order it. You can also get roasted guinea pig called *kuy* (pronounced 'kooie') in much the same manner. They are about one foot in length, skewered on what looks like a two inch diameter baseball bat, and turned by hand over charcoal. With their little faces and arms intact, they seem to stare right back at you. The meat is good tasting – somewhat like pork. The meal price in the tourist areas is between $7 and $13, which includes all the trimmings.

They use the U.S. dollar as their official currency in Ecuador since the year 2000. They had a financial crisis in 1999 and inflation took off. The old Sucre currency went from 5,000 to 25,000 to the U.S. dollar in only two months. In essence the government went wild with their money printing presses, and peoples' life savings were evaporated. The president of Ecuador was toppled and now lives in Panama with all the money he pilfered from his people. They switched to the dollar to get some sort of stability. Coins are interchangeable with U.S. coins, just the same as in Panama.

Prices are lower than in the U.S., as would be expected in any developing country. One dollar gets you a good meal with soup and juice, along with your rice, beans and meat. A day laborer can earn $10 per day for an 8 hour day. Gasoline is fixed throughout the whole country at $1.48 per gallon. But used cars are a minimum of $2000, even for older 1988 models like the Chevrolet Aska I bought. This seems high – as I traveled through Africa, top to bottom, in a car bought for only $1000.

After a couple of weeks I met a guy from England and we hit the road southward. Our first stop was in Vilcabamba, a little town that had won a modicum of fame when an actor from the *Dynasty* television show bought a place there. Seems everyone knew about this and were happy to inform you of it. There's a beautiful square in the middle of the town with big, leafy trees. For breakfast one morning we had soft avocado on fresh white bread with a pinch of salt. This was absolutely delicious, natural and healthy. We later took a walk through town and right next door to a cafe I found a small squash on a bush, picked it, walked in and asked the waiter, "Can I trade this squash for something on the menu?" When he said, "How about a bowl of soup?" I knew I was getting the skill of bartering down pat!

We were driving along in southern Ecuador and came upon a lone mule packed with bales of sugar cane clomping down the street alone, with no master or herder directing it. I thought that was strange. Then about fifty yards further down the road, there was was another fully packed mule, then another, all making their way slowly to their destination alone. This was no accident. Clearly, the mules knew where to go. The farmer had bundled the sugar cane on their backs, slapped them on the rear and sent them off to the sugar mill. How far, I thought, would those beasts of burden get in America before half were run down by cars and the other half ripped off? Yet in Ecuador they all get there in one piece, unhurried and unflustered.

* * *

Peru, $1 = 3.3 Sol

Crossing the border into Peru was a sort of culture – or currency – shock. In Ecuador the price of gas was fixed at $1.48 per gallon. Then as soon as you enter Peru where they don't produce their own petroleum, the price zooms to upwards of $4 a gallon! A good bit of advice is that before crossing a border in a vehicle, always ask about the price of gas on each side. Fill up on the side leaving, or entering, depending on the price difference. Check with as many people as possible because not everybody knows. The difference from Ecuador to Peru was huge. This explains why you don't see as many cars in the desert areas of northern Peru where gas stations are few and far between. Instead there are a lot of three-wheelers that are similar to motorcycles, almost like motorized rickshaws. You see lots of these as well in India and the Philippines. They have motorcycle engines and are very economical, and they get people around in style.

My car got twenty-four miles to the gallon, which was fairly economical. There are always people waiting for public transit so I would offer rides to them – picking up where I left off in Africa. One time I stopped and called out, "Who wants a ride?" and was rushed by a mob of people who wanted to get in. Worried they were going to stampede the car, I drove up about ten more feet and said I would take one person. One older woman fit the right profile.

She got in carrying a baby food jar that had something weird in it. She told me it was a cyst that had been removed from her abdomen, maybe an ovarian cyst, and she was taking it to a place nine hours away to get it get checked out by a cancer specialist. The only other way to get there was to take a bus, and the trip would have been pricey. It was equivalent to two or three days wages for her to pay for the doctor and the price of the transportation. It felt good to be able to help her out.

During the entire five month trip through South America, I only got stopped by traffic cops twice – both on the same day, within 20 minutes of each other in the same area of northern Peru! Maybe it was a speed trap area where they're keen on getting as much revenue as possible. One police car pulled out and followed as I was approaching a town. I went through the town and thought I'd lost them, but they kept pace and finally caught up on the far side of town.

Seeing a foreign looking white face on the guy at the wheel, all they would want was to get some money out of me. And when the cop got out and came over, the conversation was almost amusing. He told me what my speed was and went through his little book of laws and fines. He then added it up according to his own scales of 'justice' and came up with a fine of $180! That of course was the start price, a most ridiculously exorbitant one at that, to see if I'd bite. I didn't. In fact I said, "Are you out of your mind?" So he studiously checked the book again, to take up lots of time. Finally after about ten minutes of this act I just gave in and paid him three bucks, which he had no trouble taking in order to look the other way and let me go. Quite a discount, after minimal negotiations.

Then not twenty minutes later, another official palm-greaser stopped me when I was all but crawling along. He too went through the routine. I made it clear to him that, "I'm not going to pay off everybody in this country." After discussing it for a while and getting nowhere fast, I decided another kind of tack might work. In my trunk were some T-shirts from California, the kind that people love world-wide – with the names of cities and baseball teams. These come in quite handy on occasions such as this.

I went to the trunk and turned the key – but it didn't work! The cop came back and he tried, and it took us ten minutes of jimmying around to get it open. I then gave him a shirt, and one for his buddy as well, and said, "Thank you guys, goodbye." He stood there holding the shirts over his arm and it must have placated him because he echoed me, saying, "*Gracias, adios.*" By then I was pulling away.

While driving off I couldn't help but wonder why the the key hadn't worked. So I stopped the car fifty yards down the road and went back to pop the trunk again. Same problem. It took a lot of key jiggling to get it open, and when it was I noticed that two of my bags were gone! Reflecting back in time, it seemed evident that someone had tampered with the trunk and taken the bags earlier in the day at a dodgy little town. I was always careful about putting my car under lock and key in a hotel garage for the night. This particular morning I'd gone to a local Internet cafe and parked the car right out in front and kept my eye on it. When finished, I went around the corner to have breakfast and was away from the car maybe 15 minutes.

That's all someone needed. Whoever it was must have been watching me like a hawk – every minute since parking the car. When this big foreigner was away from sight, the thief pried the trunk open with something similar to a screwdriver, stole the bags, shut the trunk and ran off. And I didn't find out until eight hours later and several hundred miles away.

One bag contained a mass of paperwork from eighty different Rotary projects, as well as addresses of each local Rotary Club. Since that was the heaviest bag, the thieves probably figured that was the one that was most valuable. Not that it mattered to them, but the stuff in there was more valuable than they thought – in terms of bringing some outside help to their countries. The second bag had two cellular phones and other trinkets that I thought weren't likely worth the risk of anyone prying open a car trunk in broad daylight. As much as I had taught myself to be aware when it comes to protecting personal property on the road, you can never bend the rule, even a little. If you leave something that could look valuable in a car, keep an eye on it at all times possible or else just take it with you. Inscribe this rule in indelible ink on your hand, if needed.

* * *

The coast of Peru is almost totally desert, from the northern tip all the way down to Chile. Dirt and heat and rocks all the way. I was literally picking up people and giving them rides through the desert, making lots in terms of friendships. One of my passengers was a man named Pedro who owned a gas station, appropriately enough, and was an enormously outgoing guy. When we rolled into the capital city of Lima, I dropped off the others and he said, "Christopher, my friend, I'm going to take you to the best place I know to stay."

Lima is a huge city. About half the population of Peru lives there and I was most curious to see what the 'best' meant to an above-average Peruvian. He directed me to an area I didn't even know existed: the 'Beverly Hills' of Lima – an area known as Mira Flores. I might never have found it on my own because Lima is so spread-out. He took me to a *pension* – a family residence where they rented out rooms at nine dollars a night, which was good value for the big city. There were other wonderful people there too, including guys who taught surfing and hang gliding to tourists. Pedro was right, the conditions and people in this area were the best. I felt safe, sane and secure after my latest little disaster, the stolen bags episode. Mira Flores is like an oasis in Lima. The rest of the city can be crowded and scary, and there is a grossly high amount of traffic and noise.

Mira Flores, by contrast, is up on a cliff overlooking the Pacific. There is beautiful green grass, thick trees, and nice places to walk around and feel safe. In fact, someone left a pair of sunglasses on a park bench there and figured that was it, they had to be gone. But when he went back two hours later, the glasses were sitting on top of the bench where no one would sit on them, obviously placed there by someone who realized they'd been left by mistake. Any place else in South America it would have been someone's lucky day, finder's keepers.

We all had pizza and an unbroken supply-line of rum and colas that night. I even found a backpacker's hostel nearby that was half the price the next day – proving yet again that you can find these almost anywhere you go. There some Canadian guys were heading south too, and asked if they could come along. I said sure, just split the gas. It was a man, his wife, and their little girl, and we all had a great time together.

Driving south to Nasca in southern Peru, we viewed the world famous *Lines of Nasca* from an observation tower 30 feet in the air. These geographical artistic lines are in the shapes of animals, people, hands, even an astronaut or space alien. They are hundreds of feet long and are scattered over an area at least five square miles. They were scratched or dug into the desert floor hundreds of years before, and only discovered in the 1920's when the first plane flew over them. It is a mystery as to who created them, and how. The lines themselves cannot be more than about six inches wide, and they are not cut deep. The main highway goes right through one of the figures, and there, people have walked all over that one and scratched it away. So these are not cut into stone, yet they do not wash away with heavy rain storms. The world loves a good mystery! Could these be signals to ancient astronauts, as theorized?

After a day of venturing through the desert, my traveling companions and I took a lunch break for some fried fish at a little hut restaurant at the ocean. The owner of the restaurant said 14 Sol (the local currency, about $4) per person for lunch. I said 8 Sol is the normal price, and he said okay. It was that simple, so just remember to bargain for everything. We made fast friends with everyone there.

Following lunch we went down to the beach for swimming in the surf and tossing the Frisbee around on the shore. Great exercise. On the way back to the car, I thought I could make over the hot sand with just my bare feet. Wrong. Was scurrying from one patch of loose vegetation to another, then finally gave up and jumped in the air and landed in the sand right on my bum! Everyone up at the restaurant busted up in loud laughter, as they were all watching this spectacle. I was glad to have provided some entertainment for the locals.

Later that night at a small town, while asking for directions to hotels from three lovely ladies who were selling popcorn from a cart in the street, I had them all laughing by the end. A little flirting makes everyone happy. Shared a bottle of rum and colas with my travel companions that night. There is something special about solving the world's problems over a bottle or two!

* * *

The desert oasis town of Huacachina (say 'wa ka cheena') in southern Peru has a greenish lake with reeds, right in the middle of huge sand dunes. All the hotels have swimming pools that are just right for meeting backpacking tourist chicks from Germany, Sweden, or wherever.

The scariest thing I have done in a long time is take a dune buggy tour up and down these cliffs of sand, which can be 300 yards or more straight down! When sliding sideways while making a big left turn, I was almost certain the buggy would tip over and create massive injuries. Got close several times. Our driver was a sadistic bastard named Martin, who kept at it hot and heavy. One jump started to land sideways as well, which I thought would be a roll-over for sure, but he straightened it out all right. This type of tour could not possibly happen in a developed Western country, as the costs of insurance would prohibit it. It is like an amusement park ride... without any safety devices – an accident just waiting to happen. We tourists loved it all!

Late in the evening, back at the oasis hotel, I was woken up by barking dogs outside somewhere in the complex. After what seemed like half an hour, I had enough. I stuck my head out the window and yelled, "No!" They stopped immediately. Finally, my Spanish was actually understood! Good thing it is the same word in both languages.

The next day we pulled into the mountain town of Arequipa, Peru – the gateway to Macchu Pichu and Lake Titicaca, and a tourist town with a sizable population. Much like Cuenca in Ecuador, Arequipa is marked by a beautiful colonial-style town square, lined with rows of picturesque buildings, and has lots of cars. They have tow-away zones in the central city, but they always told me it would be safe to park five minutes in one of them if keeping an eye out. So the next morning after pulling into one of the zones – wouldn't you just know it – when I came back not five minutes later, the car was in the process of being towed away! A tow-truck had pulled in front of it and the driver, aided by a parking meter lady, had hitched the car to the truck. They were getting into the cab of the truck when I ran over, screaming, "No, no, this is my car!" They said, "Follow us," though how I could do that without a car was unclear.

"Nooo!" I wailed, and without time to think, pulled another of my Super-hero moves – jumping on the back of the tow-truck and moving the levers back and forth until something happened! Seeing this, the driver shot out of the truck looking none too pleased.

"Hey!" he was yelling in Spanish, "what are you doing on my truck?"

"I don't want my car towed!"

"Sorry, it's too late."

The meter maid came out and joined in. "Yes, it is too late to stop," she said.

"No way!" was my reply, and would lower it as the driver was trying to raise it again.

The crowd around grew quickly, watching all the commotion. This was reality-show entertainment at its best, and they were loving their front row seats! The meter maid finally acquiesced, nodding to the driver to let me unhook my beast. My hands were grimy with oil, but I drove off to the cheers of the crowd! I also flashed half a peace sign to the driver. Admittedly, I was feeling only half peaceful at this one instance.

* * *

On a mountain bus tour, the last saga of the trip back turned into quite an adventure. Local protesters had closed off the Pan American Highway in both directions. This is the main north/south route that actually runs from the top of Alaska down to Tierra del Fuego in Argentina at the bottom of the continent. These protesters were promised a water deal last year with neighboring areas, but the creeks were diverted and they never got their share of the precious water. In any desert, water is so valuable that countries even go to war over it.

We boarded a night bus at 10 p.m., drove two hours to the protest site, got out of the bus with everyone and hiked one mile in the dark to where another bus was to pick us up. We passed some protesters, who generally let us through without incident. One saw that I was a big foreign looking guy and let out a bit of a hoot, so I graciously acknowledged the reception with a casual salute. There were one-foot diameter rocks throughout the protest site and lots of torches and bonfires – plus some corn-stalks or bamboo poles that were lashed together into big X formations. These kept all the vehicles from passing.

Hundreds of trucks were lining the side of the road waiting for the stalemate to end. It reminded me of the 200 or so trucks I once saw waiting in Zimbabwe in Africa for up to four days for a ferry boat to cross the river into Zambia. Same story, different continent. Once we crossed the site, we lay down in the road together and got some sleep while waiting for our other bus to come pick us up. It came, and dropped us at our destination at sunrise the next morning.

The golf course in Arequipa, Peru has two separate flocks of sheep that graze on the course to keep it trim – as well as one cow. With the over-grown grass, you get no favorable rolls on this course: when the ball hits, that is generally where it stays. A unique feature of the course are the small lakes that are everywhere. They all have two-foot cliffs going down to the clear water, but occasionally rusty old junk appliances can be seen at the bottom of the shallow ponds. There is a natural water source from deep below, but it seems not really drinkable.

Being mid-week, there was only one other group on the course, two ladies with their caddies. They had pale features, and may have been wives of Western businessmen. The course is surrounded by slum-like houses on the hills overlooking it. People come down to use the course as a park, as in one fairway some rocks were in place that the local kids used as soccer goals.

* * *

Bolivia, $1 = 8 Bolivianos

Hi from Lake Titicaca, Peru/Bolivia

16 Feb 2006

Lake Titicaca – the famous name still inspires similar snickers years after I first heard it in my 5th grade geography class. It is the highest body of water in the world at 4000 meters (12,000 feet). I actually had my first altitude sickness here, a pounding headache that kept me awake all night. Better now, but out of breath quickly on mountain hikes. The lake is crystal clear blue, and quite cold. I managed a swim, to cool down from the bright afternoon sun so high up. Cools down remarkably at sunset. Trucha (trout) is the local food specialty, and they serve it in grand portions.

The Basilica here is famous throughout Bolivia, and people bring their cars here to be blessed to insure a safe journey. I traveled with a Danish TV film crew who were getting their boat blessed. It was a reed boat they made here on the lake – similar to the one Thor Heyerdahl once made and sailed over the ocean to prove his theories about ancient intercontinental travel.

The traditional dress of the Peru and Bolivian women consists of colorful skirts topped by a hat that is similar to a derby. They braid their long black hair in two long rows, and all have dark skin that shows their American Indian history. People in general are quiet and unassuming, and seem quite polite, respectful, and religious.

In LaPaz, Bolivia I had the honor to play golf at one of the most stunningly beautiful, as well as the highest golf course in the world. The LaPaz Country Club has lush green fairways surrounded by red and tan sandstone pillars, cliffs, and ravines. It is like playing in the Grand Canyon or Brice Canyon.

At the border of Peru and Bolivia, there is much counterfeiting of currency. I even got a counterfeit coin! You must always be on guard. Headed to Chile next.

Cheers, Christopher

* * *

Chile, $1 = 510 Pesos

The country of Chile seems to be more orderly, while in the other countries of South America there are varying shades of mayhem. You can actually drink the tap water in just about all of Chile. What a concept – the government actually providing safe drinking water for its citizens. They get first things done first, then the rest kind of flows along from there. They seem to have higher standards, while other countries are lacking.

When driving into Arica, a desert beach town at the northern border, the houses and apartment blocks are quite orderly. Even high density areas seemed nicer. You cannot just put up a shanty shack and call it home, you must build with the required permits. With this orderly Western-ism comes higher prices. Hostels are $12 per night, compared to $3 in neighboring Bolivia. Food prices are a little higher as well, but you can still find good chow. I dove into a great hot dog covered with guacamole, onions and tomatoes that had to be a foot long and piled 4 inches high with all those trimmings. Good food value for around a dollar.

I played a desert golf course using just my 7 iron. That even includes *putting* with it – yes, it can be done! No use in scratching up all my clubs on desert rocks and dirt. Played towards the end of the day, so the sun was not as hot. With no vegetation in the fairways, the ball can really roll a long distance. This course has huge rock patches with all the rocks spaced three feet apart and painted blue to indicate a water hazard, or painted green for a forest area hazard. The water hazard even has shark fins and 'danger' signs warning to stay out. Quite creative!

Colombia, $1 = 2,200 Pesos

Turning around and heading north, I retraced my steps through Peru and Ecuador until reaching the country of Colombia. Back up to the top of the continent and into the northern hemisphere, I drove safely up the coast and through the 'danger zone' of southern Colombia where FARC separatist rebels still control a large chunk of the country. After dropping off my Italian car-mates who had been riding with me from Cali to Medellin, headed north-east towards the Venezuela border alone. It was peaceful driving through the green countryside on a sunny election-day Sunday. The national election seemed to go off with no violence from insurgents, and I gave lots of people rides for short distances. The highlight for me was seeing three older ladies in their 60s or 70s walking the road. I asked for directions, then offered them a ride. One said, "*No hay platta*" (we have no money), so I winked and said all rides on election day are free! Saved them a walk of three kilometers, which is about two miles. They were so sweet.

At the sweltering humid town of Porto Berrio, after a huge chicken meal I asked where the community pool is. It was right next door so I swam my customary 10 laps, then introduced everyone there to the joys of Frisbee. Playing with a few always leads to more people joining in on the fun. I started this journey with 20 quality Frisbees that were provided by the 'Ultimate Players Association' (the international governing body for the team sport of Ultimate Frisbee), and I had been giving them away to everyone who would play with me.

The locals at the pool were eager to learn the sport, and picked up the techniques of throwing it quite quickly. Three teenage gals had a hoot, giggling all the time. At the end of the evening I was friends with everyone, including the pool owner Leonardo. He hinted that a Frisbee would be just the thing to keep his pool lively everyday. I needed a place to stay for the night, and a deal was struck as a Frisbee was bartered for a free hotel room at a classy hotel. I had to keep a straight face throughout the negotiations because I was going to give it to them for free anyway!

* * *

Colombia seems to have no major north/south national driving artery. It is all city to city winding mountain roads, and generally one lane in each direction. Getting behind a big bus or truck and stuck in a line of 10 or more cars with not much chance to pass can really teach the art of being patient.

Climbing up one huge mountain road with my car, the engine got pretty hot. Cooled it off with a water stop at the crest and was careful not to open the hot radiator cap, as I had done two days earlier. (It had blown then, and I got some scalding hot water on my arm. I was okay, though.) At the top looking down was a beautiful modern city of 600,000 people called Bucaramanga, Colombia that is surrounded by lots of green trees and mountains. Heading down the hill to the city I was reminded of descending into LaPaz, Bolivia, as both have a few similar cliffs and beautiful buildings. They may be sister cities, as this one also welcomes all to a 'City of Peace'.

At the central park I immediately found some friends and played co-ed 4-on-4 basketball, with one gal on each team. Our young lady was Andrea, and she was a tiny, sporty cutie. I was the only one to feed her the ball and encourage her to shoot. She actually made one shot, and it was only her first time playing. A group of us later went salsa dancing until the wee hours. One gal does community work with kids, and I passed her info about Rotary International – as they have grants for projects like hers. I always want to get the word out.

Ended the evening in my first dingy hostel I can remember. Cheap at about $4, but looking back, I should have gone for a better one. Got woken up by knocks at the front door of the place at least three times.

* * *

From great times, to the 'most challenging' all in just one day. Got news from a mechanic that my car may need a valve job and a ring job on the engine. At about $200, that hurts. The car clunked up a big hill for an hour, then ran rough until dark. Up in the small mountain town of Pampelonia, Columbia I got a mechanic to clean out the grotty spark plugs. While eating at a cafe next door I met some cute kids who were the family of the chef. The kids were so giddy and giggly at the sight of this big foreigner. I get that all the time – ear to ear smiles all around. They even practiced their English with me.

Upon leaving, a man and his wife asked if I needed help finding a hotel room. I said sure, if they knew an economical one. They jumped in the car and took me to the top ritzy hotel in town, which cost about $20 per night. I was used to about a third of that price. It was raining, my car was acting up, and I was getting frustrated – plus, I could not understand them. Finally after getting another decent hotel ($5), I took them back 'home', or at least I thought so. The next place turned out not to be their home – but another hotel! They did not realize I had already decided on the last one, I was just trying to get them to their house.

And to top it off, I hit a curb and popped my tire. Having to change that tire in the rain, I was *not* happy. A security guy was bicycling around blowing his whistle to tell all that everything is all clear, at 11 o'clock at night. Believe it or not, this is not unusual, and it goes on all night long. I think that is the stupidest thing to do in the middle of the night, and I told him to shut up. In so many words. He then brought some soldiers around, and I told them he is an idiot. They had guns and it might have gotten ugly.

But I was in a cranky matter-of-fact, tell-it-like-it-is kind of mode. To make a long story short, they must have sensed it, and they got right down to work and helped me get that tire off! By the way, it was stuck and it took two hours. In the rain. There were handshakes and high-fives all around when we finally finished! Being proud soldiers, they even refused my ardent offers of a tip for their kind service. What great guys. After all this on a rainy night, my big quilt to snuggle under back at the hotel saved the day!

Venezuela,

$1 = 2,150 Bolivares (official rate), $1 = 2,500 Bolivares (street rate for cash)

Crossing into Venezuela, I purposely held off buying gasoline in Colombia where it is around $3 per gallon because I heard gas is cheap in Venezuela. I had no idea how cheap. In Venezuela gasoline is 20 U.S. cents per gallon!! They are big international petroleum producers, so they literally give it away to their own people. You can fill up your whole tank, then drive around for 300 miles, then fill up the tank again, and the price of those two tank-fulls is less than the price of one Big Mac! Want a real cheap date? Take her for a long ride in the scenic countryside.

But it comes at a price at the border towns. Because Colombians want the cheap stuff too, they have gas lines of cars going around three blocks or more! I have not seen people waiting in cars for gas since the 1970s. People wait two or three hours in line, and you can only get gas two days a week according to your license plate. I could not get any gas that first day, but had to wait one more. The price is fixed by the government at 70

Bolivares (their currency) per liter, and you can only buy the equivalent of six gallons at a time. There is a huge black market in gasoline, with people offering 25 liters for 25,000 Bolivares. That is 1000 per liter, or almost 20 times the official price. This had been going on for at least six years, and someone should have been able to fix it by then. The border guards all have hoses and check the tank levels (using these as dip sticks) on all cars going out of the country, as you can only go out with a minimal amount. Even letting the price rise at the borders to half the neighboring countries would help clear up some of the lines.

I had to stay overnight in my car the first night to protect it. Ironically, it was empty. Ran out of gas because of the license plate rationing. Plus, in the middle of the night I had to punch a kid who tried to break into my car – while I was in it! He came around twice, so he was probably not the sharpest tool in the shed. I twisted his arm and threw him to the ground while stepping on him to keep him down, and was half asleep when all this was happening. He later came back and threw a rock at the car, but missed. I waited for him to come back again, but he must have gone on to easier prey. Be aware.

Found out later the gas lines are just at the border towns in Venezuela, because of the big price difference. The rest of Venezuela is okay, and they even let the tourists like me skip the lines. A soldier just waved me to the front of the line, and did not care about my license plate.

I met a cutie named Milagros (means 'Miracle' in Spanish) at the border town of San Antonio. She lives in the nearby big city of San Cristobal, and wanted to practice English. Why not! For the week I spent there, she came to all the Rotary parties with me and helped lots with translating. We went on a picnic that Sunday in the mountains with the Rotary Club, and had great soup of chicken and veggies that was topped off with fresh avocados and sour cream. Just mix them in! All the kids and even some of the adults at the picnic had a great time playing sports – traditional soccer and the curiously new Frisbee. Being a special buddy to all those kids, a few practiced their English with me. One young guy even wanted to give me his 'dog tags' from around his neck as a gift! I was so touched, but politely declined as it had his blood type on it and may have been important for him as identification. The big Rotary formal dinner celebrated 10 years of the building of their Medical Center. Milagros looked awesome by my side!

Stayed in San Cristobal for a week to get that major valve job engine work done on my car. The guys who lived at or hung around at my *posada* (guest house) were a hoot! It was like living back at the fraternity house. They all cracked jokes about each other, even saying, "He is gay" or "He is a mother f...r" once in awhile. That was the extent of some of their English language skills. Luis had lived there a year and is a government civil engineer. He has three ex-wives, and is proud of his successful sons. He is lively and a hell-raiser, and took me out for a fancy steak dinner (complete with a mariachi band) when I left. Jesus is the manager and the cook. Not as much an English speaker as Luis, so I really learned a lot of Spanish from him. Edgar and Carlos rounded out the group.

Baseball is the national sport of Venezuela, and is much bigger than soccer. We all watched the final (live on TV) of the World Baseball Classic at San Diego, California from 10 p.m. to 3 a.m. Lots of rum and colas all around. I put together a $5 betting pool of 100 squares (10 x 10), with each square costing 100 Bolivares (about 5 cents). Luis bought lots, and won just about everything. I gave Jesus 10 squares, as he had no money. Winners were paid at the end of inning 2, 4, 6, 8, and at the final score. Japan beat Cuba 10-6, and everyone loved it!

* * *

Heading into the ranching country around southern Venezuela, I met a great Rotarian guy named Adalberto when staying at his hotel in Santa Barbara de Varina. He looks like John Denver! His son Alberto is successful with cable TV in Miami, Florida and was home for a visit.

They took a group of 16 of us out for pizzas and beer, and the excellent food was served in a real snappy atmosphere: palm trees, cave entrance, swimming pool. Adalberto had his pistol in his belt just in case, as armed bandits are a problem throughout the area.

The next day we helped fix broken water pipes at the old folks home (*casa viejos*) that the Rotary Club sponsors. They provide three free meals per day to 40 seniors. The lunch they served was heavenly: big huge beef neck bones with mouth-watering meat hanging off them. Ample amounts of marrow reminded me of the line in the movie *Dead Poets Society* that we should, "...suck the marrow out of life..." I surely have had my share! Plus the homemade strawberry yogurt was the sweetest ever tasted. I was loving it all!

We played dominoes and chatted in Spanish with those old folks, as I could even carry on a decent conversation by now. Being tall, I picked some really big avocados for everyone off the top of their large tree. After a nice half day visit to the countryside I said my goodbyes to Adalberto, and upon leaving his driveway saw the bloody results of a highway robbery.

From the Caribbean Coast of Venezuela

28 Mar 2006

Greetings from Caracas, the capital of Venezuela on the Caribbean Coast! A place where the price of gasoline is fixed at less than 20 US cents per gallon around the whole country.

But people still carry pistols in their belts for protection in more rural areas. It is like the wild west all over again. In the south of the country I saw the bloody body of a dead man riddled with bullets on the side of the road, with a pistol still lying right next to him. I had been in the same spot not more than 5 minutes earlier. Not knowing if he was the victim of a robbery or the actual robber himself, I did not stop to ask questions. The area has successful ranchers, and people who want to kidnap them for their cash. All windows on newer vehicles are tinted, to insure more anonymity for the number of passengers inside.

This really shows how easy it is to get caught in a desperate situation, so one must always be aware of the surroundings. For those rebels around us who want anarchy, Venezuela is the place for them. No-one seems to obey traffic laws. It is not uncommon for someone to drive down a one-way street in the wrong direction, and no-one seems to care. People stop at a red light briefly, then drive right through. Police even wave them along, or look the other way.

My car broke down in a seedy area of Caracas – at night! Everyone was saying I better get out of there fast, before all the shops close and anything goes. I made some quick friends who helped me push the car to an overnight guarded parking spot. We became good friends and spent a couple of days together. There are good people everywhere, you just have to look.

The Caribbean water is clear and I am headed for Trinidad next. Cheers, Christopher

* * *

In the town of Guiria (say "wier-ee-ya"), the road ends in this most north-east corner of Venezuela. I checked out boat rides to Trinidad, the island nation four hours away by ferry. The only public transportation operates on Wednesdays, meaning I would have to spend at least a week there, plus another five days in Guiria waiting for it. The price is 400,000 Bolivares ($161). I checked with fishermen who may want another person along on their daily trip, but they all thought I wanted a chartered boat and quoted me prices around $1000. No, thank you.

One captain of a boat full of drunk guys was saying "no problem," but would not give me a firm price – which *is* a problem. An English speaking (barely) guy jumped in my car, and we headed off to where I could park my car safely for about four days. Cheap and safe, he said, and his friend came along, too. We stopped at a government truck depot across the street from where they work. The guy in charge said it would be okay to park there if we got permission from the top guy. My 'friend' said the top guy's house is only five kilometers (3 miles) down the road. Lets go! We went in that direction until I realized all the houses ended and we were headed out into the jungle. I turned the car around, came back to a gas station, and said one of them must wait here – so the one in the back seat got out. The other then asked me for money for more beers, and when I said no he also started to get out. He then turned around, got in my face, grabbed my sun glasses and ran away! The whole thing was all a set-up to rob me! It could have been much worse with two of them out in the jungle in the middle of no-where.

So I ran after the guy a bit, but went back to lock my car. His friend was still around so I fronted up to him and said that since his friend is gone, he is now responsible. I grabbed his baseball cap in much the same way as his friend had grabbed my sunglasses. He would get it back when I got my glasses back. It was duly dropped off with the town police, who know the place where they work and would sort it out.

The next day was Sunday, and I spent a great day at the beach with a friend named Delvalle and her family. We had met earlier while singing Karaoke songs together at a disco. The beach had sun, palm tree shade, and lots of crystal clear water. At the beach bar at the end of the day, I thought I recognized that sun glass thief from the day before! When asked where my sun glasses were, he answered only in Spanish that he did not understand. Not absolutely sure if it was him, I let it go – but kept an eye on him the whole time. When he left I followed him out just to see if he would do anything to my car, but nothing came of it.

A good rule of thumb is to avoid the a-holes of this world, and seek out nice people. There are so much more of the latter.

Guyana, $1 = 190 Guyana Dollars

The people of the country of Guyana are more relaxed, it seems. I came to the jungle town of San Martin, Venezuela which is on the river border with Guyana, and this village has 800 people who are mostly English speaking Guyanese. Indeed, Guyana is the only English speaking country on the South American continent. Black, Latino (brownish), and Indian people are all mixed together. I could leave my car out on the street all day and night, and return to find it in the same condition. Maybe it is just the small town atmosphere. I met a black man named Flavian on the main highway, and gave him a ride 70 kilometers through the jungle. It felt so great to speak English again! The road started out with two lanes, one in each direction, but the jungle has encroached on both sides, and one lane is the norm. Sometimes jungle vegetation scratches both sides of the car. Flavian introduced me to Annie and her family who are part Indian, and she is an elder with her Seventh Day Adventist Church. I bought a huge four pound fish, fresh from the river, and a three liter bottle of cola that served 15 people in that house. They let me set my tent up on their back patio area a few nights.

I took a boat across the river (one minute ride) to Guyana, the 96th country I have visited world-wide. In my three days there we did lots on the river, including visiting a dredge that was mining for gold and diamonds on the sand bar that was no-mans-land in the middle of the river between both countries. The river is brown and shallow with a quick current, and maybe two hundred yards wide. San Martin is a 'dry' church town, so we went over to the Guyana side for beers with lots of rowdy black miners. Everyone around works the mines – on the river or in the jungle. I wanted to see how they process gold dust using mercury to bring it all together, but only got the oral explanation. Possibly, they keep their gold secrets away from outside prying eyes.

Being back where they speak English, you can joke with people a bit more. That is the subtlety of language – you can express ideas more deeply, not just the basics of who, what, and where, when you have a lack of deep knowledge of the local language. I was at a shop with my friend Flavian, and he introduced me to all the people hanging around on the front porch. One older lady was quite outspoken about her church teachings. I have learned to listen a lot when this happens, as there is no winning an argument when discussing religious beliefs. She had three young boys line up for me and recite from memory a creed they were taught in Sunday School. It was a lot, but the boys made it through all right. When they finished and as I was politely getting into my car, the lady said that beliefs are very important.

Without missing a beat, I added a quote from a bumper sticker I once read: "Everyone has got to believe in something. I believe I'll have another beer!" Everyone cracked up in laughter, even the older lady! I really like getting reactions like that, as it is giving them something special to remember. Be gracious.

* * *

Happy Easter from Guyana

13 Apr 2006

Greetings from Guyana, the only English-speaking country on the mainland of South America. Famous for the forced mass-suicide of 914 people in the jungle religious commune of Jonestown back in 1978. Locals all seem to have a story about that.

It sure is good to speak with people on the street who can actually understand me! They have a heavy Caribbean Jamaican-type of accent to their English, and it can be hard to understand sometimes. But at least we can communicate, and that is saying a lot. Not having to piece together sentences to get a point across is quite refreshing. However, when they speak among themselves in their local slang, they lose me straight-away. It is broken English like the kind you get right out of the ghetto 'hood' in some parts of our US inner cities. They seem to understand each other quite well.

Everyone in the area seems to be a miner – searching for gold and diamonds. Went out on a dredge in the middle of the river to see how it all works. The sound of the engine on the dredge is deafening, and it goes for 23 hours a day (1 for maintenance), 7 days a week. All mud and rocks are thrown against a sifter, and minuscule amounts of gold are harvested. Running the engines is economically feasible because of the low price of gasoline here. Also, gasoline smuggling is big business here too.

Had some great fish dinners from the huge fish taken out of the jungle river. No piranhas (fish with razor sharp teeth) in sight yet, so it is safe to do a lot of swimming to keep cool. All the best for a happy Easter season. Cheers, Christopher

At the Guyanese pub across the river, I was the only white guy around. All the black miners throw their money around with reckless abandon. They buy a case of beers at a time and then give them out to everyone. Both in Guyana and in Venezuela there is a habit of opening a new beer, then spilling out a bit before starting to drink. It is like blessing the ground. Then when finishing, they pour out the last sip on the ground, as well. Quite wasteful if you asked me, and these are people who do not have much in the first place. Why waste the little things they do have? Just try wasting things like that in a country known for frugality such as Scotland. They would probably shoot you!

I taught Frisbee to everyone in the village, then gave them the disk when I left. It is my own way of saying, "Do this in memory of me." Quite religious in its own way. While swimming at the river landing with the locals, there is a strong current just a few yards away from the safe 'swimming hole' area. Towards the end of the day the Frisbee got into that current, and with limited daylight we lost sight of it. I swam out into the strong current, similar to a couple of times before, but this time just could not see it! I swam to the shore, ran to where a small boat was just coming in, and asked for the captain's help. We ended up going down river a half mile and finally saw the white disk in the murky brown water. Grabbed it and saved the day! We could not believe just how fast that thing traveled, and were really lucky to find it. That was the community gift, and they got it safe and sound.

* * *

Back in Venezuela at the City of Guayana (not the country Guyana), there are lots of modern amenities – more than I have seen anywhere in South America. This is a company town, with CVG company being the backbone of it all. It stands for Corporation Venezuela Guayana, but one guy joked that it is so big that it could be the Central Venezuela Government! They do mining of iron ore, as well as hydroelectric dams. The mall here has all the modern Western fashion shops. All names of shops are in English, and the locals do not really know or care what they mean. They just buy there, all the same. One shop is called, "As seen on TV." I explained that one to a friend, and it was quite a revelation for her – "So that's what that means!" All fast food shops are Western prices, which means I would probably not shop there (can get better local values right outside the mall, and I can get these back home anyway), but many people do. TGI Fridays, Papa John's Pizza, Wendy's Hamburgers, etc. All are there.

The private Italian-Venezuelano Club is like paradise! About eight swimming pools spread over a huge area of green grass and manicured gardens. The beach area along the river lake is full of palm trees and speed boats, and lots of restaurants abound. Pizzas there are a fraction of the price back home, so I had lots. There is a nine hole par-three golf course that is well manicured. The club has a discotheque, and tennis and soccer facilities, as well. Lots of beautiful people and their kids are hanging around in swimsuits. The Coronoko Golf and Country Club has nine regulation holes that you play twice for a par 72. I played golf here four times with friends who made me feel like one of the members. One guy even gave me two clubs (older ones, but nice ones) to help replace clubs stolen from me way back in Peru.

'Semana Santos' is Holy Week just before Easter, and in Venezuela they get the whole week off as vacation. The traffic on the streets is lighter, and the city of Guayana seemed deserted as the people head for the coast to escape the heat. I met a German man named Horst who spent 15 years in New Jersey as a construction remodeling company owner. He did not pay his company taxes and someone turned him in, so he had to leave. Now he has a $1000 a month pension from the German government, and lives like a king on two million Bolivares a month. He says young ladies come up to him all the time, and he wines and dines them. When he takes them home and pays for their company, he says he is helping the local economy. He likes the lifestyle, but worries about the crime; and says he likes the USA better. I told him to ask the IRS how much they want, then settle with them – as they are businessmen, too.

The cars in Venezuela include an extravaganza of huge 'muscle' cars of the 1970s and 1980s – big Pontiac GTOs, Chevy Novas, Ford LTDs, and much more. They all seem to have big fat tires and mag rims, and are in various stages of disrepair. Some are rusted out, while others have dents and missing panels. Lots of body and paint work is needed, but some also look surprisingly 'hot'. Since gas is so cheap, you can have an old car with a bad engine – just keep buying oil every other day. There are oil stands that sprout up along all the highways everywhere, and I visited them regularly. My shiny red Chevrolet from Ecuador fit right in.

It seems like I was getting used to having my car broken into in South America – twice in Peru, twice in Venezuela. At the time of the last break-in, I really did not think I had anything more of value to steal! I was wrong. My tent had been with me for six years over five continents; funny they did not steal the tent poles along with it. Tough luck for them! But the two golf clubs that were just given to me, and were now gone – that kind of hurt. Belts, shoes, and shirts were also pilfered. The hat and sun glasses are the ones to replace first and foremost, as the heat and the sun's glare here can really get to you quick. Let your guard down once, and you get stung. I feel stupid about the break-in, as it could have been prevented. There was a security guard in the area, and I could have slipped him some cash to watch it along with the other ones he was watching. He probably let the robbers ransack mine, as it was not under contract with him. Live and learn.

When looking for a hotel late in the evening I saw a man in a shop and stopped to ask for help. He saw the car stop, and went and got his shotgun. My broken Spanish was not helping, so I stayed far enough away so as not to make him nervous. These are wild-west days, where anything can happen. A friend from Rotary changed some traveler's checks for me, and handed me a stack of bills worth 1,700,000 Bolivares. Yes, that is 1.7 million. First time I have ever been a millionaire, all for just $700! He told me to be careful, and he held up one 50,000 bill ($20). He said people here will kill a man for just one of these, and I had a whole stack of them that would choke a horse. Be aware.

* * *

Tucacas beach on the northern coast of Venezuela was everything my friends said it would be. Clear blue water, and you can see the reefs underneath the surface throughout the bay. Palm trees all over the place, mangroves around as well, and the sand is clean. The beach is supposedly closed for cleaning on Mondays, but they must have finished already as the gate was wide open. Had a whole beach for myself and one other family who was there, too.

A scuba dive shop owner who is a white guy from Guyana living in Venezuela 26 years said he has reservations about the current Hugo Chavez government. Most business owners seem to think the same way. They think Chavez wants to start a class war, helping the poor at the expense of the better-off. They worry that Chavez sends the message that it is okay to rob someone in order to feed a family. Business growth is stifled as people wait to see what would happen after the next elections. I said you cannot just put your life on hold like that, as there were similar sentiments in Zimbabwe in Africa with dictator Robert Mugabe – and he is still in power four years later. Here, there is a real fear of violence in the streets, and most believe Chavez will only leave power by force. Some businessmen have contingency plans to relocate to Colombia (of all places!) once the bullets start to fly. One guy described how 5000 people died in two nights of rioting back in the 1980s. The soldiers shot them to maintain order after the government ordered price rises on basic foods – say, 300% price rises overnight! The natives can be restless.

I met two German traveling carpenters at the local backpacker's hostel. Their tradition of apprenticeship is to go out into the world for three years and work in various countries – leaving with $5, and returning with $5 three years later. They work for food and travel expenses, learning carpentry and survival skills along the way. They travel in their traditional German old-style leather outfits, complete with white shirt, a tie, and hat. Of course they get lots of stares from everyone, and giggles and squeals from groups of kids. They say they get used to it.

Their names are Ben and Volcker, the latter which is pronounced like 'Fokker'. I told him about the comedy movie with Ben Stiller called *Meet the Fokkers*, and how everyone in America laughs at the similarity of his name and another famous word. He now loves it, and suddenly understands why Yanks tell all their friends, "Hey, this guy's name is Fokker!" in such a robust way! We shared a dinner together with two French cuties, as well. You have kindred spirits when you go over zany stories with other fellow travelers.

At the most northern part of Venezuela on the peninsula of Cabo San Ramon, there is a big modern lighthouse made out of stone cut from the native rock. It is either dead coral or magma flows of igneous rock. Walking over it is tricky, and driving on it is hard on the tires. They cut it into bricks about one foot square, then mortar them together to make a wall. It looks like the pattern on a giraffe's neck, and all the houses are made the same way. It was eerily quiet at the point of land's end, almost like going through a ghost town. I found a restaurant that had cold beer, but no other food or soft drinks until the weekend crowd comes in. A three day weekend (May Day for workers) was coming up, so there should be more people then.

The desert of northern Venezuela is peaceful in the early morning before the hot sun takes over for the day. There is a gentle breeze blowing and you can keep the windows of the hotel open to let it flow through. The town of Coro and the whole northern state of Falcon reminds me of Arizona, with cactus sprouting up everywhere and mixing in with the green thorn trees for an interesting combination.

I spent the night at the Dunas (dunes) Motel, which is a 'love shack' type of hotel where you might take a girlfriend to make out. These types are bright and modern with nice tiles everywhere, and water that flows cleanly. You drive right up to your door, then pull the garage door down behind you. Others have a curtain that shields your car from any curious 'lookie-loos' so privacy is assured. There are about a half dozen of these hotels on the outskirts of town, so business must be booming. It is 15,000 Bolivares for a four hour period, and I gave 20,000 for the whole night ($8). These hotels can be seen all over Latin America, and they are great values. Just negotiate the rate for the full night. There is always cable TV, with a few English channels as well. They all have clean sheets and modern conveniences, and some have Jacuzzis for a relaxing spa.

* * *

Greetings from Lake Maracaibo!

17 May 2006

Having just spent the last two weeks in Maracaibo, Venezuela I have completed the bisection of the country from east to west, and north to south. With transportation costs so low (gas, tolls, etc.) it is easy to cover a lot of ground. Lake Maracaibo is a huge fresh water lake that connects to the Caribbean sea. A lot of Venezuela's oil reserves come from here, and the area seems to have a higher rate of affluence than the norm. Perhaps that is why the local state here always has rumblings of wanting to break away and be autonomous or even independent from the rest of the country.

The president of Venezuela, Hugo Chavez, has been in the international news lately for his outspoken anti-western stances. He likes to align the country with others such as Iran, Cuba, and North Korea, which shows where his views lie. He is a 'power to the people' populist, and a champion for the impoverished masses. The country is deeply split when his name comes up. Most agree that he will not be leaving power any time soon unless by force, and people are preparing for any and everything.

Price inflation here is rampant. I collect coins and came across a coin from 1990 about as big as an Eisenhower silver dollar that was worth

5 Bolivares. Back then you could buy a nice meal at a restaurant with it. Today, 16 years later, you need 5000 Bolivares for that same meal. That same size coin is now 500 Bolivares, and it will only buy you one third of a can of Coke. If going from 5 to 10 is 100% inflation, then from 5 to 5000 is off the board! Fiscal responsibility is a sign of good government management. It is sadly lacking here.

They call this time of year the rainy season here (their 'winter' time), but it does not rain all the time. The cloud cover cools everything down, making it much more pleasant for golf! Earlier in the year the heat and humidity could be quite sweltering, and this is a welcomed break.

All the best! Cheers, Christopher

* * *

The endpoint of my South America trek – and of this book – once again confirmed the law of last-minute hassles. I had made it to Maracaibo, the second-largest city in Venezuela. The city displays none of the ubiquitous billboards of President Hugo Chavez seen throughout much of the rest of the country. They have a more regional 'go it alone' type of pride.

Knowing the trip was coming to an end, I sold my car to a fellow traveler, a British guy who was a good friend. I didn't quite break even, but it was a good deal for us both, and I was glad he could now have the freedom to travel the country cheaply and in style. We took a road trip to Caracas, from where I would catch my flight home.

During the interim few days, however, being a Western traveler without wheels seemingly gave the signal to certain people to let the rip-off games begin. For no apparent reason at all, three days in a row I had the misfortune of being stopped on the street by the Caracan police – who saw me as a prime target of opportunity to get their palms greased.

The first time it happened, when three cops stalked and then surrounded me as if I were public enemy number one, I protested that I wasn't doing anything except ambling down the street. Ignoring this, they ordered me to show them my paperwork, which they inspected with furrowed eyebrows and grim looks. Not good enough, they said, before going through my wallet, money belt and every item in my pockets looking for who knows what they could use to say something was out of order. This went on for an inordinate amount of time in front of a small gathering of shop keepers and other passers-by. Finding nothing, I'm sure to their dismay, one of the cops said, "Okay, senor, you can go."

We weren't quite through with each other just yet, though. They had put my items from the search onto the hood of an adjacent car. As I was putting some of my stuff back into my wallet and money belt, my pen rolled from the car to the ground.

The humiliation of this whole interlude had stuck in my craw. Why should these guys get off so easily? And so, almost reflexively, I threw down the gauntlet. "Wait a minute," I said to the leader, "You just badgered me for twenty minutes for no good reason. So, since you put that pen on the car, why don't you pick it up for me?"

Refusing to comply, he simply stood inertly, saying nothing and trying to regain some of his previous smugness. As for me, I couldn't possibly give in, either. I added, "I'm not going to pick it up, so how are you going to return to me my property?"

So we stood there, nobody making a move to bend, for what seemed like an eternity. The people on the street watching were intrigued. The cop and the gringo locked in an endless stare-down at the OK Corral. Finally someone blinked, and it wasn't me.

"Here," the cop said, taking another pen out of his pocket, "you can have my pen instead." Figuring that was the start of a victory in this

Mexican stand-off (or rather *Venezuelan* stand-off), I took the pen, but wasn't finished yet. Feeling my oats, I said, "Now I have a few questions for you." I then asked each of the three cops their name and badge number, and then proceeded to interrogate them for another ten minutes. It was a case of what's good for the goose being good for the big American traveler.

"What is your height and weight?" By now their smug looks had turned to looks of confusion. No-one had ever put them on the spot like this. Perhaps out of shock, they actually became less belligerent and more uncomfortable by the minute. I had plenty more. "Any tattoos or distinguishing marks?" I was thorough, and calmly wrote down everything. When they scoffed, I simply wrote down, "Refuses to answer."

I was really pushing it, too. "Home address and telephone number?" I could have gone on for more, but they must have had other tourists to harass, and departed. The crowd seemed to be incredulous. It was their show for the day.

Two other similar routines from two more sets of Venezuelan cops happened over the next two days. This had to be officially sanctioned from higher ranks. Each encounter ended the same, with the cops finding nothing to use as a lever to pry out money, and me duly interrogating them right back.

That was pushing the envelope on the law of last-minute hassles. I couldn't get onto the plane fast enough, before something really bad happened. In retrospect, these incidents were a microcosm of the travel experience: standing up for what is right. I thought of how close to the edge of the tightrope I had come over the past decades of travel through the Third World. But here I was, hale and hearty, content with having given more than a few native rip-off artists as much trouble as they gave me, yet easily able to distinguish between the chaff and the wheat in the Third World.

The latter, wherever the road had lead, was being able to see, touch, and live the Third World Experience: its glories, its potentialities, its natural gifts of physical resources – and most of all, its people. These memories would linger the most, stoked by continuing correspondence and meetings with literally hundreds of friends I had made along the way.

The best part of all? Knowing that more friends are there to be made whenever restless feet hit the beckoning road once again.

Crispy fried grasshoppers in Borno State, Nigeria.

Sipping from a coconut in Goa, India.

EPILOGUE

What can be learned from all these pages? What is the brick and mortar common to each place visited? What were the lessons that went beyond being able to spin Mark Twain-like tales of weeks and months on the long road less traveled? It would be impossible to piece all of the ordered and disordered thoughts together in a few pages, since new and different aspects and meanings can be realized nearly every day. Still, there are some observations I would like to share, by way of placing a few signposts in the turf for others to follow on their own journeys. These may increase understanding of what is found, and how to deal with it.

I hesitate to call these musings baubles of wisdom, but rather informed tidbits that are common reference points for surviving the Third World. They are influenced by my own learnings as a humanitarian, and based not on the obvious and cherished differences between people in developing nations, but on their intrinsic kinship – with everyone on this one world.

* Always give something first in order to receive something in return. Show that you care. I do little chores everywhere, and make it a habit to pick up trash that is not mine, in the spirit of making things a little better. This is something that was learned in Scouts a long time ago. When finishing camping trips we would put everything away and then

police the area, taking away all our trash and others' too. Always make something a little bit better than it was before first coming upon it.

* Establish a rapport with people. Talk to them, mingle with them, get to know them, ask questions. I travel only with the most basic of maps primarily because I love talking to people, and asking for directions is an effective way of getting to where you want to go. People love to help. Locals hold travelers in great esteem, like visiting dignitaries. Return that respect. That will break down barriers with warp speed.

* Don't be afraid to pick up natives if you're driving, or to hitch a ride with them if you aren't. The notion of giving or getting a ride from strangers doesn't carry the same stigma that it does at home in the 'civilized' countries. When hitching a ride I always tell the driver a story, possibly a story of far-off lands, that will make them laugh and enjoy the experience of riding with a Westerner. They will treasure that experience all their lives.

* Realize that prices are very cheap in developing nations. The answer as to why is not as simple as many Westerners believe. Economists will give you long, boring dissertations about supply and demand, suppressed markets, poor economic working conditions. Few experts, however, bother to consider the psychological factors of the people who work for incredibly low wages. They also live on the same incredibly low wages. They make a living and earn their daily bread. Westerners also lament – sincerely or otherwise – about Third World people "having" to live on two dollars a day. Recently former President Clinton, in speaking of his Global Initiative program to aid underdeveloped nations, said exactly the same thing. His heart was in the right place, but his perspective wasn't. One could speak with pity that people in those regions "have" to live on a minuscule wage – or with envy that they "get" to live on it.

There is a subtle but meaningful difference between those terms. The difference being Third World folks have no problem living on what they need, not obsessing on what they don't need. If two dollars is what they are to get, two dollars is all they will spend. Economic progress will, and should, improve wages and living conditions, and these people are working hard to achieve that evolution every day of their lives. However, let us not overlook the refreshing, almost unheard-of lack of avarice they demonstrate in daily life. They are earning future wealth with the common sense they display today.

* The Third World needs to develop a sense of safety and security. When this happens, economic development and standards of living sky-rocket. This is where a Westerner's perspective can contribute to progress in a way more valuable than dropping a few bucks into a supermarket slot marked "Save the Children." Because what really can save the children is by making it possible for the children's parents to provide for them. This can be done by stressing the importance of people being protected by their own governments. We, of course, take our security and our safety for granted. For most of us, our safety is automatic, and expensive, in the taxes we pay for our police forces and our military. In the Third World another reason why prices are so low is that they don't have a comparable amount of security. That, I believe, is the biggest problem facing people there. The biggest gift any government can give its people is to be tough on crime. This includes government corruption, which is a whole chapter in itself. A safe place is a successful place.

The best example of this could be the contrast between South Africa and Venezuela. There once was a very heavy-handed venal system of apartheid in South Africa. Because of the very strict police presence, everybody had grown to expect that breaking the law has consequences. The same holds true for today, long after the racist barriers fell. Black, white or otherwise, you don't bribe the police and you pay parking tickets on time. It's not a police state, but a police-conscious state. The people believe in a strong government that can keep order – not in the dictatorial sense found all too often on the same continent, but one dedicated to enforcing the rules of law.

On the other hand Venezuela is a rich oil producing country, but they don't have an effective level of security. The government tries to help poor people by throwing money at a problem, but they don't have the strong will to have a police presence where lawbreakers are punished and lawful citizens are rewarded. Thus, people see they can get away with crime and they disobey even elementary things, starting with the basics like traffic laws. They are by far the worst drivers I have seen: willfully not stopping at red lights, or commonly passing on the road shoulder. And their economy is in shambles. Play connect-the-dots and you can see the problem, and how to fix it.

* Explain to Third World citizens how much alike we are to them. Stereotyping isn't a one-way street. Just as Westerners can ascribe certain assumptions to them – possibly the wrongful that they are lazy, ignorant and without skills – they can similarly look upon us with a kind of misplaced awe. I have heard many times around the world that everyone in America must be a millionaire, and thus everyone must be happy as a lark. They didn't say this in envy, but in fascination, an image carved by the television programs that make their way to them in which all the characters live in nice places and have nice cars, yet never seem to do any work for a living.

For those who say that, I would say to them, "Listen, there are a lot of people in America who are struggling to keep their head above water, living on credit cards, borrowing from Peter to pay Paul half the time. They're not as happy as you think." My own observation, having lived in both places, is that there is a delicious irony beneath the stereotyping: Americans would absolutely love to have things that are common in the Third World, such as nice fruit growing off the trees, warm sunshine, a peaceful tropical paradise. It is the way of the world that everybody wants what they don't have. Most people yearn for the excessive things found in developed countries. Who wouldn't? But people in developing nations live their lives daily with the peaceful things they have that Westerners yearn for. So it's a trade-off. Shakespeare once wrote that if a man earns 100 pounds a year and spends 105, he's an unhappy man. Subsequently he can be quite content by earning 100 pounds and spending only 95. In the Third World, I would venture to say that the common people rarely spend more than they have.

One can use the example of a car as an analogy of what life is, or should be, all about. Because life is like a car. All you really need to get by are four wheels, an engine and a steering wheel to get you going in the right direction. We like the other things that go along with it: fancy leather bucket seats, air conditioning, stereo, all the good stuff. Given our economy in the Western world, we are able to have all those cool things, but we don't really need them. In the developing nations, folks do quite nicely with the basic essentials. They would like to have the bucket seats, but realize they don't really need them to get to the next village.

A parallel can also be drawn between what life was like in the West a hundred years ago and what life is like now in the developing countries. Developing people now get by on the utensils that were regarded as 'luxury' items back then. Transporting back in time, we would see ourselves then as 'Third World.' The point being, people all over the world are working on the same blueprint as we did. And given the fact that they started later, having lived under colonial regimes and not getting their independence until the last half-century, they are actually working on the blueprint we had two hundred years ago. In that light, the progress they have made has been truly remarkable. Be aware, then, that Third World people are working to get to where we are, and not resigned to living in the past. That should be lesson one.

* Spread the way of thinking that everything we do is based on improving ourselves. This also has everything to do with economics,

and is a subject studied around the world. The inescapable conclusion is that you improve a country's economy only by improving yourself. From the moment we get up in the morning we work to improve the community by helping ourselves. I stress this concept to other people so that they can be aware of the communal effect of their own productivity. Laziness is not acceptable, as crime stems from the myopic way of thinking of taking short-cuts to riches. There are no short-cuts, just lots of hard work.

Sometimes you have to be cruel to be kind. Even if you have to rock the boat to get beggars to be productive, do it. They may have just given up, and need a constructive kick in the pants. I will listen to our own inner-city pan-handlers, then give them a low-cost shaving razor. That should improve self image, and it gets their attention. I then give them a plan. They can trade their old clothes at a second-hand store run by a charity (they won't be turned away if they are sincere); then can go out and get the *worst* job possible, and work up from there. You must start somewhere. Drum it in that they (and only they) will make life better, for themselves and everyone around them.

* Stand up for yourself. This is something you have seen already, that is part of my personality and has served me well. There is an element of con artists and predators world-wide seeking the prey of a rich Westerner. By standing up for yourself and not letting people rip you off, you are weakening their ability to rip others off. They will get the message that tourists are not weak and soft, and will not pay up on the spot to relieve themselves of pressure. (There are exceptions to this rule, as you will also see. You don't want to invite or incite trouble from the wrong people, those who will go beyond scaring you and will actually hurt you. It's a judgment call, something that will become clearer with practice.)

Along the same lines, speak up and spread good values because people will look up to you and think of you as a kind of Plato dispensing wisdom. Teach them what you know, be it how to fix a car engine or how to speak and read English. Every little bit makes a difference. Learning is power and the more power people have, the more they will control their own lives – by speaking up for themselves. Those with the loudest voices are going to rule. My dream is that everybody world wide will have a voice. And we, in our own small way as visitors, can help give them that voice.

* * *

* Everyone has their own beliefs. This is coming from a guy from California where kooky beliefs sprout up like wildflowers. When being criticized, that is when people dig in their heels and do it ten times more (or louder) just out of spite. Some ascribe to the bumper sticker that says, "The more it offends you, the better it is for me." Just let them go on their merry way. The world is too big a place. However, when they attack groups (say, the Scouts) who are doing good, they place their own values over what is best for society. Without standing up for universal ideals, it is an example of the inmates running the asylum. Be aware.

* Try to make sense of what you've seen. Think about even the most trivial of scenes and what they say about the people you come in contact with. The best time to do this sort of meditation might be at night while unwinding from a day of exploring – or cheating the odds against survival. If you can't get to sleep, use this time to think – Lotus position optional.

Don't lose sleep trying to get to sleep. Sometimes getting to sleep can be difficult even at the best of times – say, in your own comfy bed at home. Then throw on top of that some strange surroundings on the road, or if your bed is a grassy meadow and the four walls are the sides of a tent. I happen to find that to be adventuresome and invigorating, but am still not always the type who can fall asleep instantly. So I tell myself that sleep is a state of mind, to be mastered with a few tricks of the brain matter. It is a state of deep rest. Keep eyes closed and tell yourself you will rest like this until the sun comes up if need be. You probably worry about all the things to be done, and are afraid of forgetting something important.

What to do? Keep a pen and piece of paper next to the bed and write down what is on your mind, then tend to it tomorrow. Do it with the lights off and eyes closed, as it is actually fun to decipher and rewrite ideas the next morning. Tom Peters, the author of *In Search of Excellence*, wrote: "What gets written down gets done. What gets paid for gets even more done." Write down ideas, then check them off upon completion. It is a rewarding feeling to turn thoughts into valuable life experiences.

* Tell people wherever you are to get down to basics. Stop worrying about the things you cannot change, and work on what is most important to you. It is no exaggeration saying there are only three things I generally keep track of: 1) the number of hours of sleep each night, which is between seven and nine hours; 2) the amount of money made or spent that day; and 3) my golf score. By keeping sights on these basic things, I don't worry about other things that are out of my control.

Those in the Third World usually have this perspective, which is why they have far lower rates of heart disease, cancer, hypertension, digestive disorders, diabetes, and mental illness – the earmarks of human laziness and over-consumption in the 'civilized' Western world. They keep stress out of their lives, eat fresh and wholesome foods, don't smoke cigarettes, and keep active not as a choice but as a necessity. Again, the basics. Don't ever tell me we can't learn from the Third World. In fact, what we can learn can save our lives.

* Be active as a way to being involved. I try to do one sport every day – even a small activity such as throwing the Frisbee, as you've seen.

Something like that keeps me physically fit and my mind occupied, builds camaraderie with other people, and is just plain fun. My Australian mates have a saying: "I'm here for a good time, not a long time." We can enjoy what we have and what we are doing, or we can obsess on the bad things in life and be miserable. Guess which option is healthier?

* Try to surround yourself with a positive vibe. I taught myself how to windsurf while studying in Germany by going over to people on the lake and saying, "Hi there, can I borrow your windsurfer for a few minutes while you are not using it?" Almost always, they would say, "Sure, go ahead. Do you know how to do it?" I'd say, "Naturally," but in reality was learning on the fly. It wasn't just that they were nice people, which they were, but a sunny demeanor sure helped. I learned from that. People will judge you by your attitude and your approachability, and that breaks down barriers. It is how friends are made in the farthest corners of the world.

Minds are easily influenced, so try to stay positive. You won't always get the positive vibe in return, so if you don't, try to forget it. Don't let others put negative thoughts in your head. You wouldn't let someone dump trash in your living room; same goes with your mind.

* Leave a mark wherever you go. Remember, people in the Third World will remember you. As a visiting Westerner, you will be treated as a rock star. And just as I still recall so clearly my one fleeting brush with a real rock star – Rod Stewart on the streets of London – the natives of these lands will be able to describe everything about you twenty years from now. That being the case, you may as well leave them something good to remember.

* Understand that people do value what they have in the Third World. In this day and age, in the so-called 'advanced' countries, we have lots of nice things. We've gone beyond how difficult it is around the world to

feed and clothe and shelter ourselves. We take those things for granted, and the result of this pampered life is that we think too much about minute things – come to think of it, we think too much in general.

We've got too much time on our hands, and so we act as magnets for sometimes illusory problems, those that cause us neuroses and anxieties that others have no time to even think about. The contrast is stark: we have psychologists by the boatload, yet in the Third World there are almost none. The people there are simply too busy getting the basic necessities of life. The more we get back to basics, the more we avoid the need to pay head shrinkers.

* Have a working understanding of exchange rates in every country, because they can vary tremendously from one to another. Always check prices for essential items at the borders, to get the best values on both sides. Gasoline will be a big expense when driving, but also keep in mind things such as haircuts, clothing, and even vaccinations. Are you going to get shots at home where they're more expensive; or do you want to get a haircut for fifteen bucks, or fifty cents?

Of course, it also works in reverse. When buying high-tech items such as a computer or a cell phone, you can get them at home for a song but if you try to buy them in the Third World it may cost you an arm and a leg (comparatively), and the thing might likely be close to obsolete already. Other specialty items might be as simple as a pair of size 12 sneakers. Needing to buy a new pair in Peru, I found they do not generally have sizes that large there, and had to pay a premium.

* Practice 'opposite-think.' By this I mean challenge yourself to think in ways totally opposite to what human nature would dictate. This is particularly trenchant for those looking to boost economic conditions in the Third World. It is easy to want to throw money at a perceived problem because you "feel sorry for them." Be careful with what you do, as this just might compound the problem. It can create people

waiting around for more handouts. Giving to a beggar makes him a better beggar, and robs a local artisan who wants to be productive and actually earn your money. A better way might be to provide services and ideas that would allow locals to get their own small businesses up and running.

Not to get too preachy or Pollyanna about it, but 'opposite-think' applies as well to basic human values. A holy man like Jesus practiced it simply by refusing to hate others, even those who harmed him. You may not be able to love your enemy, but you can challenge yourself not to make enemies.

Perspective is everything. I was helping some volunteers put a newsletter together for an organization that was helping to develop electricity grids world-wide. The people were altruistic types, and one day we sat for an hour listening to one guy go on and on trashing big businesses and big banks, skewering everybody involved who he claimed were out to screw the downtrodden masses. Finally, I had to say how full of it he was. "Listen, you've got it all wrong," I said. "Everybody's not out to screw the little man. The best businesses are the ones trying to lower their prices as much as possible, because they know that if they benefit you, they benefit themselves. The smart people will go to them, get better value, and the company will also prosper."

This shows how business people think, and it may be opposite to what might be perceived. This approach is rooted in solid supply and demand economics, but is also humanitarian in its results. By gaining these ideals, developing countries will get a leg up sooner than even they may realize is possible.

* Look optimistically at the future of the developing world. A parallel drawn is that we in America were not much different during early stages of our history than people are now in the Third World. So why should

it be hard to believe that these developing nations are tracing a path no different than our own?

Just as America did, developing countries still face many obstacles, to be sure. The biggest obstacle is perhaps in the form of their own leaders, many of whom condone bribery and seek to keep themselves in power above all else – no matter how many of their own people must suffer for it. But then, we too were once ruled by a king, until the founding fathers understood that we all must live in the same house. We changed for the better, and others can change too. For example, Israel became a thriving oasis in the middle of a desert, while its neighbors who have a lot more natural resources still live much the same as 2000 years ago, and seethe with envy.

Still, people can learn to see the light of reason and reality. We can plant seeds by showing that governments can be wiser, and that they can set up the ground rules to help people help themselves. There is a fine line between not interfering with sovereign nations' trade markets, and rewarding dictators for their bad behavior. But at least let us encourage some good behavior. All government programs can be reviewed for improvement.

One example might be health care. When living in Australia, I went to the doctor all the time because universal health care meant never paying extra for it. The system was set up to be abused. In America, where people are responsible for themselves, I've gone next to never. By allowing more medical schools to be opened here or reviewing barriers to entry, the supply of doctors would rise, and allow the costs of medicine to naturally come down in an orderly way on its own. (The same theory correctly says the price of apples comes down when there are more during apple season.) This is not about welfare or government handouts. It is about smart, common sense economics.

Governments must be wise to set up programs designed to be an incentive for people to be productive for society. If offered the choice of free money or having to work for a living, it is probably a no-brainer for the average basic person which one to choose. This will undoubtedly continue until a small businessman who needs willing workers successfully sues the government for unfairly competing with his business.

* Remember, your voice can become a voice for many. Tell people throughout the world that their opinions and ideas have resonance and meaning, and embolden them to present their ideas to others around them. That will build chains, and when many chains are long enough they will become interconnected and eventually strangle the dictators of the world and their assassins hiding in the shadows. That will be when the warm light of shared progress will burn brightest, and also when the term 'Third World' will become a third-rate anachronism.

I will end these pages as they began, with overriding guidelines for surviving travel in the Third World. This will govern most everything to be faced out there, and produce rewards and memories for a lifetime.

Be aware, be gracious – and, most of all, be there.

* * *

The Donkey Theory
– Anon.

One day, a farmer's donkey fell into an abandoned well. The animal cried piteously for hours as the farmer tried to figure out what to do.

Finally he decided that the animal was old and the well needed to be covered up anyway, so it just wasn't worth it to him to try to retrieve the donkey. He invited all his neighbors to come over and help him. They each grabbed a shovel and began to shovel dirt into the well.

Realizing what was happening, the donkey at first cried and wailed horribly. Then, a few shovelfuls later, he quieted down completely. The farmer peered down into the well, and was astounded by what he saw.

With every shovelful of dirt that hit his back, the donkey was doing something amazing. He would shake it off and take a step up on the new layer of dirt. As the farmer's neighbors continued to shovel dirt on top of the animal, he would shake it off and take a step up. Pretty soon the donkey stepped up over the edge of the well and trotted off, to the shock and astonishment of all the neighbors!

Life is going to shovel dirt on you, all kinds of dirt. The trick to getting out of the well is to not let it bury you, but to shake it off and take a step up. Each of our troubles is a stepping-stone. We can get out of the deepest wells just by not stopping, never giving up! Shake it off and take a step up!

Remember these five simple rules:

Free your heart from hatred.
Free your mind from worries.
Live simply.
Give more.
Expect less.

OH YEAH,..........ONE MORE THING.

The donkey kicked the crap out of the guy that tried to bury him.
Which brings out another moral for this story:
When you try to cover your ass, it always comes back to get you.

Wide open African highways of Mozambique.